Good Cooking

ALASTAIR

A COMMON READER
Pleasantville, New York

ALASTAIR LITTLE
KEEP IT SIMPLE

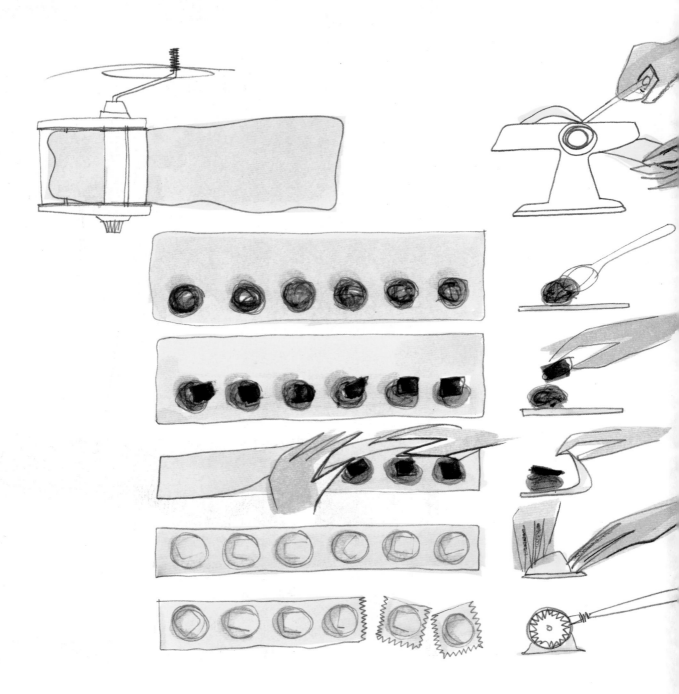

ALASTAIR LITTLE

KEEP IT SIMPLE

**A FRESH LOOK AT CLASSIC COOKING
BY ALASTAIR LITTLE AND
RICHARD WHITTINGTON**

**PHOTOGRAPHY BY DAVID GILL
ILLUSTRATIONS BY BRIAN MA SIY**

**THE OVERLOOK PRESS
WOODSTOCK · NEW YORK**

For John Lincoln and Pippa Whittington who separately, and in their different ways, gave more to this book than we can say.

Of the very many people who helped in the process of making this book, we would especially like to thank the following: Lewis Esson, whose indefatigable and good-humoured quest for accuracy made him our ideal editor; Juliet Peston, whose creative cooking has impacted on many of the recipes; Brian Ma Siy for his extraordinary illustrations; David Gill for his luminous photography; Janey Suthering who proved that making food look as good as it tastes is an art; and, last but by no means least, Anne Furniss, Paul Welti and Mary Evans for their considerable efforts in making this a very different book.

First published in the United States in 1994 by
The Overlook Press
Lewis Hollow Road
Woodstock, New York 12498

Text copyright © 1993 Alastair Little & Richard Whittington
Photography copyright © 1993 David Gill
Design and layout copyright © 1993 Conran Octopus

Library of Congress Cataloging-in-Publication Data

Little, Alastair
    Keep it simple : a fresh look at classic cooking/
Alastair Little, Richard Whittington.
p.   cm.
1. Cookery. I. Whittington, Richard.   II. title
TX714.L575   1994
641.5-dc20   94-19090
                                        CIP

Printed in Singapore
ISBN: 0-87951-547-3

Editor and Project Manager *Lewis Esson*
Editorial Director *Anne Furniss*
American Editor: *Norma MacMillan*
Art Director *Mary Evans*
Design *Paul Welti*
Editorial Assistant *Penny David*
Indexer *Hilary Bird*
Food for Photography *Alastair Little* with *Jane Suthering*
Styling *Sue Skeen*
Alastair Little Portraits *The Anthony Blake Photo Library*
Production *Julia Golding*

Typesetting *The R & B Partnership*
Color Separations *Chroma Graphics (Overseas) Pte Ltd*
Printing *Kim Hup Lee, Printing Co Pte Ltd Singapore*

Contents

Preface

Escoffier's famous dictum "*Faites simple*" is frequently quoted but mostly ignored by chefs, who are craftsmen rather than artists and understandably obsessed with technique. What does "keep it simple" mean? I do not intend to dwell in detail here on the philosophical complexity of an apparently bald statement, but some explanation is in order.

Simple food does not necessarily mean quick food or even easy food, though it can be both. Keeping it simple means being pure in effect – finding natural rhythms and balances, allowing food to taste of itself. Simple food does not hide behind a sauce of concealment, nor is it a contrived picture on a plate. It is a picture, but an honest one that has no pretensions. Being simple is not allowing the pursuit of change for its own sake, though it does mean the occasional introduction of new elements to give a freshness to dishes that have grown tired from popular abuse. Being simple certainly means ruthlessly cutting away inessentials to get at the essence of a dish. It is never tricky or crafty and it must never be deceitful.

All history is revisionist, and nowhere is this more true than in the writing of recipes. Look at the way classic dishes are redefined as tastes change. For there is nothing new in food; only altered perceptions, shades of redefinition, and rediscovery. I have been dubbed a "food fashion leader," a term and concept that I dislike, preferring to see the trends that develop as natural, no more than reflections of a continuous voyage of improvement. I go on learning and out of that process my cooking changes.

Professional cooking is full of tricks and short-cuts. In a busy restaurant, cooking to order is an intensely pressurized business, and the old adage "keep out of the kitchen if you can't stand the heat" refers to the pressure more than the temperature. It is something you either love or hate, but cooking in this way has nothing whatsoever to do with cooking at home. A chef chops at dazzling speed because he does not have the luxury of time to work in any other way. If the time is available, it does not matter that it takes you 15 minutes to slice a carrot into the finest *julienne*, for it is ultimately the quality of the end-result that counts, and not the rapidity of its execution.

When your days are spent in the preparation of food rather than eating it, the danger of technique-driven cooking is ever-present, for it is all too easy to take your eye off the ball and think that faultless execution of a complex procedure is an end in itself. Perhaps (wrongly) this may be the case in a catering college, but not – we hope – in either the restaurant or the domestic kitchen, where the taste of the food on the plate should always be the primary consideration.

The person eating the end-product is ultimately interested in taste first, texture second, and appearance third. Our enjoyment of a meal is affected by a number of other factors: the company we are in, the ambience of the dining room, the quality of the service, and the wines we drink. Are we hungry or have we lost our appetite? The person making the dishes for the customer to eat may think he shares the same priorities, but it is easy to slide into a diametrically opposite position. A good chef tastes, tastes, then tastes again; but this is not the same as sitting down to consume not one course but three. The sensory perceptions are different when dealing with a sip as opposed to a plateful. The strength of salt in a teaspoonful of food may seem right to somebody working in a kitchen (where you lose salt from the body with the intense heat and physical activity), but becomes unbearably dominant after several mouthfuls. This is an enduring problem, rarely mentioned but nonetheless profoundly significant.

Some tricks of the trade are worth adopting into the domestic environment, others can be ignored because they have been developed to alleviate certain problems peculiar to the restaurant kitchen. For example, the reason you rarely find a proper risotto in a restaurant is not because it is difficult to make, but because it demands at least 20 minutes of non-stop concentration by one person to prepare it correctly. Cooking one portion to order at a time is simply not viable, so you often find chefs make an enriched rice pilaf that can be held when finished, and then heated through with more butter and Parmesan stirred in at the last moment. The result is rich and tasty but not a risotto.

This book is really about the practical transfer of what I have learned in 20 years of

cooking professionally into a domestic context. Encouraged by the interest of several publishers and critics, I had thought about writing a cookbook for several years. When I sat down in the limited time I had free from the kitchen, however, the vision I thought I had clouded. Too many chefs were writing books in a spirit of mutual masturbation and I was determined that I would not go down the same depressing route. I wanted to write a book for people who cook at home for the love of it, yet this was something I had not done myself for a very long time. I knew I had something different to say, but wondered about how to say it in a way that made sense for the keen amateur. (I do not use that word in a pejorative way, for I believe that you can often eat better in a private house than in any restaurant, and that there are certain dishes that will always work better at home.)

I decided that the answer lay in working with somebody who had skills complementary to my own, but who understood better than I the realities of the domestic kitchen. Somebody who could say when something would not work and remind me of the limitations of domestic ovens and deep-fryers. Somebody who had read as many cookbooks as I had and shared my vision of what was good and what bad. Somebody I could cook with at home, reworking recipes to develop consistent and achievable results. Somebody who wrote for a living and cooked for joy. That somebody was Richard Whittington, and out of our collaboration a very different book has emerged from the one first mooted.

The experience of going back and looking again has revealed much received wisdom and given me time to reconsider a number of unwarranted assumptions. There has been a reverse migration out of the collaboration, which has put new dishes on the restaurant menu. It has also been fun, something the exigencies of professional cooking rarely allow. I hope that the result will give you some of the pleasure it has given us in creating it.

ALASTAIR LITTLE *February 1993*

Introduction

Shopping for Quality

Buying good food is the first step toward a delicious meal on the table, yet many people dread shopping, resignedly girding up their loins for the inevitable supermarket trek, which is undertaken ritualistically at the same time and place each week. A list is produced and ticked off as the shopping cart is pushed and shoved around the aisles of the huge store. It becomes a bad-tempered chore, encouraging tunnel vision and menu repetition.

In an ideal world we would shop every day, visiting the specialists who strive for perfection in their chosen area of food marketing: the fishmonger, the butcher, baker, greengrocer, specialty store, game dealer, and cheese-monger. However, this is unrealistic: Convenience is a fact of life, and I am not going to paint some idealized picture about food shopping, for reality dictates that we make compromises. Supermarkets are, after all, generally beneficial, but they are better at some things than others. They have excellent wine and the best possible range of dried and canned goods, as well as the essential tedium of household necessities. However, buying good fresh fish is difficult enough at a decent fishmonger, let alone at the shopping park giant.

It is a salutary thought that the fish caught in Penzance on Friday probably does not reach the city fishmonger until the following Tuesday or Wednesday. This is disgraceful, and it is not much better in towns nearer to the sea. When you think that we are an island with nowhere that distanced from the coast, then we compare unfavorably with the majority of Europe, for the provision of fresh fish here and the lack of choice is nothing short of scandalous for an island nation.

This is our own fault. We do not demand and, as with the politicians who represent us, we get precisely what we deserve. When we ask for something and are told that there is no call for it, we should not wipe our mouths and turn away, but make the point that we are demonstrating that the demand exists. If we manage to persuade a shopkeeper to buy a case of whatever it is, then we should be prepared to give our continued support by going back and buying that item on a regular basis. There is no point whining about poor quality and lack of service after the event. If we are only reactive, standards and choice do not improve as they should. Squeezed harder and harder by the retail combines, the small shopkeeper needs our support to survive, but that survival is not a right. It must be earned through exceptional service, and we must expect to pay a premium for it.

I am not suggesting you approach the retailer in a combative mood, but rather be prepared to negotiate. You want to develop a relationship with your supplier from which you will both benefit. Once the relationship is developed, the added value is immediately apparent. Many local stores will deliver. It may not say so on the window, but it could be practical for your telephoned order to be sent to your home. Once you trust the quality and the consistency, you do not have to go into the store and select for yourself. In the restaurant I do my ordering over the telephone: The idea that chefs are at the markets in the early hours prodding the vegetables is a myth. I work until after midnight, so please do not expect to find me engaged in jolly banter with my suppliers at five in the morning.

Quality of service is not selling at a discount, but rather about adding value. Harrods food halls in London have a reputation for excellent meat and fish, yet not everything costs more and all the cheap cuts are available. On a smaller scale, when you go to a local butcher (as opposed to a supermarket), do not give your business to a chain that offers everything pre-packed, but to a retailer who buys and hangs whole carcasses and deals with customers as individuals with different requirements.

Ideally, when you buy a chicken or duck it should not be drawn until the moment of purchase, because the flavor will be better and you want the giblets, if possible. If you want marrow bones – or fresh side pork or caul fat – then he should be happy to supply them, for he has bought a whole carcass and is in business to sell all of it, not just the prime cuts. Good meat needs to be hung for lengthy periods in cold storage to develop flavor and texture. This takes up space and demands refrigeration, and both cost money. As the meat matures, so it loses moisture and with that weight. If you understand this, then you begin to understand the price-to-quality relationship. But in every case you have to be ready to go in and fight the consumer's corner.

Fruit and vegetables are now flown in from all over the world and we are spoiled for choice, but whenever possible I still prefer to cook whatever is in season locally. The idea of eating strawberries out of season that come from thousands of miles away is frankly ridiculous. On the other hand it is nice to be able to have green beans, snow peas, and decent tomatoes throughout the year; but never lose sight of the seasons and the natural rhythms they impose on our diet.

Never buy too much of anything only to keep it in the refrigerator for days on end. The kind of refrigerator most people have at home may slow down decay, but the effect is limited. If you can shop twice a week rather than once, then do so.

Judging Quality and Freshness

How do you determine what is good and what bad, what is fresh and what past its best?

Fish is the easiest to assess. The scales will reflect light and be filmed with a slightly slimy sheen; the eyes will be clear and transparent, while the gills will be bright red. Above all, it will not smell even slightly fishy. If it does, then it is no longer fresh.

Meat is more difficult, but when buying beef look for a dark red color with the fat tinted with yellow. If it is too bright then the meat has not been hung for long enough. There is a pernicious practice in some supermarkets of lighting food displays in a way that intensifies the color, so be on your guard and examine the meat away from the cabinet.

When buying **lamb,** look for a deep pink color. If it has started to go gray and sweaty then it has been exposed to temperature fluctuation in its cut form and may have been in and out of the cold store for several days.

Pork, too, should be pink and firm to the touch with the fat very white. The trend toward producing leaner pigs is unfortunate for, without sufficient fat, pork will be dry and tasteless. On the subject of fat it is worth remembering that here is where the flavor of the meat resides. If you are worried about saturated fat, then eat smaller portions of meat rather than buy meat from which fat content has been deliberately reduced.

All meat should smell sweet when you buy it (though game has its own distinctive odor) – another reason for eschewing plastic-wrapped cuts that prevent you from smelling them.

Chickens should always be free-range for the best flavor and texture, quite apart from the nightmare of intensive-farming conditions, which should put anybody off eating poultry raised in this hellish way. When buying from a poultry dealer you can look at the feet and beak as indicators of quality, the former ideally being pliant and the latter shiny and dark (this applies equally to **turkeys, ducks, guinea fowl, and game birds**).

For the real flavor of true, grain-fattened, free-range chickens, try French imports like the quality-controlled *label rouge*, black-legged birds and *poulets de Bresse*. These are usually brought in for restaurants, but your butcher will find a wholesaler in the market who can supply them for his shop. He will have to buy a case of them (usually a minimum of eight), but if he is reluctant to risk the investment it is worth saying you will take them all if he finds he cannot sell them. They freeze well, or you can buy together with friends.

When buying **salted and smoked meat products**, always discuss with your butcher or meat man how salty the cure is, and buy unsmoked slab bacon or salt pork for cooking in stews or with beans.

white bread flour
self-rising flour
"OO" (double zero) pasta flour
potato flour/starch
semolina/farina
quick-rise dry yeast
spaghetti
lasagne
ditalini, macaroni, and other dried pasta
Basmati rice
risotto rice
couscous
different varieties of dried beans
dried chick peas (garbanzos)
lentils
polenta/cornmeal
dried mushrooms
granulated sugar
confectioners' sugar
golden raisins
extra virgin olive oil
sunflower oil
oriental sesame oil
chili oil
sherry vinegar
balsamic vinegar
white wine vinegar
red wine vinegar
rice vinegar
Colman's mustard powder
Dijon mustard
Lea & Perrins Worcestershire sauce
good-quality tomato ketchup
mushroom ketchup
Thai fish sauce
Kikkoman soy sauce
hoisin sauce
oyster sauce
mirin
sake
brandy
dry sherry
wasabi
five-spice powder
star anise
whole nutmegs
paprika
cumin seeds
coriander seeds
saffron threads
turmeric
dried chili flakes
freeze-dried oregano
freeze-dried bay leaves
Maldon sea salt

Stocking the pantry

The pantry should not be constructed to support a nuclear bunker, for many products deteriorate markedly with the passage of time. Olive oil, rice, and flour are cases in point. Items that I would always keep in stock are listed in the margin.

If you don't make stock all the time, then cans of **chicken bouillon** can be added to a list that grows alarmingly. That little lot will set you back a considerable sum but, of course, you do not have to have everything on it before you reach for a skillet. In an ideal world, though, your cupboards will groan with most of the items since all can be found in the recipes of this book.

Some of these items need to be considered in more detail:

Seasonings

The bald description **salt and pepper** in a recipe can cover a multitude of sins. At worst the salt will be mined and contain additives, while the pepper will be a moldy sneezing powder. I always use English Maldon sea salt, which is as fine as any from France, and recommend that you keep this on hand in your kitchen in a stoneware crock as this keeps it dry. Using this pure flake sea salt, you do not find any need for a salt mill, but at home you should use a mill to grind peppercorns fresh for every application.

In the restaurant kitchen the sheer scale of usage demands that both salt and pepper are on hand in open containers; however, the black peppercorns are ground fresh daily. We use an electric mill for this purpose and the pepper is not ground to a uniform dust, but to a point where both coarse husk elements and grains are produced. These are then put into a fine strainer and the coarser parts retained for pepper crusts, the *mignonette* pepper of dishes like *steak au poivre*.

White peppercorns are also available and are pungent in a slightly different way from black peppercorns, but their use is largely cosmetic – as in a white sauce to avoid any visible black flecks. This is not an issue with me. You can also buy multicolored peppercorns of green, white, black, and pink, though to be accurate the pink are not true peppercorns but a type of berry. They have a nice aromatic quality, but if you can produce freshly milled black peppercorns to order you really need not worry about the fancier variations.

Sichuan peppercorns are something very different and have no substitute. They are the red-brown dried berries of a plant found only in Sichuan province of western China.

Herbs and spices

We tend to use fresh herbs; in the case of **oregano,** however, dried is actually preferable and the freeze-dried version is best of all. Other herbs to keep dried (but used circumspectly) are **bay, sage, and thyme.** Otherwise I have yet to be convinced that even freeze-drying produces any other edible herbs.

Most aromatics (i.e. spices and other flavorings) are also used dried: **cinnamon, nutmeg,** and **vanilla beans**, for example. **Saffron**, the stamens of a species of crocus, is the most precious aromatic of all, and indispensable in *risotti*. Turmeric is not a substitute. Saffron is so expensive you are unlikely ever to store enough for it to get a chance to deteriorate.

As a general rule with all dried herbs and aromatics, however, keep them in small quantities. There is no scarier sight in the domestic kitchen than a wooden rack of herb and spice jars, their tops dusty with age and their contents of archaeological rather than culinary interest.

Oriental ingredients

Several Chinese products feature in my food. **Star anise** has an unmistakable licorice flavor and is essential when making a soy master stock (see page 20) for Chinese braising of meat dishes. **Five-spice powder** is incredibly aromatic and one of the tastes that shouts China. It contains star anise, cloves, fennel seeds, cinnamon, and Sichuan peppercorns.

Chili oil I make myself by putting sliced hot red chili peppers and seeds in a bottle of sunflower oil and leaving this at room temperature for a month. You can speed the process by putting the chilies in a saucepan with the oil and heating gently, then letting this cool before bottling. **Sesame oil** is a Chinese ingredient made from roasted white sesame seeds. The sesame oil that features in Middle Eastern food is made from cold pressed seeds and tastes rather different. **Chinese red vinegar** and **rice vinegar** have unique characteristics and are milder than their Western counterparts.

Black beans are salted fermented soy beans with ginger and you can buy them packed in brine or dried. Fry them with oil and garlic and you have instant black bean sauce. Though, as a fresh vegetable, **pak choi or bok choy** does not go in the pantry, I mention it here because of its Chinese origins. I love these greens, which you will find cropping up in my recipes at regular intervals. **Dried tangerine peel** is a favorite Oriental flavoring ingredient of mine. Ordinary fresh citrus peel will do at a pinch, but it won't impart the same sweet intensity.

Fish sauce is used in Cantonese cooking, but is more central to Thai and Vietnamese food. It is made from fermented small fish and squid and is powerful stuff. **Hoisin** is a sweet dark-brown sauce most familiar to us with Peking duck in pancakes. It is made from soy beans, garlic, chili, sesame, vinegar, sugar, and salt. **Oyster sauce** is an excellent sauce that can be used to give depth to meat as well as fish dishes. I like it in steak and kidney pudding. Take care when buying that you are getting a sauce made from oysters and not one that is "oyster-flavored."

Chinese cooking uses a lot of **soy sauce**, but I prefer the Japanese product to the Chinese. Soy sauce is a culinary gift of great value and is made from fermented soy beans and salt. I always use Kikkoman, which is the most expensive but quite simply the best. Nobody is paying me to say so, though I use so much of it I could perhaps have my jacket sponsored by the company with Kikkoman decals like the racing overalls of a Formula One driver.

I am also indebted to Japan for **wasabi**, the exuberantly hot green horseradish powder without which sashimi would be unthinkable. I also love shredded **daikon**, the large white radish that provides texture and garnish to so many dishes, though I have to confess it does not have much flavor. **Mirin** (a sweet rice wine) and **sake** (the rice wine) with a flavor reminiscent of sherry, both feature in Japanese braising. The intensely flavored **bonito flakes**, which can add flavor to many dishes as well as entertain guests by dancing in the serving dish (see page 123), are dried shavings of tuna flesh. The same dried fish forms the basis – with nori seaweed and soy sauce – of the tasty Japanse stock **dashi**, which is conveniently available in powdered form.

Nowadays, large supermarket chains carry an amazing range of such ingredients. Should you have difficulty in obtaining any, however, most big cities have excellent specialist Asian supermarkets and there are also good mail-order suppliers.

Anybody keen on Indian food and making their own **masalas**, the particular mixtures of spices that differentiate curried dishes, will also want to have a range of spices to do so: including mustard seed, fenugreek, cardamom, and tamarind. These and coriander, cumin, cloves, and peppercorns play distinctive roles in that complex and regional cuisine. As a general rule I would not use ready-made curry powders, just as I would not use pre-mixed *fines herbes* or bouquets garnis.

For no good reason I can think of, I have never cooked Indian food though I love to eat it. Perhaps it is because its flavors are so dominant they do not sit easily in an eclectic menu. Of course, many of the spices people think of as being Indian are found in other cuisines and some of them, like chilies, came originally from Mexico.

Italian influence

Analyzing where the contents of my pantry come from I find Italy more than any other country as major contributor. The influence of Italy on contemporary cooking is enormous. Fresh pasta and polenta are staples of today's global kitchen. Olive oil, seafood, and tomatoes, once typical of Southern Italy, are now the *lingua franca* of healthy eating from Canberra to California. Remove Italy from the culinary melting pot and you remove one of its most important constituents. Internationally the food of the South currently holds sway, but a richer balance is to be found in the *risotti* and *ragù* of the North, the cured pork products like salamis and the world-renowned Parma ham that are a gift to the instant first course, and Parmesan, one of the most wonderful cheeses ever created.

Cooking without good **olive oil** is to me unthinkable. In my childhood only the privileged few even knew about olive oil and most Italian restaurants in London cooked with mean substitutes. Today there has been a joyous revolution and even supermarkets and neighborhood stores offer consumers choice. You can find oils from France, Greece, and California, but for me the finest are Italian. Indeed, if one edible substance can be the essence of Italy then it is olive oil, of which the country produces about one-third of the world's output. It is difficult now to imagine cooking without it, never mind a salad dressed properly in anything else. However, the wide availability of first-pressing olive oil outside of Italy is a very recent phenomenon, as is an understanding of the different grades and styles.

Italy has six official grades starting with *olio di oliva extra virgine* – the cold first pressing from green (unripe) olives – down to *olio di oliva*, a blend of clarified olive pulp residue and a little virgin oil. The best is not to be wasted on cooking and the estate-bottled oils like Colonna are too expensive to abuse. The delicacy and intensity of the viscous green-colored, estate-specific oils make them a perfect dressing by themselves on hot or cold dishes.

Entire books have been written about olive oil. There are so many to try and enjoy that the only thing to say is explore them for yourself and use what suits your taste. Remember, however, that while it will not have an adverse effect, using extra virgin oil when frying is a waste. Always try and keep a slightly less fruity and more acid oil for cooking.

If tempted to buy a lot of good oil because of discount opportunities, also keep in mind that after 18 months or so it will begin to deteriorate, an inevitable process that can only be slowed by refrigeration. Low temperatures do no harm to the oil, though it will solidify. If this happens all you need to do is return it to room temperature and it will clear and become fluid again. This solidifying when cold is why olive oil does not make a good marinade in the refrigerator.

There are also olive oils that have been steeped with strongly flavored additives, like lemons and *porcini* mushrooms, to take on their flavor. The most successful of these is truffled oil, which uses *tartufi bianchi* to make it incredibly fragrant.

Another Italian original that has pride of place in my kitchen is **balsamic vinegar**, which comes from Modena and is made from grape juice infused with herbs. The vinegar is aged in oak casks with all the care usually reserved for noble wines. It is consequently expensive and you can find balsamic vinegars that cost more than a *grand cru* wine. I do not believe that the most expensive marks really live up to the price. Shop around and try different labels. Some supermarkets are importing in bulk and selling own-label balsamics that offer excellent value.

In many ways this is the ultimate vinegar, with an incredible fragrance and a complex and powerful taste that has a sweet, intense edge. A balsamic vinaigrette is the perfect foil for slightly bitter salad leaves like radicchio. A tablespoon in a slow-cooked stew works its own unique magic. Boiled meats like ox tongue benefit from having balsamic vinegar dripped over them. However, because this vinegar is so identifiably itself, you should exercise caution in its use: It is easy to overpower dishes with injudiciously large applications.

Italy also gives us the ingredients for fresh pasta and it is worth searching out the **"00" (double zero) extra fine flour**. I now also buy pasteurized eggs in cartons; these are brilliant in pasta dough. **Risotto rice** is an Italian Arborio or similar (Carnaroli, Vialone, Roma, and Riso Baldo, for example), which are available in some Italian grocers. Arborio is now widely obtainable in supermarkets, but try the others for comparison if you find them in the stores. This rice will cook in about 20 minutes, absorbing stock, wine (when used), and butter without going soft or breaking. You cannot substitute any other sort of rice. Do not buy risotto rice in large quantities because it goes stale.

No kitchen can function in my view without good quality **dried pasta**. The choice is so large it is bewildering, but I would always have fine spaghetti, a shell-type pasta like *conchiglie* for stuffing, a soup pasta like *ditalini*, and lasagne sheets. **Polenta**, yellow cornmeal for making the savory porridge that has become so popular, is a staple for any pantry.

Italy also provides me with most of my **dried legumes**. Great dishes can have humble origins: Pasta e Ceci (see page 144), *tonno con fagioli*, or just beans with nothing more than a lemon and oil dressing, perhaps a few leaves of basil to lift them or chives to add an edge. Dried beans actually contain more protein by weight than meat and there are many varieties to choose from. Borlotti, cannellini, and fagioli di Lamon are all delicious, each with its own slight but distinctive taste variation, and I would always keep several varieties in the cabinet.

Perhaps more than anywhere else in the world, Italy is the home of the **wild mushroom**, and mushroom gathering is a national pursuit. There is nothing like the freshly picked wild porcini (cèpe), but when dried they can still lift dishes that if made with cultivated mushrooms alone would be merely insipid. Soaked for half an hour in warm water and then carefully rinsed to remove any grit, only a very small amount will contribute a powerful flavor to a mushroom soup or risotto. The liquid in which the *porcini* have been soaked is also used as a flavoring stock, again after careful straining.

No discussion of Italian ingredients would be complete without some mention of the **white truffle** – the *tartufo bianco*, the most precious fungus of them all – for it is very rare and cannot be cultivated. I use them in the restaurant and, for a special treat, would certainly serve them at home. Mentioning them is about as close as most people will come to truffles at today's prices, which make them more expensive than gold. You have to ask whether any taste justifies such expense, but there are plenty who will say, "absolutely."

The description of food always risks hyperbole, but when one says that the scent of the truffle is extraordinary this is an understatement. Some find it repellent, and it was illegal to carry truffles in Italy by public transport – the smell is so all-pervading that if the airtight containers (in which it is essential to carry them) were to break, the odor would be overpowering. So strong is the smell that it can be used to advantage. Place a truffle with Arborio rice in a jar in the refrigerator and the flavor perfumes the grains. Truffles stored with whole raw eggs will empower them with some of their magic.

The best way to eat a white truffle is raw, sliced with a special truffle slicer in wafer-thin shavings over potatoes or eggs or risotto. The price of truffles has made them a much sought-after commodity and, as the three-month season begins in October, a clandestine trade takes place across borders with all the trappings of drug dealing. Chefs meet with underground suppliers in parking lots at dawn and transactions are strictly in cash. If you have never tasted white truffles, then there is a strong argument for doing so at least once. But beware: If you fall under their spell you could find yourself with a dangerously expensive habit to support.

In the Refrigerator and Freezer

Italy is also the producer of **Parmesan cheese**, another staple that features widely in my cooking and far and away the nicest of the so-called *grana* or grating cheeses that include grana padano. Parmigiano-Reggiano is the best of the Parmesan cheeses, which are produced only in the area around Parma, Reggio Emilia, and Modena, and are so valuable people actually trade in Parmesan futures.

It takes 686 quarts of cows' milk to make one 75-pound cheese. These great wheels of Parmesan are salted in a heavy brine for 25 days and are then shelved and turned daily for four months before being moved into cool, airy storage to mature for two to three years.

At this point, when the wheels are first broken open, you have the best eating cheese I know and you can buy it from good Italian grocers like Camisa in Soho, around the corner from my restaurant in London. The cheese is not cut, but levered away from the main block in chunks using a special sharp trowel.

It will keep well in the refrigerator, wrapped in foil. Grate it fresh for cooking or to strew over hot dishes or shave it in curls using a potato peeler to go on salads or cold meats.

A very different Italian cheese that demands careful shopping is **Mozzarella**. A mild-tasting, white, soft and fresh curd cheese, it is lightly brined, then packed in its own whey and keeps for up to two weeks in the refrigerator. In its truest form it is made from the milk of water buffalo, though these days it is more commonly made from cows' milk, in which case it should be called *fior de latte* and is, honestly, not as good. Italians are very competitive about Mozzarella, sneering at people who eat it when it is more than a day old. This is all very well if you live in Southern Italy near to a water buffalo farm, but rather difficult for the rest of us.

On the multinational semi-perishable front, I would always have unsalted Normandy butter, English farmhouse Cheddar, free-range eggs, plain yogurt, and crème fraîche in the refrigerator. Pancetta (Italian unsmoked bacon) and ham live here too and contribute richly to other dishes in disproportionately small amounts. When buying full-fat soft cheeses like Brie, do not refrigerate them but keep them somewhere cool and well-ventilated, for violent chiling will ruin the cheese.

Onions, potatoes, carrots, and garlic should be bought weekly, green vegetables and salad leaves only when you want to use them. If you have room, keep all of these in the refrigerator, but leave tomatoes out to ripen.

Freezers do not feature large in my life, but people get awfully attached to them and being rude about their contents can chill the atmosphere as well as the food. I hate those chest freezers in which people lose things, creating burial dumps of ancient stocks, ugly stews, and assorted bits of long-dead animals. For the record, freezers are not cryogenic environments, which allow items to be removed in a pristine condition at some date far in the future. Things still deteriorate, albeit more slowly, and you must be ruthless in using them or throw them out within weeks rather than months.

I would tend to limit freezer items to won ton skins, Chinese pancakes, sourdough bread, puff pastry, tart shells (see page 25), frozen raspberries, coffee beans, and lots and lots of ice. If you must, a bag of frozen leaf spinach and another of petite peas make emergency vegetable rations.

In summary, if I have one key message about shopping then it is not to buy food with rigid meal plans in mind. Be open and be flexible. Let the seasons be your guide and buy the fresh food that looks, smells, and feels the best. When it comes to your stored food, be tough: use it or lose it.

Basic Batterie de Cuisine checklist

Knives:
small vegetable knife
all-purpose knife with a curved blade
boning knife
ham slicing knife
carving knife
heavy chopper
strong serrated knife

Pots and Pans:

*several heavy steel saucepans with
    lids (including 3-quart, 2-quart, and
    1-quart capacities)*
*blanching basket (to match largest
    saucepan)*
2 large and heavy frying pans
iron omelet pan
iron crêpe pan
4 small blini pans
*3 heavy casserole dishes in different
    sizes (one large round and at least
    one large oval one)*
several heavy metal roasting pans
heavy ridged iron grill pan
several nonstick metal loaf pans
2 large colanders
*4-6 nonstick sheets (baking sheet,
    cookie sheet, jelly roll pan)*
*2 springform cake pans (8 inches and
    one 10 inches)*
2 metal tart molds of the same size

BELOW *Using a knife and skewer to
prepare Hasselback Potatoes, see page 132*

Batterie de Cuisine

Keen cooks need no encouragement to spend money on the utensils that allow them to indulge their passion to the full, but in reality one can get by with a fairly restricted *batterie de cuisine*. Indeed, analysis of what is used in people's kitchens usually reveals that only a small percentage of items are employed on a regular basis, with many things generally remaining in cabinets gathering dust. On this subject I recommend – if you have not done so already – the standard kitchen practice of hanging as many pots, pans, and utensils as possible from hooks. You can then see at a glance where things are and they are much easier to get at than when they are buried in a cabinet or drawers.

Let us begin with knives – surely the single most important purchase the cook is likely to make. I make very few references to knives in the book, since they play a part in virtually every cooking process. No reference has therefore been made to knives in the utensils section of each recipe unless a very specific type is required. Knives, too, are very personal things. Indeed, chefs do not share knives in the professional kitchen and everybody is encouraged to have their own set.

Restaurant kitchens often have knife grinders who call on a regular basis, but I have had bad experiences with them and always sharpen my own. A steel is used to keep an edge sharp, but knives do blunt past a point from which a steel cannot bring them back. For home use, I recommend the use of oil whetstones or water stones. I assume that you will keep your knives sharp, for blunt knives are useless and dangerous.

Good knives are expensive, so it is a good idea to buy one knife at a time, spending as you can afford. The knives listed in the margin I regard as the minimum requirement for the serious cook. Sharp knives should never be kept in a drawer, but on a magnetic knife rack or in a wooden knife block. This is for the sake of both the knives and the fingers of those reaching into drawers. While not essential, a tomato knife is a very handy addition since, surprisingly, tomatoes blunt the sharpest knives very quickly. Although not strictly speaking knives, I list a potato peeler here and a wheel pasta cutter. A good sturdy pair of scissors is a must and poultry shears are also very useful.

You need a variety of saucepans ranging from very small to very large and including 3-quart, 2-quart, and 1-quart capacities. I like heavy steel pans with lids. This is one area where it is difficult to have too many. One pan should be a large pan that you will probably use exclusively for blanching with a blanching basket of a matching size. A double-boiler is also a good idea, though not essential: You can put a bowl into a saucepan and achieve the same results.

Baking dishes are terribly important and you will need heavy casserole dishes in three sizes. I like Le Creuset best and suggest one large round enameled iron dish and at least one oval one for roasting meats and poultry. Standard metal roasting pans are always useful and a deep one can double as a water bath. The heavier they are the better for even heat distribution. Earthenware dishes are always useful, particularly those that will sustain high heat and double as serving dishes on the table.

Richard has a turntable in his kitchen that contains the following (all of which have been used in the preparation of the recipes in this book):

12 wooden spoons in different sizes
metal skimming spoon
3 pairs of tongs (one pair sprung)
slotted pancake turner
various rubber spatulas
long metal spatula
scissors
poultry shears
assorted cookie cutters
mandoline grater (invaluable, as an adjustable blade lets you select precisely the fineness of slice)
cheese grater
potato peeler
cheese slicer
pastry brushes in different sizes
metal chopsticks
larding needle
cherry/olive pitter
ice-cream/sorbet scoop
potato masher
bulb baster
rolling pin
nutcrackers

The domestic broiler is very good for cooking fish, but is not ideal for things like steaks. For this a heavy, ridged iron grill pan works best and has the benefit of searing instantly with an attractive striped patterning. When choosing a grill pan be sure the ridges are raised sufficiently from the base of the pan to ensure grilling rather than frying.

You will need large and heavy frying pans. Trying to cook without them would be very difficult. Nonstick pans are good news as long as they retain their nonstick qualities, but in my experience they do not. You should also have an iron omelette pan, an iron crêpe pan, and four small blini pans. A wok is a nice thing to have, though often impractical if you have an electric range. Their size also makes them greedy of limited cooking space. A lot of things that the Chinese cook in woks can be cooked in a heavy frying pan. I love to use steamers and prefer the inexpensive bamboo variety you can buy in Asian markets. They do not live long, however, and you may prefer to invest in the more expensive steel varieties.

Terrine molds are not essential, but they look nice on the table and the thickness of the china plays a functional part in distributing the heat evenly. They also come with lids. However, you can use nonstick metal loaf pans to good effect and I recommend you have some of these even if you never bake bread in them.

I could not imagine a kitchen without colanders. I use them constantly and think you should have at least two, and the larger they are the better.

Nonstick baking sheets, cookie sheets, and jelly roll pans are multi-purpose and I suggest you have at least four and as many as six. They are useful for so many things (the least of which are making cookies and jelly rolls): They are good for putting things in as you prepare them, for roasting in… for just about anything you care to mention. Supermarkets sell them, they are cheap, and you can never have too many.

You will want to have springform cake pans and metal tart molds with detachable bases. Start with two 8-inch and 10-inch ones.

Whisks crop up all the time and you will need at least two: one large, one small.

Strainers are vital and you will need to have at least three: conical, round, and fine. A tea strainer is also useful. A coarse woven metal "spider" for lifting things out of liquid is another helpful addition. Asian markets sell cheap ones to use when deep-frying. In these wonderfully inexpensive markets you can also find lots of other cheap kit for Japanese and Chinese cooking, like sudare mats for rolling sashimi, dipping bowls for serving sauce, chopsticks, and big serving platters.

You will want to have heavy-duty chopping boards. Professional kitchens no longer use wooden chopping and cutting boards, but they are still the nicest surfaces to work with and you can use them at home. Take obvious hygiene precautions, like not cutting the children's sandwiches on a board on which you have just dissected a raw chicken. A separate chopping board for garlic is a good idea. You only have to sit a sweet pastry tart on the spot where you have been smashing garlic to get that point forcefully.

Pasta should feature on a regular basis, so you will want to have some large basin-shaped dishes for tossing and serving it, which will also do just as well for tossing salads. You can never have too many bowls in the kitchen. Small and medium sizes are great for so many things. You will also find useful as many plastic boxes of different sizes with lids as your space allows, for refrigerator and cabinet storage.

In these pages you will find frequent references to salad spinners. I could not imagine kitchen life without one. I would also find life without a food processor and an electric mixer tricky since the two do different jobs. A portable electric mixer is always in use. If you want to make your own pasta, then you will also have to have a hand-cranked pasta machine. I also use a blender a lot; and a coffee grinder for grinding spices rather than coffee beans.

Nice but inessential are: an ice-cream freezer, a fish kettle, a pizza stone, and a barbecue. If you have the space, a second oven will make all the difference. The new generation of convection, broiler, and microwave combination ovens are brilliant.

This list stops here, but yours need not. For example, a decent espresso machine will not set you back too much. Your *batterie de cuisine* can grow as long as your pocket and space allow. You can, however, be ruthless and minimalist and cut back to the bone, for good cooks produce good food with even limited kit. Nevertheless, with developed skills the more functional equipment you have, the more you can achieve.

Mise en Place

This is a book that sets out to prove that a competent and enthusiastic amateur cook can achieve professional results at home. If I have something different from most chefs to offer you – in a world where chefs' books are published at an astonishing rate – then it is because I am largely self-taught and did much of my experimenting and growing up in the kitchen by reading what other people had written and then trying it for myself. Today I believe that the crossover between restaurant and domestic kitchens is becoming ever more significant.

The transfer of skills from the professional kitchen to the domestic is possible because, in reality, the cooking techniques are no different from those employed at home. What tends to be different is the restaurant approach, which is of necessity more structured and organized. At the heart of this is the practice of *mise en place*, literally "put in place," without which no restaurant kitchen could survive.

Mise en place means doing everything that can be done in advance. Its reality is entirely practical and the complexity of activity ranges from peeling potatoes to making sauces or, indeed, entire dishes. You do not wait until people sit down to eat before cooking the *daube*. The cold salmon must have been poached some time before and left to cool. This may seem to be stating the obvious, but you only have to think about some of the dinner parties you have attended to realize that this most basic principle is frequently ignored.

Consider a stir-fried dish. It takes two minutes to cook but the preparation – the careful shredding of the vegetables and laying out of the other ingredients so you can cook it that fast – may have taken an hour… an obvious example of *mise en place*. Not so obvious is the use of blanching, refreshing, and holding, standard professional techniques that fall within *mise en place* and can usefully be transferred into the domestic environment. For this reason, most of the recipes in this book have a Mise en Place section, listing all the pre-preparation which may be executed before tackling the actual method.

On the larger scale, if food can be cooked and reheated without detriment to its texture or flavor, then you do so. There is often confusion between the freshness of produce before it is cooked and the freshness of the finished dish. Throughout the book, wherever appropriate, I highlight Holding Points that indicate stages at which the preparation and/or cooking of a dish may be paused and ingredients kept in a cool place or refrigerated anything from a few hours to a day or so. The dish may then be finished fairly effortlessly and speedily while guests are gathering.

Mise en place is an approach to cooking where you think and plan ahead. In an area where the actual cooking and eating take place during relatively short periods, you adopt a long-term view. Gravlax (see page 74) takes five days to pickle, therefore you count back from the point when you intend to serve it and make your preparations accordingly. If everything is in its place before you begin – from having the colander strategically placed in the sink ready to drain the pasta, to having all the ingredients chopped or otherwise prepared before you begin cooking – then you are going to make the best use of the time available and you will constantly be reminded of what you need to do. If you invite your guests at 8:00 for 8:30, then you do not want to sit down at the table with everybody the worse for wear at 9:30. *Mise en place* will help you hit those critical deadlines. You will be more relaxed and the food will be better as a consequence.

Most of us cook because we want people to approve of what we have done. It gives us pleasure to give pleasure to others at our table, but this should not be showing off, and cooking at home should never be competitive. We all get things wrong and accidents happen, but they are more likely to happen to those who forget simplicity and approach dinner parties as if they are going for a guide rating, attempting over-complicated dishes they have never cooked before, and agonizing over last-minute and unnecessarily fussy presentation.

Mise en place is absolutely central to everything you can achieve in the kitchen and is the single most important advice I can offer you. Embrace it and your horizons will broaden, there will be more hours in the kitchen day, and your execution will improve.

Basic Recipes & Techniques

For some time I resisted having such a section in this book, but as time went on it became obvious that it would be much easier – good *mise en place* – for the reader to have all those things that cropped up in recipe after recipe assembled together in one identifiable place.

STOCKS

No cook should attempt to function without good stocks. It is in classic French cooking that we find the art of stock-making at its most advanced. Without a range of stocks there could be none of the sauces associated with *grande cuisine* – *glace de viande, demi-glace, chasseur, duxelles, espagnole, gibier, jus de veau lié, poivrade, suprême,* and *velouté.* Fish sauces, e.g. *fumet de poisson,* are all based on fish bones and trimmings.

The base stocks are called *fonds: brun,* made from beef, veal, and raw ham; *gibier,* a selection of game; *blanc,* veal and chicken. In the classic tradition, stocks are elevated works that call for expensive ingredients. According to Escoffier a *fond blanc* needs four raw chicken carcasses and $3^1/2$ pounds of veal shank to yield just $1^1/2$ quarts of stock.

At this point most people laugh and reach for a bouillon cube, which is unfortunate because excellent stocks can be made for pennies. Your butcher will give you beef bones and chicken carcasses and although professional kitchens use raw ingredients for stock-making, no such constraints need to be imposed on the private cook. Every time you roast a chicken you have the wherewithal to make a chicken stock, particularly if you always buy free-range birds, which have a superior flavor. Vegetables and herbs play an important part in all stock-making, with onion, carrots, leeks, and celery taking key roles.

Stock-making demands discipline and an understanding of how different flavors combine and contribute to the end result. Stock pots are not receptacles for kitchen garbage, nor should the stock pot be left to simmer endlessly on the range.

The following recipes are not cast in stone. What you have on hand will provide acceptable variations on a theme.

Fond Brun

If you have a roast cut on the bone, like rib of beef, then you have an excellent basis for a stock to make the next day. When buying the roast, ask your butcher for some marrow bones or any beef or veal bones he has on hand. If the bones are large, ask him to saw them into smallish pieces. This recipe makes about $2^1/2$ quarts.

Cooking

Preheat the oven to 450°F. Put the bones in a roasting pan and roast them until they brown and fat runs out.

Peel and coarsely chop the onion and carrots and fry them in some beef drippings (or the fat that has exuded from the bones) until nicely browned.

Put all the browned bones and vegetables in a large pan with $4^1/2$ quarts of cold water and bring to a boil. As scum comes to the surface, lower the heat and skim carefully.

After the first skimming, throw in a handful of ice cubes or pour in $1^1/4$ cups of cold water, bring back to a boil, and skim again. Repeat this 3 times.

Add the remaining ingredients, lower the heat, and simmer uncovered for at least 8 hours, and as long as 12. It must not boil or the glue element will be extracted from the bones, which will cloud the stock and give it an unacceptably bony flavor.

Ingredients

$4^1/2$ pounds beef bones or a mixture of beef and veal bones

1 large onion

6 ounces carrots

2 bay leaves

bunch of parsley

stalk of celery

1 thick slice of unsmoked bacon

10 whole peppercorns

Utensils

roasting pan

frying pan

stock pot

strainer

saucepan

Obviously there will be evaporation, so add more water from time to time. However, experience shows that after skimming and once you have achieved the barest simmer (steam coming off the surface, but no bubbles rising) this amount of stock can be left to cook overnight without drying out and burning. (Before doing so, however, it is a good idea to make the stock for the first time during the day, then you can work out whether your range will let you leave a pot simmering all night without your sitting bolt upright in the early hours wondering whether you can smell something burning.)

Strain the stock into another saucepan and let it cool. Refrigerate once cool. The stock will then gel and any remaining fat will solidify on the surface – this can then be removed before use.

The stock will keep indefinitely if boiled up twice a week. It also freezes well: Try reducing it down by about half and then freezing it in ice-cube trays; the cubes can then conveniently be used 1 or 2 at a time.

Fond Blanc (Chicken Stock)

Traditionally, fond blanc *is made of near equal weights of chicken carcasses and veal shank; but forget the veal, chicken stock is what you are after – fond blanc de volaille. If you are roasting a bird, then reserve the giblets and cut off the wing tips and pope's nose first. These will provide the raw element of your stock ingredients. This recipe makes about 7 cups.*

Poaching a whole chicken as for Chicken Broth with Parsley Pasta (see page 72) will, of course, give you a perfect chicken stock, as will a classic poule au pot, *while Bollito Misto (see page 172) will give you the best veal stock of all.*

Cooking

Once you have carved the bird, chop the carcass and put it with the giblets and other raw ingredients in a large saucepan. Cover with cold water.

Bring to a boil and skim carefully, lowering the heat to a bare simmer. Add the remaining ingredients and simmer 3 or 4 hours. Strain into another saucepan and reduce to about 7 cups. The stock will keep indefinitely if boiled up twice a week. It also freezes well.

Fumet de Poisson (Fish Stock)

Unlike meat-based stocks, fish stock is never simmered more than half an hour, otherwise the fish bones break down and make the stock bitter. The ingredients are never expensive, but should be heads, trimmings, and bones of white fish like cod, whiting, or flounder, or a mixture. Any fishmonger will be pleased to give you these. This recipe makes about 1 1/2 quarts.

Cooking

Put all the ingredients except the lemon juice into a saucepan together with 1 1/2 quarts of water. Bring to a boil and skim.

Lower the heat and simmer 20 minutes. Add the lemon juice and continue to simmer 10 minutes longer. Strain and use at once, or let cool and then refrigerate for no more than 1 day.

Ingredients

giblets, trimmings, and carcass from 1
    roaster chicken
2 or 3 carrots
1 leek
1 onion
1 celery stalk
bouquet garni of thyme, bay, and
    tarragon

Utensils

2 large saucepans
strainer

Ingredients

3 1/2 pounds fish trimmings and bones
1 onion
2 ounces mushroom stems
10 parsley stems
1/2 bottle (about 1 1/2 cups) of dry white
    wine
6 peppercorns
juice of 1/2 lemon

Utensils

large saucepan
strainer

Ingredients

2¹/₂ cups good soy sauce
1¹/₄ cups sake
1¹/₄ cups mirin
6 star anise
2 ounces fresh gingerroot
2 garlic cloves
1 large hot red chili pepper
4 pieces of dried tangerine peel

Utensils

large saucepan
strainer

Ingredients

1 or 2 stalks of celery
2 or 3 carrots
1 onion
2 tablespoons sunflower oil
1 bay leaf
1 glass (²/₃ cup) of white wine
1 can of chicken bouillon

Utensils

large saucepan
strainer

Soy Master Stock

This delicious, aromatic, and easy-to-make stock is used for Chinese-style braising of beef and chicken. The quantities given here make about 2¹/₂ quarts.

Japanese Kikkoman soy sauce is the best, but it is too expensive for use in such quantity. Buy an imported Chinese brand from an Asian market where they sell soy sauce in quart bottles (and larger) very cheaply. Sake is a dry rice wine rather like sherry, while mirin is a sweeter rice wine; both are Japanese but used widely in Chinese cooking and widely available in Asian markets, as are star anise and dried tangerine peel.

Cooking

Put all the ingredients into the saucepan with 5 cups of water and bring to a boil. Lower the heat and simmer 30 minutes.

The soy master stock will keep in the refrigerator indefinitely if you strain it, store in a clean lidded container, and remember to boil it up twice a week.

Quick Stock

But what if you have no chicken stock in the refrigerator? Then substitute a light stock based on a can of chicken bouillon.

This recipe makes about 1 quart.

Mise en Place

Coarsely chop the vegetables. Heat some sunflower oil in a saucepan, and brown the vegetables and bay leaf.

Add the wine and bubble the mixture for a minute.

Put the canned bouillon in a large measure and add enough water to make slightly more than 1 quart of liquid (to allow for evaporation). Add to the saucepan.

Bring to a boil, lower the heat, and simmer half an hour. Beware of the salt content of canned bouillon, which tends to be high. Experience with your preferred brand will tell you whether or not you should dilute to taste. After half an hour, strain and return to the saucepan.

If you have any scraps of cooked chicken or the carcass of a previously roasted chicken lying about, then add to the stock. No need to skim, but extend the cooking time to an hour from the point when the liquid comes to a boil.

Ingredients

1 onion
1 carrot
1 stalk of celery
4 pounds lamb bones, chopped small
bay leaf
1 glass ($^2/_3$ cup) of dry white wine

Utensils

roasting pan
slotted spoon
wooden spoon
strainer
stock pot

Ingredients

2 carrots
1 stalk of celery
2 onions
2 pounds fish trimmings
1 bottle (75 cl) dry white wine
    (it doesn't matter if it has gone
    vinegary)
2 tablespoons white wine vinegar
bay leaf or kaffir lime leaf
few parsley stems
12 black peppercorns
1 tablespoon sea salt

Utensils

*fish kettle or pan large enough to hold
    the whole fish (e.g. big Le Creuset
    casserole)*
small saucepan
fine strainer

Lamb Stock

This rich stock has such a distinctive flavor that it can only really ever be used with lamb dishes. This recipe makes about 5 cups.

Mise en Place

Preheat the oven to its highest setting • Chop the vegetables into a mirepoix.

Cooking

Brown the lamb bones and vegetable mirepoix with the bay leaf in a roasting pan, turning occasionally and carefully to avoid splashing hot fat on yourself. When done, the bones will be a golden brown and there will be a pool of hot fat in which the lamb bones are caramelizing. Take out of the oven and let sit 5 minutes to cool slightly.

With a slotted spoon, transfer the bones and vegetables to a stock pot. Pour the fat away and deglaze the roasting pan with the wine and an equal quantity of water (boil vigorously, scraping with a wooden spoon until all the caramelized elements are incorporated). Pour the contents of the pan over the bones and vegetables.

Add just enough water to cover (for a quick stock like this, which is almost a gravy in itself, be careful not to overfill the pot – the water level should barely cover the bones). There will be an immediate precipitation of discernible fat on the surface. Skim this off, then bring to a boil, simmer, and skim again.

Let simmer 1 $^1/_2$ hours. During simmering, small amounts of cold water or handfuls of ice cubes can be added to encourage more fat to rise to the top for skimming. Strain into another saucepan and reduce if necessary.

This stock will keep indefinitely if boiled up twice a week, and also freezes well.

Court Bouillon

This aromatic liquid is mainly used for the poaching of fish and seafood.

Mise en Place

Prepare the vegetables: Peel the carrots and cut them into rounds about $^1/_8$-inch thick. Slice the celery stalk into thin pieces. Peel and finely slice the onions.

Cooking

Put all the chopped vegetables and the remaining ingredients into the fish kettle or large pan. Add 2 $^1/_2$ quarts of water, place over medium heat, and bring to a simmer (if using a fish kettle use two burners). Simmer for 20 minutes.

Remove from the heat and let cool to room temperature. Adjust the seasoning, if necessary. The liquid should be acid and salty; adjust with more salt and vinegar if necessary.

SAUCES

Sauces are so important to so many dishes that, in general, I have left them with the appropriate recipe. Some are used so often, however, or are so classic and lend themselves to such wide use that they are given here for easy reference.

Vinaigrette

Ingredients

1 tablespoon wine vinegar
$^1/_2$ teaspoon salt
$^1/_2$ teaspoon pepper
4–5 tablespoons extra virgin olive oil

A vinaigrette is the simplest salad dressing of all and nothing can improve on its effect. The ingredients must be of the best quality, as a vinaigrette is not an emulsified sauce but a light amalgamation in which the elements cling only briefly together. Always make vinaigrette fresh for every salad: The habit of making a dressing and keeping it for long periods in a bottle is abhorrent.

A classic vinaigrette contains only wine vinegar, extra virgin olive oil, sea salt, and freshly ground black pepper. The variations in flavor come from the type of vinegar used and the ratio of vinegar to oil (I use one part vinegar to four or five of oil). Experiment with different vinegars in combination with different salad leaves.

Preparation

In the salad bowl put the vinegar, salt, and pepper and stir vigorously with a wooden spoon until the salt has dissolved. Always do this before adding the oil. Now beat in the oil until the elements have combined.

If you leave it to sit too long it will separate, so stir again just before adding the leaves. Always toss the salad to coat each leaf with a thin film of vinaigrette only just before eating.

If you have made the right amount of vinaigrette for the salad, none will be left in the bottom of the bowl, but every leaf will be dressed.

Mayonnaise

Ingredients

2 large egg yolks
1 teaspoon salt
$^1/_2$ teaspoon pepper
1 $^1/_4$ cups sunflower oil
2 teaspoons Dijon mustard
juice of 1 lemon
some boiled water, still warm
1 $^1/_4$ cups extra virgin olive oil

Utensils

portable electric mixer
bowl

There is something magical about mayonnaise. When you look at the ingredients before making it – egg yolks, olive oil, lemon juice or wine vinegar, salt… and pepper… perhaps a little mustard, a spoonful or two of water – out of their amalgamation comes one of the great cold sauces, a flavor without which summer would be incomplete.

There are purists who claim that true mayonnaise must be made by hand in a stone mortar with a wooden spoon. This is time-consuming and the mayonnaise is prone to separation during the early stages. True, food-processor mayonnaise is a poor imitation of the real thing; but mayonnaise made using a portable electric mixer is excellent, and I would challenge anybody to tell the difference between one made in minutes using a mixer and one made by hand. I accept that, given the time, there is an almost sensuous pleasure to be had from making mayonnaise the old-fashioned way: It is an elemental process that is deeply satisfying. However, I do not have the half-hour needed to indulge myself in this way.

Classic mayonnaise is made using only good-quality olive oil, but I find it tastes far too strong and prefer to use a combination of equal quantities of extra virgin olive oil and sunflower oil. The quantities given here are for $2^1/_2$ cups of mayonnaise. In fact, two egg yolks will hold more oil than that, but the color is important.

Eggs should not be used straight from the refrigerator. Take care, however, that the ingredients are not too warm, or you will have difficulty getting the emulsion to bind. Should it separate, just put another egg yolk into a second bowl and beat the curdled mixture into it, starting with a few drips until it holds and then pouring more generously.

Preparation

Separate the eggs and put the yolks into the bowl with the salt and pepper. At full speed, beat the yolks and begin adding the sunflower oil a few drops at a time, until it starts to thicken.

Then start to pour the oil in a thin stream until all the sunflower oil is incorporated. The mixture will now be very thick, so beat in the mustard and half the lemon juice before adding the olive oil. If still too thick, add the rest of the lemon juice and some boiled water, a tablespoon at a time. When you have incorporated all the oil, taste and add more salt and pepper if needed. The final consistency should be that of heavy whipping cream.

The mayonnaise will keep in an airtight jar in the refrigerator without deterioration for 48 hours. In reality it will keep much longer, but there is nothing to be gained from this and the raw egg element suggests that speedy consumption is desirable.

Ingredients

3 shallots
2 sticks (1 cup) unsalted butter
¼ cup Muscadet or other very dry white
    wine
¼ cup white wine vinegar
½ teaspoon salt

Utensils

heavy saucepan
wire whisk

Beurre Blanc

For no good reason this has become a "restaurant sauce" and has taken on mythical degrees of difficulty in the popular culinary imagination. It is conceptually a difficult construction only because we doubt that it can work: a small reduction of shallots, wine vinegar, and white wine into which a lot of unsalted butter is whisked to produce a creamy emulsion. People get nervous… where is the egg yolk or the flour, they wonder? In reality, ½ pound of butter is a fairly restrained volume to incorporate: Once started the emulsion will take much more. The stopping point is therefore an emotional rather than a chemical one.

Brittany claims this sauce for its own, though you will find it proclaimed as a local specialty throughout the Loire Valley. It goes beautifully with any simply cooked fish, whether poached or pan-fried. Muscadet works particularly well both in the sauce and to drink with the finished dish, while Brittany has no similar wine to offer. Wherever it originated, it can be yours.

Mise en place

Peel and mince the shallots • Cut the chilled butter into 8 pieces.

Cooking

Put the minced shallots into the saucepan with the wine, vinegar, and salt. Bring to a fast boil, then reduce to a simmer, stirring from time to time until all you have left is a mush of shallots and a film of residual liquid.

Take off the heat for a minute to let the base cool a little. Then put in one piece of the butter, place over low heat, and whisk vigorously until they combine and there is no visible element of butter.

Add the rest of the butter a piece at a time, adding the next piece as the last disappears into the sauce. After the last piece is just incorporated, remove from the heat and continue to whisk 5-10 seconds. It will be creamy with a discernible body. Serve immediately.

With practice you will find you can add much larger pieces of butter after the first lump has emulsified. The first time you cook it, however, go more slowly and remember always to keep the heat under the pan low.

Pesto

Fresh basil is a joyous herb that has a powerful smell but does not taste pungent. Our new-found ability to buy basil most of the year is a great bonus. Obviously it is cheaper in the summer, when it is not flown in from such great distances, but is still too expensive from most food markets. Basil is a great addition to most tomato dishes.

Basil leaves should always be torn rather than chopped, as they bruise and discolor very easily. Carefully stored in a plastic bag, fresh basil will keep in the refrigerator for up to 3 days, but throw it away as soon as it starts to discolor. Old basil is foul basil, and will make you think of tom cats in a most unpleasant fashion.

One of the best ways of serving basil is in pesto — one of the great pasta sauces, made from basil, Parmesan, and pine nuts pounded together. (Incidentally, pesto should always be served with dried rather than fresh pasta.) When making pesto, use only the freshest of basil and the best Parmesan cheese you can get hold of. Never, under any circumstances, use ready-grated Parmesan cheese bought in a package or drum. One shudders to think what pesto made from old basil and ready-ground Parmesan cheese would taste like.

Don't worry if you don't use all the pesto you make immediately; it is a very versatile sauce with many other uses. Try adding it to mashed potatoes to give them a different dimension, or bake some on halved tomatoes in the oven with fresh bread crumbs to make a light and delicious gratin.

Pesto will also keep in a canning jar in the refrigerator at least one month without deterioration, provided the surface of the pesto is covered with a thin film of olive oil and the jar has been properly sterilized. (A dishwasher is sterilizer enough, though don't put the rubber ring in or it will stretch — wash it separately by hand). Also, pack the pesto down with the back of a

Ingredients

2 large bunches of basil (enough to fill
 the processor loosely before the
 leaves are chopped)
5 1/2 ounces best Reggiano Parmesan
 cheese (in a piece)
1 cup pine nuts
2 large garlic cloves
about 1 1/4 cups extra virgin olive oil
sea salt and pepper

Utensils

food processor
clean jar(s) for storage

clean metal spoon to make sure there are no air pockets.

Try the same technique using fresh mint leaves to replace the basil. This makes a fabulous sauce to accompany cold roast lamb or as a dressing for boiled new potatoes.

Mise en Place

Rinse the basil very carefully and gently. Then dry it in a salad spinner or pat dry gently with paper towels. (If the leaves are very fresh, there is no need to wash them, but this is a matter for personal preference.) Tear the leaves away from the stems and discard the stems • Break the cheese into pieces that will go down the feed tube of the food processor • Put all the ingredients next to the processor.

Preparation

Turn on the machine and process the cheese, dropping in one piece at a time until it has a uniform texture about the size of coarse bread crumbs. Do not over-process at this point because there should still texturally be an identifiable cheese element in the finished sauce.

Add the pine nuts and garlic and process again, briefly. Add the basil and process briefly. Then, with the machine still running, add the olive oil in a thin stream until you have a coarse paste.

Taste and season. Process once more, adding the remaining oil until you have a texture that is spoonable but quite runny. Check the seasoning one last time and add a little more salt if you think the extra oil has cut the edge.

Serve at once with hot pasta (spaghetti is perfect), or store in the refrigerator as described, covered with olive oil in sterilized jars. Once these are opened, use within 2 or 3 days.

DOUGHS & PASTRIES

Pasta

Two hundred years ago pasta became a popular everyday food in Naples, which to this day remains the center of excellence for dried pasta – most notably, spaghetti. Dried pasta is not inferior to fresh; indeed some pasta, like spaghetti, *penne,* and *ditalini,* should always be dry. Currently, however, fresh pasta is in vogue and a universal expectation in good restaurants. Recent times have seen freshly made ravioli stuffed with exotic and expensive ingredients like langoustine and truffles as the signature dishes of many world-class chefs.

The main thing about pasta is that it is a great leveler and often the simplest pasta sauce is the most delicious. Fresh tagliatelle, piping hot, tossed with a little butter till it glistens, and then served with Reggiano Parmesan cheese grated from a piece of the whole cheese is nothing short of sensational. Pasta has substance and flavor but does not dominate, providing the perfect stage on which a sauce can perform to best advantage. It is the food of the poor and of the rich. Once it was a phenomenon of Southern Italy; today it has conquered the world.

If you have never considered making your own pasta, then now is the time to begin. Ideally you will buy a pasta machine – once a piece of kitchen exotica, but now widely available and not expensive. There are electric machines on the market, but these *are* expensive, so start with a hand-cranked machine.

Once you get the knack of feeding the dough through the rollers, your family and friends may begin to wish you had not become quite such an enthusiast, as fresh pasta inevitably crops up with great frequency once you find out how easy it is to make. Here are two recipes: One uses a food processor, the other is mixed by hand. With the latter you may be surprised by the quantity of eggs.

If you can find it, Italian "00" (double zero) grade extra fine flour is the one to use; otherwise use all-purpose flour from any supermarket. Bread flour is too difficult to work with, while durum flour needs factory equipment and is out of the question in the domestic environment.

Basic Homemade Pasta

This basic homemade pasta dough (Pasta Fatta in Casa) is inexpensive and suitable for a wide range of purposes. As it is easy to handle and dries quickly, it is particularly suitable for ravioli.

Mise en Place

Sift the flour and put it into the processor. Add the eggs and process until it just starts to form into a ball.

Shake a little flour on a work surface and knead the ball of dough by hand for 5 minutes or so until it is smooth and elastic, adding a little more flour if it sticks. Try kneading it 100 times – experience shows this takes 8 minutes and is very good exercise for the pectorals.

Wrap the dough in plastic wrap and let it rest in a cool place for at least 1 hour or up to 3, but no longer.

Rich Pasta Dough

This dough is used for pappardelle *and rich* ravioli *or* tortellini, *but it also makes the most sensational* tagliatelle *for use in recipes where the pasta is the main point.*

It is obviously expensive to make, but dries well. So if you have some left over dry it by simply hanging it over a broom handle or drying rack for an hour. It will then keep a week or so in the refrigerator. What you will have re-created will be the finest quality commercial egg pasta.

Mise en Place

Sift the flour into a bowl and add the egg yolks and the whole egg. Mix in with a fork until it starts to gather into a loose mound. It will seem very dry at this point.

Transfer to a work surface (do not flour the surface) and knead about 10 minutes. This is hard work but must be done by hand. A food processor will not do the job and you will get much satisfaction from transforming flour and eggs into something delicious with your hands, an elemental sense of achievement such as a potter must feel on throwing the first pot.

If, after 4 minutes, the dough shows no sign of forming a ball, sprinkle it carefully with 1 tablespoon of water. (Egg yolks have almost no liquid and vary in size even within a standard grade). When the dough is ready it will be smooth, with a yellow satin sheen to the surface.

Wrap it tightly in plastic wrap and let it rest it in the refrigerator 1 hour before use.

Pâte Sucrée Tart Shell

These delicious crisp, sweet pastry shells are useful for all sorts of fruit tarts. The quantities given make 3 shells, so it is a good idea to make extra and freeze them. They cook beautifully straight from the freezer.

Mise en Place

Dice the butter into small cubes.

Preparation

Put the sugar, almonds, and flour into a food processor and turn on at full speed for a few seconds. Add the butter dice and work again until just blended in. The mixture will resemble fine bread crumbs.

Add the egg and extra yolks, the lemon zest, rum, and a minute pinch of salt and work again until the pastry balls.

Scrape this out onto a sheet of plastic wrap and roll up the wrap to form the dough into a cylinder with a diameter of about 2 inches. Chill at least 2 hours. (Because of the high butter content this pastry can be kept in the refrigerator for a week and freezes well.)

Ingredients
3¹/₂ cups flour (see previous page)
5 large eggs

Utensils
flour sifter
food processor

Ingredients
3¹/₂ cups flour (see previous page)
15 egg yolks, plus 1 whole egg

Utensils
flour sifter
large bowl

Ingredients
2¹/₂ sticks (¹/₄ cups) butter
³/₄ cup sugar
1 cup ground almonds
3¹/₂ cups flour
1 whole egg, plus 2 extra yolks
¹/₂ teaspoon grated lemon zest
1 teaspoon rum
pinch of salt

Utensils
food processor
spatula
three 10-inch loose-bottomed metal tart molds

The dough is impossible to roll out, so cut thin disks off the end of the cylinder and overlap them slightly to cover the bottom and sides of each tart mold, pushing down with your fingers to make as even a pastry shell as possible. It should be slightly more solid around the edges and pushed right up to the top as it will shrink slightly as it bakes. Be careful to press into the corners, so there is no air between the mold and the pastry.

OTHER USEFUL TECHNIQUES

Blanching Vegetables

Vegetables are blanched for several different reasons – mostly either to part-cook because the ultimate cooking technique would otherwise take too long (or fail) to make them tender, or to cook the vegetables ahead of time.

Certain vegetables definitely benefit from a brief blanching process before being incorporated into dishes. For example, fine sliced leeks blanched for 1 minute, refreshed, and then gently stewed with butter 5 minutes are better than leeks cooked without the preliminary blanching. Large green peas also benefit from the same procedure, though they need longer cooking in the butter. Also, should you be faced with the ghastly prospect of peeling pearl onions in large quantities, try blanching them 60 seconds before refreshing and then peeling. This simplifies matters enormously and stops you crying.

The technique of blanching vegetables briefly in boiling salted water and then refreshing them in ice water to stop the cooking process is central to the mise en place in the professional kitchen. The vegetables are then held until needed in the refrigerator. All that needs to be done to bring those vegetables back to pristine, just-cooked perfection is to dip them again in boiling water for a few seconds. It is a technique that buys you time, keeps the range clear, and helps you get food on the table on time.

Most green vegetables and small root vegetables, like new season's bunched carrots, are best cooked by blanching. The principle is to use lots of fast-boiling water which has been quite heavily salted. What does "heavily salted" mean precisely? Like many chefs I am over-fond of salt and in an ever more nitrophobic world I am aware that this can cause problems. However, blanching involves a brief exposure to salt followed by a plunge in cold unsalted water to refresh, which, coincidentally, removes much of the salt. Salt impacts on the color – keeping green vegetables green – and helps retain the nutrients. I would say, therefore, that salting at 1 tablespoon for every 1 quart is about right.

Method

Three-quarters fill the pan with cold water. Cover with a lid and bring to a fast, rolling boil (this is critically important as blanching is not poaching – it is a short and very fast process, which preserves the freshness of the vegetables).

Put the vegetables into the basket and lower into the fast-boiling water for the requisite time (see left). Do not cover.

When done, immediately remove the vegetables and plunge them straight into the bowl of ice water. Leave until cold, then drain (do not leave in the water for too long as this leaches out flavor).

You can blanch up to 1 pound of vegetables at a time. If you try more than this amount, you will lower the temperature of the boiling water sufficiently to slow the cooking process and this will cause the vegetables to lose color and absorb too much salt.

Utensils

large pot (minimum 3-quart)
blanching basket (pasta basket) or spider
large bowl of cold water

Blanching times

Different vegetables have different cooking times and it is difficult to be absolutely precise, but here are some guidelines:

spinach: 60 seconds
hearty greens (collards): 2 minutes
Savoy cabbage (inside leaves): 2 minutes; (outer leaves): 5 minutes
broccoli florets: 3 minutes (less salt is important here)
cauliflower florets: 3 minutes (less salt is important here)
asparagus (thin): 3 minutes; (fat): 5 minutes
thin green beans: 4 minutes
green beans (sliced): 3 minutes
fresh fava beans (unpeeled): 3 minutes
snow peas: 2 minutes
green peas (petite peas): 2 minutes
scallions (whole): 2 minutes
baby leeks: 3–4 minutes
bunched carrots: 4–10 minutes (depending on size)
new potatoes: 10–15 minutes (depending on size)
baby beets: 10 minutes
turnips: 10 minutes

Making Risotto

Risotto is the stuff of which myths are made. The way some people go on about it you would think this a very witches' brew of complexity, involving left-hand stirring counterclockwise in a rare copper pan. Do not let such nonsense put you off. Any mystique can be cheerfully bundled to one side, for making a perfect risotto does not take special skill, simply an understanding of the processes involved and an equally clear understanding of what a risotto is not. As there are several risotto recipes in this book, I thought it would be useful to give here a very detailed treatment of the procedures and ingredients involved.

There are a number of criteria that define a true risotto. Firstly, the rice must be an Italian Arborio or similar (see page 12). The cooking process is fixed too. Butter is melted in a heavy pan, and chopped onion is gently fried in it until translucent. The dry (unrinsed) rice is then sautéed over low heat until it is shining and slightly translucent. As you do this you can hear the rice "clicking" against the side of the pan. It is important not to use too high a heat because the butter must not burn. High heat can also make the rice go hard. Butter is invariably used and not olive oil, since the provenance of this dish is essentially Northern Italian, but olive oil is more appropriate for a fish or seafood risotto, a Southern influence.

Next, simmering stock is added, a ladleful at a time, and stirred in until it is absorbed. You must stir constantly, being careful to work the wooden spoon against the outside bottom edge of the pan, or the rice will stick. This is why a flat-bottomed, sloping-sided pan is better for the job than one with vertical sides, and a frying pan is unsuitable. It is important that the stock is kept close to a boil throughout, or the cooking process will be interrupted. If using wine, put it in before the stock. Adding it toward the end of cooking would make the risotto taste disgusting. Cook over medium heat. Too high or too low a heat and the rice will mush.

Taste the rice after 15 minutes. It should be cooked *al dente*, i.e. just tender but still with a bit of bite – but not under-cooked. It may need as much as another 10 minutes of cooking. If you are using saffron threads, add these in the last few minutes of cooking. Do not add too many threads or you will end up with a beautifully golden risotto tasting of dry-cleaning fluid. If you run out of stock before the risotto is done, simply add some boiling water. The consistency is all-important: It should not be too soupy, but have a creamy, moist texture, with every grain separate yet all held together in a harmonious unity. Also remember that the rice continues to cook after it is taken off the heat.

At the end of cooking most *risotti*, more butter and some Parmesan cheese are usually stirred in. Taste for seasoning after adding the Parmesan and add salt and pepper as you see fit. The saucepan is then covered and left to stand off the heat for 3 minutes. Give it a final stir and serve immediately, in large warmed soup bowls.

Home-Dried Tomatoes

Commercially produced sun-dried tomatoes have enjoyed a honeymoon period where people have eaten them because it was fashionable to do so. Many of the brands are literally disgusting, with a leathery texture and a rank taste. Home-dried tomatoes, by comparison, are altogether nicer. The word "dried" is somewhat misleading, for they are not dried to the extreme degree of sun-dried tomatoes and are still quite soft to the bite. The procedure involved is so simple and the end result so good, I guarantee you will be a convert after the first time you make them. They are brilliant in a quiche, tossed with fresh pasta, or in a salad… the uses are endless.

Use plum or roma tomatoes, which are now available for most of the year. When you buy them they will almost certainly have been held at a low temperature and will not be ripe. Spread them out on a flat surface in a warm place to ripen. Never put tomatoes in the refrigerator. They will just sit there sullenly like red and pointless bullets. Avoid those horrid greenhouse tomatoes like the plague. It is one of life's great mysteries that something that looks like a tomato should taste of nothing at all and move from a state of inedible, rock-and-water nastiness to going bad without ever passing through a stage of ripeness.

When the tomatoes are dried, use them at once or pack them in jars and cover with good olive oil. They may then be stored up to six months without refrigeration, as long as the jars are

Ingredients

about 16 plum tomatoes (see right)
about ¼ cup olive oil
salt
about 1 tablespoon sugar

Utensils

you can now buy excellent knives for slicing tomatoes; if you do not have one, use a small very sharp knife
2 baking sheets

scrupulously clean and the tomatoes completely covered.

Use as many plum tomatoes as you feel like drying. A word of warning, however: Do not try to dry too many at once. Alternatively, experiment with longer drying times. As a rough guide, 16 tomatoes will produce two baking sheets of dried halves.

Mise en Place

Preheat the oven to 300°F and drizzle olive oil over the baking sheets • Cut the tomatoes in half longitudinally. Slide the knife around the inside of each half to remove the pulp and seeds, leaving you with something that resembles a small boat.

Cooking

Arrange the tomato halves on the sheets so that they are not touching. Dribble a little more oil over the top and sprinkle sparingly with salt and sugar. Dry in the oven for about 45 minutes. Remove and let to cool. Taste one, eat the tray, and start again.

Vanilla Ice Cream

Should you make your own ice creams and sorbets? And, if so, do you need to buy an expensive machine to do the job? Five years ago I would not have hesitated in saying yes to both questions, but now, in the age of the widely available Häagen-Dazs (marketed as post-coital) and other excellent ice creams, and with the wide availability of good sorbets, I am not so sure. If you intend to make and serve ice creams and sorbets on a regular basis, then I still say buy a machine, but with the proviso that this must be one of the heavier-duty and more expensive models. Cheap small-volume units are just not worth the trouble and do not produce acceptable results. Anyway, it is possible to make decent ice cream by hand, using a whisk or portable electric mixer. When freezing your homemade ice cream, never keep it more than 48 hours or it will have lost its magic.

There are dozens of recipes for vanilla ice cream, a joy in its own right and the basis for most other flavored ice creams. This version is based on that of the great Swiss chef Frédy Girardet. I like it because it uses fewer egg yolks than usual, but delivers a beautifully rich-tasting ice cream nonetheless. The recipe makes about 2$^1/_2$ pints.

Ingredients

2 vanilla beans
6 egg yolks
1 cup sugar
2 cups whole milk
2$^1/_2$ cups heavy whipping cream

Utensils

flat white plate
bowl
saucepan
fine strainer
ice-cream machine (or heavy-duty plastic bowl that will fit in the freezer)

Mise en Place

Split the vanilla beans longitudinally, then, using a table knife, strip out the seeds. (Do this on a white plate so you don't lose any) • Separate the eggs and put the yolks, sugar, and vanilla seeds in a bowl, then whisk just enough to amalgamate.

Cooking

Put the milk in a saucepan with the vanilla beans and heat until just below boiling.

Then whisk the hot milk into the egg and sugar mixture. Put the mixture back into the pan over medium heat and cook, stirring constantly, until it achieves a coating consistency (the mixture holds to the back of a spoon). Do not overcook.

As soon as this consistency is achieved, remove from the heat and stir in the cream. This will have the effect of stopping the cooking and cooling the mixture.

Pour through a fine strainer into the ice-cream machine and churn. Despite what some instruction books say, there is no need to wait for the mixture to cool completely. Indeed, by some strange quirk of physics, a hot mixture will turn into ice cream faster than a cold one. (Retrieve the vanilla beans, rinse, then dry and store in a jar of sugar.)

To make the ice cream by hand, pour the finished mixture into a heavy-duty plastic bowl that will fit in your freezer (it should be about half full). Let cool completely (for obvious reasons, never put a hot object into your freezer), then chill 30 minutes in the freezer.

Remove and whisk until smooth. Return to chill 15 minutes longer. Remove and whisk again. Repeat this process until the mixture becomes stiff and difficult to whisk. At this point the ice cream is stable and will freeze as ice cream without too many ice crystals.

Serving Food

The theme of this book is simplicity; both in terms of the food, which should ultimately taste of itself, and, where possible, in its execution. It follows that presentation of food and its service should follow the same rules, for I dislike the whole business of painting pictures on plates. The only people who do this well are the Japanese and even then the impression that all Japanese food is painstakingly arranged is inaccurate. Food has its own innate presentation just as it has its natural seasonal rhythms. To me, anything that forces it to change its nature is wrong. There can be no absolute rights and wrongs here; no black and white "do this" but "don't do that," and my kind of food would look plain silly or pretentious if it were not put on plates in a simple way.

Any discussion of how we present food needs to be addressed historically, culturally, philosophically, and practically. Looking back to certain periods in history we can identify times when grandiose presentation took precedence over flavor and season. The banquets of ancient Rome, the feasts of Tudor England, the dazzling table of *Le Roi Soleil,* and the introduction of the so-called "Russian service" in the last century, when food for the first time was presented on individual plates in separate courses, all made statements that went beyond serving good food. Here was food as a complex mixture of messages, where the guest was being told of his or her importance, witness the cost and the trouble taken, while the host was demonstrating his or her generosity. More recently, *nouvelle cuisine* heralded a deliberate attempt to promote appearance on the plate, frequently at the cost of value and taste. What started out as an admirable initiative to move restaurant food away from the excessive richness of *cuisine de luxe* soon deteriorated into farce. Here was food imitating fashion, a miserably inadequate construction of clashing flavors, vivid colors, and undercooked vegetables arranged by hand on an oversized plate.

It is much easier to say what is wrong in the way food is served than what is right. The fewer items on a plate the better for me. What more does a decent stew need than a mound of perfect mashed potatoes beside it? The old British working class tradition (which still exists) of the Sunday roast accompanied by roast potatoes, mashed potatoes, cabbage, cauliflower, sprouts, carrots, and gravy is, in its way, sending the same messages as the overblown banquet: Here is plenty, heap your plate high, and eat till you drop. A kind thought and sound ingredients, but too many of them.

We also see the middle-class phenomenon of compulsive garnishing, the "ghastly parsley" syndrome, by which every dish bar the dessert is relentlessly strewn with the strong-tasting herb. As a rule, garnish only when the taste and texture add to the dish. I now use only flat-leaf parsley when cooking and, infrequently, as a garnish, finding it superior in every way to the curly variety of my childhood. I also use chives quite a lot as a garnish; otherwise the food must stand by itself and be counted.

When taking food to the table I frequently put out large bowls for people to help themselves. This is not a general rule, and whether you do so or not depends on the formality of the occasion and how well you know your guests. Friends eating at the kitchen table would doubtless find the sight of you carefully putting their food on individual plates entertaining, but it hardly seems to add much to the occasion. Really one uses common sense: A fragile fillet of fish is best put on the plate by the cook, but why should people not help themselves to however much they want if the dish makes this appropriate?

I also happen to like plain white plates, bowls, and soup plates – the slightly dished, deep plates that are perfect for things like risotto. Olive oil comes to the table in its own bottle with a pourer because I am proud of the quality and people like to see the label. Parmesan cheese is brought to the table in a piece for people to grate or cut for themselves. Knives and forks should look like knives and forks, large and plain. There was a grim period when Scandinavians tried to redesign knives and forks and came up with things like gardening implements for Trolls. Best forgotten.

I like simple food. Why should it not be simple on the plate? Who wants mutton dressed as lamb?

Spring

Spring is a season of rebirth and awakening. The rites of spring are celebrated Swedish-style with peppery nettle soup, the new lamb, the first baby beets. Sea bass is given a delicate Cantonese twist in a heady mix that includes delicate blanched spinach, while the freshest raw fish is served in Japanese sashimi. Desserts provide rich and comforting counterpoints – crème brûlée, sweet tarts, and unctuous homemade ice cream.

First Courses
Tagliatelle with Bacon and Scallions
Nettle Soup
Shrimp Won Ton with Dashi
Sashimi
Salade Niçoise
Risotto with Asparagus
Spaghetti alla Genovese
Sauté of Lambs' Sweetbreads with Peas and Mint

Main Courses
Salmon Cutlet with Herb-Dressed Sorrel
Sliced Sea Bass with Soy and Shredded Vegetables
Poached Halibut on the Bone with Hollandaise Sauce
Oxtail Stew with Basil Dumplings
Filet Mignon with Polenta and Salsa Verde
Roast Rack of Lamb with Flageolet Purée
Beijing Crispy Squab with Chinese Seaweed
Sauté of Chicken with Morels

Vegetables
Gratin Dauphinois
Boiled New Potatoes
Baby Beets and Scallions Stewed in Cream

Desserts
Crème Brûlée
Pear and Almond Tart
Lemon Curd Tart

FIRST COURSES

Nettle Soup

From time to time people come into the restaurant trying to sell me unusual herbs they have picked…. something I tend not to be very enthusiastic about, preferring to telephone my greengrocer. A number of chefs, like Michel Bras, make a point of incorporating wild plants into their cuisine and are often photographed out gathering nature's bounty from fields and hedgerows, usually in dazzling whites (perhaps to prevent hunters shooting them by mistake).

One wild plant of which I am inordinately fond is the first young stinging nettle of spring, dazzlingly green and with a unique peppery flavor. I am not sure I like the idea of London nettles, which may already have been inspected by dogs in a way that does not stunt their growth but certainly puts me off.

This soup is actually from a Swedish recipe, in which country its consumption with soft poached quail eggs is a rite of spring, conjuring up images of Bergman movies and beautiful Nordic types gathered sexily around the table. I had had various stabs at making this dish, with varying degrees of success, until I was introduced to the real thing at a Stockholm restaurant called KB, from where I gleaned the following recipe. They use chicken stock, but I like it just as well made with water. I specify a blender rather than a food processor, because I find it produces a less gluey purée.

This technique of making soup works equally well with spinach, lettuce, parsley or broccoli. The potato, leek, and onion mix is the basis for so many soups. On its own, it is the classic soup, potage bonne femme, and delicious in its own right. Chilled, with cream stirred in and topped with chopped chives, it becomes vichyssoise. Using this base, I once made five soups in ten minutes during a television demonstration.

Ingredients (for 4)

1 large onion
2 large potatoes
1 large leek
1 pound young stinging nettles
4 tablespoons butter
2 1/2 cups chicken stock or water
salt and pepper
1/4 cup crème fraîche, to serve (optional)

Utensils

two large saucepans
rubber or surgical gloves
pasta or blanching basket
blender

Mise en Place

Put plenty of water in a large saucepan and bring to a boil • While the water is heating, dice the onion, potatoes, and leek • Wearing rubber gloves (or surgical gloves, which make you feel X-rated), strip the leaves off the nettles. Wash them and put them in the blanching basket.

Cooking

In the second pan, melt the butter over low heat and sweat the vegetables in it for 5 minutes. Cover them with stock or water and simmer until just cooked.

Blend the contents of the pan until smooth (holding a cloth over the top to avoid getting splattered with hot purée) and return to the rinsed-out saucepan.

Dip the basket of nettles in the large pan of fast boiling water for 60 seconds. Refresh in cold water and pack into the blender while still wet. Blend to a purée.

Add the nettle purée to the basic vegetable mixture in a proportion of roughly 2 tablespoons of nettle purée to 1 ladleful of potato mixture. Taste and season with salt and pepper. If the soup is too thick, add a little more water as necessary.

Heat through gently, stirring, but don't boil or you will lose the vivid green color.

Serving

Serve in 4 warmed soup plates. If you want to garnish the soup, float a spoonful of crème fraîche on top of each plateful.

Tagliatelle with Bacon and Scallions

At the end of our morning writing sessions, Richard and I usually repaired to the kitchen for an impromptu lunch of whatever combination of food his refrigerator provided. On one occasion this turned out to be bacon (Mr Cutting, his local butcher's finest unsmoked), a bunch of scallions, fresh supermarket tagliatelle, extra virgin olive oil, and Reggiano Parmesan cheese. It tasted awfully good, even with commercial fresh pasta, but it would have been even better with the real thing, and I put it on the restaurant menu that evening.

Ingredients (for 4)
8 scallions
8 thick bacon slices
2 ounces Reggiano Parmesan cheese
1 pound fresh tagliatelle (see page 25)
extra virgin olive oil
pepper

Utensils
large saucepan for the pasta
grater
broiler pan and rack
colander

Mise en place
Put 2½ quarts of salted water to heat • Preheat the broiler • Clean the scallions, removing roots and outer skin • Cut any rind off the bacon • Grate the Parmesan.

Cooking
Broil the bacon until crisp; set aside but leave the broiler on and broil the scallions until lightly charred, turning once. When the bacon is cool enough to handle, cut each slice into 6 pieces. Mix the bacon pieces and scallions. Keep warm.

Cook the pasta in rapidly boiling water until just *al dente*, about 4 minutes.

Drain the pasta in a colander and return it to the pan. Pour in a little olive oil, stirring and tossing. Return to low heat on the rangetop, add the bacon and scallions, and mix. Heat through 1 minute.

Serving
Serve in hot bowls, with the Parmesan cheese added to taste at the table. Grind some black pepper over each helping (it will not need salt).

Shrimp Won Ton with Dashi

This dish uses two ready-made items to great effect: won ton skins and packaged dashi broth. Won ton served in even very good Cantonese dim sum restaurants tend to be rather coarse and basic, both in terms of taste and of appearance. Here, using the best raw shrimp and carefully balanced flavorings, a much more refined and subtle result is achieved.

Won ton skins are sold in packs of fifty or one hundred, but you can freeze what you don't use up to six weeks – after that they become brittle. If you can't get hold of dashi you can serve a light chicken or clear fish broth instead.

Ingredients (for 4)

two ¼-ounce sachets of dashi (see
 page 11)
24–30 won ton skins
flour, for dusting

FOR THE FILLING:

1 pound large unpeeled raw shrimp,
 defrosted if frozen
1-inch piece of fresh gingerroot
1 shallot or small garlic clove
small bunch of fresh coriander
 (cilantro)
1 tablespoon dry sherry
1 tablespoon Kikkoman soy sauce
1 egg white
salt and pepper

Utensils

large bowl
colander
food processor
two large saucepans (one for the
 dashi and the other for cooking
 the dumplings)
baking sheet
pastry brush
spider or slotted spoon

Mise en Place

First prepare the filling: Peel the shrimp. Using a very sharp knife, slice down the back and remove the intestinal vein. Rinse the shrimp under running water, then soak in a bowl of cold salted water 20 minutes. Swirl around with the fingers, rubbing the shrimp gently. Drain in a colander and rinse again under cold running water. This procedure will make the shrimp taste much sweeter and removes any musty taint from the flesh • Mince the ginger and shallot or garlic • Pick over the coriander and remove stems. Coarsely chop about 1 tablespoon of leaves into the food processor and add the shrimp and all the other filling ingredients. Process to a coarse paste: Ideally you want pieces of shrimp bound together rather than an over-worked paste. Season.

Put a large saucepan of salted water on to heat, and make the dashi according to the instructions on the package using 1 quart of boiling water.

Make the won ton: Shake some flour on the baking sheet to prevent the won ton skins sticking and tearing. Put some cold water in a cup or small bowl. Dealing with the skins one at a time, place each on the floured sheet and brush around the edge with a little water to moisten. Be careful not to make it too wet. Put a heaped teaspoon of the filling into the middle of the skin. Draw up two opposite corners and pinch together. Now take the third corner up to the middle and pinch at the top and along the edges to seal. Repeat with the fourth corner. You will now have a neat dumpling that looks like a priest's biretta. Depending on the size of each spoonful of stuffing you should end up with 24–30 dumplings. If not cooking immediately, you can keep them in the refrigerator up to 4 hours. Do not freeze as the shrimp may already have been frozen.

Cooking

Always cook the won ton in lots of water. If you cook them in the broth, the flour will cloud it. When the water has reached a fast boil, put in all the won ton and return to a simmer. They will bob to the surface. Check none have stuck to the bottom. If any have, push them gently with a wooden spoon to release. Poach 3–4 minutes. Drain the dumplings using a spider (see page 16) or a slotted spoon.

Serving

Serve in large, plain, warmed soup bowls with the hot dashi poured over. Scatter a few coriander leaves over each and offer more soy sauce at the table.

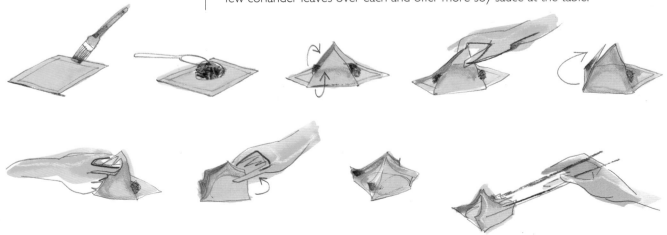

Sashimi

I believe I was one of the first non-Japanese chefs to serve raw fish in the Japanese style in London. Fifteen years ago there were few Japanese restaurants, and sashimi and sushi (see page 187) had yet to become fashionable internationally. Ten years ago sushi bars were all the rage on the West Coast of the USA, and we are now just starting to see a new generation of cheaper Japanese fast-food outlets gaining the same kind of popularity in Britain. Leave sushi to the professionals, however, as it is far too difficult.

There is a mystique and a formality surrounding sashimi. In Japan, special schools teach the art of preparing, slicing, and presenting raw fish. At this level sashimi is a refined and esoteric form, but this should not put you off serving raw fish at home. There is no real mystery — just the freshest fish, the sharpest knife, a clean chopping board and the essential accompaniments: wasabi (Japanese green horseradish) and Kikkoman soy sauce. An attractive serving plate is integral to the presentation.

The following recipes describe 4 different types of sashimi, each of which may be served as a first course — but for a really spectacular feast serve all four.

Willow-Pattern Sashimi

This gets its name from the fact that the slices of fish should be thin enough for you to be able to see the pattern of the serving plate through them.

Ingredients (for 4)

*1 very fresh sea bass, weighing
   about 2 pounds
1 cucumber
sea salt
sugar
¹/₂ tabelspoon wasabi powder
   (Japanese green horseradish, see
   page 11), to serve
Kikkoman soy sauce, to serve*

Utensils

*strong tweezers or electrician's pliers
parchment paper
razor-sharp knife
blue-patterned serving plate
   (preferably willow-pattern)
5 shallow dipping bowls (see page
   16)
4 sets of disposable wooden
   chopsticks*

Mise en Place

First prepare the fish: Ask your fishmonger to scale, clean, and fillet the bass and remove the pin bones, or do it yourself using a small pair of pliers or strong

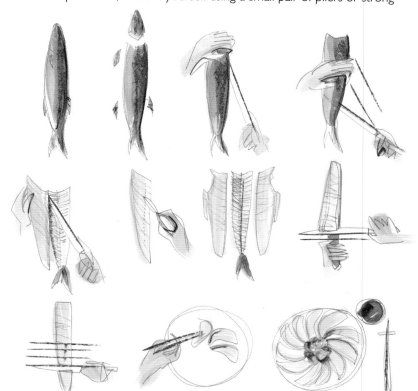

tweezers. Skin the fillets and pat them dry with paper towels. Salt lightly, wrap in parchment paper, and refrigerate up to 2 hours. Also chill the serving plate.

Peel off alternating strips of skin along the length of the cucumber to give a decorative striped effect and then cut the cucumber into very thin slices. Sprinkle with a little salt and sugar and leave 1 hour • In one of the 5 dipping bowls, make some wasabi paste by mixing the powder with an equal amount of cold water.

Preparation
Unwrap a bass fillet and lay it on a chopping board with the head facing your preferred hand. Slice as thinly as you can, cutting at an angle of 45° through the fillet. Each slice will have a remnant of the skin, which will show as a pink membrane.
   Rinse and gently squeeze the cucumber slices and pat dry with paper towels.

Serving
Heap the cucumber in a mound in the center of the chilled serving plate. Then arrange the bass slices, slightly overlapping, in a circle around the cucumber. Serve accompanied by the soy sauce and bowl of wasabi.
   Using chopsticks, each guest mixes a little soy sauce and wasabi in the bottom of their bowl and then helps themself to slices of fish to dip in this mixture – followed by some cucumber salad to help assuage the hotness of the wasabi.

Scallops with Spinach Oshitashi
Spinach oshitashi is a dish served in its own right in Japan as an appetizer, but I prefer it in combination with scallops.

Mise en Place
First prepare the spinach: In a large pan of boiling salted water, blanch the spinach 1 minute. Refresh in cold water and drain. Gently squeeze out residual water and fluff up the spinach with a fork.

Prepare the scallops: Clean them, then slice each one, across into 3 rounds.

Trim the scallions and cut them across into very thin rounds • Squeeze the lemon into a small bowl and mix the juice with 4 times as much soy sauce.

Serving
Dress the spinach with the soy and lemon mixture. Using the metal ring to shape, form a round of spinach on each of 4 plates, positioning it slightly off-center.
   Arrange the scallop slices overlapping on top of the spinach. Sprinkle with the scallions and bonito. Serve with wasabi and soy sauce as above.

Tuna Domino Sashimi
Fresh tuna is one of the most sought-after fish today, and Japanese buyers comb the world for the best of the global catch – the most vital consideration is freshness.

Mise en Place
First prepare the fish: Trim the fillet into a neat brick shape and cut away any bloody meat. Wrap in plastic wrap and refrigerate until ready to serve. Then slice the tuna into domino-sized pieces.

Ingredients (for 4)
1 1/2 pounds fine leaf spinach
8 very fresh scallops
2 scallions
1 lemon
Kikkoman soy sauce, to serve
1 tablespoon bonito flakes (see
   page 11)
1/2 tablespoon wasabi powder, to
   serve

Utensils
large saucepan
colander
razor-sharp knife
small mixing bowl
4-inch metal ring or cookie cutter
5 shallow dipping bowls
4 sets of disposable wooden
   chopsticks

Ingredients (for 4)

*1 very, very pink tuna fillet, weighing
about 1 pound when trimmed*
*1 pound daikon (Japanese white
radish, see page 16)*
*1/2 tabelspoon wasabi powder, to
serve*
Kikkoman soy sauce, to serve

Utensils

razor-sharp knife.
5 Japanese dipping bowls
*4 sets of disposable wooden
chopsticks*

Ingredients (for 4)

*4 cleaned squid bodies, each
weighing about 4 ounces*
4 sheets of nori seaweed
1 tabelspoon wasabi powder
4 scallions
Kikkoman soy sauce, to serve

Utensils

razor-sharp knife
5 shallow dipping bowls
*4 sudare (bamboo sushi mats, see
page 16)*
*4 sets of disposable wooden
chopsticks*

Peel and slice the daikon into the finest julienne • Rinse briefly and drain • In one of the small bowls, mix the wasabi to a thick paste with an equal amount of water.

Serving

On each of 4 round plates, arrange 6 pieces of tuna to look like a stack of dominoes that has fallen over to one side of the plate. Pile a neat mound of daikon to one side of that. Finally, composing a suitable haiku, place on each plate a marble-sized piece of wasabi paste to produce a harmonious yet asymmetrical triangle.

Serve the soy sauce in individual small shallow dishes into which wasabi is mixed to individual preference. Eat the sashimi with chopsticks.

Squid Roll Sashimi

Some people find the idea of raw squid unattractive, but it is delicious and has the most unusual texture that contrives to be both resilient to the bite and meltingly tender.

Mise en Place

First prepare the squid: Cut along one side of each of the squid bodies and open out. (There is a line like a seam running along the back of the squid: Cut along this.) Clean the squid very carefully, using a blunt knife to scrape the inside free of all ink, membranes, and innards. Turn over and repeat the cleaning process for the outside skin, peeling away the outer membrane. Wash the squid thoroughly. Trim the opened squid to the largest rectangle you can cut. (Freeze any trimmings and squid tentacles for use in a fish soup.) Score the outside of the squid in a neat, close criss-cross pattern, taking care not to cut too deeply.

Prepare the nori: Cut a rectangle to the same size as each of the pieces of squid and toast them by holding over the lowest flame for a few seconds until crisp. If you do not have a gas range, then put it under a low broiler – but take care, as it burns very easily.

In one of the small dipping bowls, make some wasabi paste by mixing the powder with an equal amount of cold water • Clean and trim the scallions.

Preparation

With a long end of each nearest you, place one of the pieces of squid, cut-surface down, on the sushi mat. Lightly smear the top with a little of the wasabi paste and place the matching nori sheet on top of it.

Position a scallion across the sheet just in from the edge nearest you and, by lifting the mat, roll the squid and nori into a tight cylinder around the scallion.

Unwrap and move this roll to one end of the mat, then roll a second time inside the mat. Squeeze and press to firm up. Repeat with the remaining squid bodies and filling, then refrigerate 5 minutes.

Unroll the mats and remove the cylinders. Cut these across into slices about 1/4-inch thick. These will look like mini jelly rolls. The end ones will be a little too untidy for a formal presentation, so eat these yourself.

Serving

Build a neat pile of the rolls on each of 4 plates (preferably not round) and serve with soy sauce and the remaining wasabi as for Willow-Pattern Sashimi.

Salade Niçoise

This once-famous dish has fallen into disrepute, as abortive and rather nasty versions have been served in questionable homage to one of the most original dishes to have evolved in Nice. I like to serve it in the restaurant with seared fresh tuna steaks, but there is nothing wrong at all with using good-quality canned tuna in olive oil.

For me, a good Salade Niçoise prepared from the freshest ingredients will always be redolent of Provence. You can almost hear the cicadas. Well… almost.

Ingredients (for 4)

12 new potatoes
1/2 pound extra thin green beans
1 head of lettuce, preferably romaine
4 large plum tomatoes
4 fresh eggs
2 ounces canned anchovy fillets in oil, drained
20 pitted black olives
4 fresh tuna steaks, 3 ounces each, or 1/2 pound best-quality Spanish or Italian canned tuna in olive oil, drained
extra virgin olive oil

FOR THE ANCHOVY DRESSING:
1 egg
1 garlic clove
1 handful of flat-leaf parsley
2 ounces canned anchovy fillets, drained
juice of 1 lemon
1 tablespoon tomato ketchup
1 cup sunflower oil
5 tablespoons extra virgin olive oil
black pepper

Utensils

2 or 3 saucepans
large bowl
food processor

Mise en Place

Prepare the vegetables: Boil the new potatoes in salted water until just tender. Cook the green beans in fast-boiling salted water. Test after 3 minutes. If not done, check again after another minute. The current fashion for near raw beans is, in my view, wrong. They should not be woody, but *al dente*. When done to your liking, drain the beans and plunge them into cold water • Trim the lettuce, discarding the outer leaves. Wash and spin or pat dry • Slice the tomatoes in wedges.

Boil the eggs for 6 minutes. Remove the pan from the heat and let the eggs to sit in the hot water 2 minutes longer, then refresh in cold water for 3 minutes. Drain, shell, and cut the eggs into quarters.

Make the anchovy dressing: Put all the ingredients except the oil in a food processor. Process to a smooth paste and then add sunflower oil and olive oil in a thin stream through the feed tube, until the dressing is the consistency of heavy whipping cream. Season with black pepper.

Put the potatoes, lettuce, beans, anchovies, and olives into a large bowl. The amount of lettuce you use should be about half the volume of the whole salad. Pour over 4 tablespoons of the anchovy dressing (the rest will keep well in an airtight jar in the refrigerator for several days) and toss thoroughly to coat • If using fresh tuna, preheat a hot broiler or grill pan.

Cooking

If you are using fresh tuna, brush the steaks with olive oil and sear under a preheated hot broiler or on a grill pan for 60 seconds on each side. The tuna should be pink in the middle.

Serving

Heap equal amounts of the salad on 4 plates. Arrange the tomato wedges and egg quarters around the outside. Put a tuna steak on top of each serving or flake over the canned tuna. Drizzle olive oil over the top and serve with the best bread you can buy.

This is one of those dishes where a good, dry rosé makes the perfect accompaniment. The very best rosé is Château de Sours, which is made by an Englishman, Esme Johnson, who turned to viticulture very successfully after selling Majestic Wines in England. Strangely, this wine is not from Provence, but from Bordeaux and is technically called a *clairet*.

Risotto with Asparagus

Risotto with asparagus (con asparagi) is my choice as the nicest vegetable risotto. The asparagus tips are reserved to be served still al dente (i.e. tender but still firm to the bite), while the rest of the asparagus cooks until it has almost dissolved. Once I had this risotto at a well-known London restaurant, with only a very small amount of the new season's asparagus in it. I later wondered whether I was seriously ill because of the extraordinarily powerful aroma that accompanied micturition. For my fuller treatment of the cooking of risotti see page 27.

Ingredients (for 4)

1 pound young green asparagus
1 carrot
bay leaf
2 onions (one large, one small)
4 tablespoons unsalted butter
1 1/2 cups Arborio or other risotto rice
1 glass (2/3 cup) of dry white wine
salt and pepper
2 ounces Reggiano Parmesan
cheese, to serve

Utensils

2 large saucepans
strainer
large heavy-based pan for the risotto, preferably with sloping sides (see right)
potato or asparagus peeler

Mise en Place

Make a vegetable stock: Put 1 1/2 quarts of water in a large pan and bring to a boil. Peel and trim the asparagus. Put the trimmings in the boiling water together with a diced carrot, the bay leaf, and the larger of the two onions, peeled and quartered. After it returns to a boil, bubble 20 minutes and no longer. Strain into another saucepan and return to a boil.

Peel and mince the smaller onion • Cut off the tips from the asparagus and blanch these briefly in the vegetable stock (say 2–3 minutes, no more). Remove and reserve • MInce the asparagus stalks and poach them in the vegetable stock until tender. Remove and reserve.

Cooking

With the vegetable stock simmering gently on the stove, melt the butter in a deep heavy-bottomed pan with sloping sides over medium heat, then sauté the minced onion until translucent. Add the minced asparagus stalks and sauté with the onion over medium heat about 2 minutes. Add the unrinsed rice and continue to sauté, stirring to coat with the butter and onion mixture and being careful not to brown by using too high a heat. It is at this point that you should hear the rice "clicking" against the side of the pan as you stir. Add the wine and boil 1 minute, stirring all the time.

Add a ladleful of simmering stock and stir until it is absorbed. As soon as it is, add another ladleful and continue to repeat this process until the stock is nearly finished. Throughout the cooking of the rice, you must stir constantly, being sure to push the spoon firmly – but not roughly – against the sides and bottom of the pan to prevent any rice from sticking.

After 15 minutes, taste: The rice should be *al dente,* i.e. tender but firm to the bite and not chalky. If insufficiently cooked and there is no stock left, add boiling water a half ladleful at a time until it is.

When you are satisfied that the risotto is cooked, draw the pan off the heat. Do not, however, grate the Parmesan cheese, or mix it in when cooking is completed.

Serving

Serve the cooked risotto in large, warmed soup plates, apportioning the asparagus tips equally, and finish by shaving over curls of Parmesan cheese using a potato or asparagus peeler.

Spaghetti alla Genovese

Spaghetti simply dressed with pesto is delicious enough, but in this refreshingly different variation on the theme the pasta is balanced with sliced new potatoes and extra fine green beans. These slightly surprising additions give a depth and difference to the dish that is quite remarkable and out of all proportion to the simplicity of the ingredients.

Commercial pesto, sold in small jars, is universally disgusting in our experience and the real thing is very easy to make as described on page 23. Do not be tempted to use more than about one tablespoon per person: it has a very strong flavor and the pasta is just as important as the sauce.

Ingredients (for 4)

10 new potatoes
$1/4$ pound thin green beans ("haricots verts")
$3/4$ pound spaghetti (this is a generous serving for 4, but provides standard Italian first course portions – you could use less)
$1/4$ cup Pesto (see page 23)
salt and pepper

Utensils

large saucepan
pasta or blanching basket or colander
large bowl
tongs

Mise en Place

Both vegetables can be prepared well in advance and held: In a large pan of boiling salted water, cook the potatoes until just tender. Refresh in cold water and let cool slightly. When cool enough to handle, peel and slice to the same thickness as the beans. Trim the beans, cut into 1-inch lengths, and blanch in well-salted water for 3 minutes. Drain and refresh by dipping briefly in a bowl of ice water to stop the cooking process.

Put as large a pan of lightly salted water to heat as you can for the pasta. Remember that it may take 20 minutes to bring such a large pan of water to a fast, rolling boil, so don't leave this to the last minute. Put a colander in the sink ready to drain the pasta as soon as it is done.

Cooking

When the pan of water is at a good rolling boil, feed in the pasta by the handful. Never cut or break pasta. The longer it is, the better it tastes. Feed it in slowly, pushing it to coil around the pan as it softens. When it is all under the surface, stir immediately to separate the strands and make sure none sticks to the bottom. Return to the fastest boil you can maintain without the water boiling over.

While the pasta is cooking, put the sliced potatoes, beans, and pesto in a warmed serving bowl and mix well. Add some freshly ground pepper to give it an extra lift. Have the bowl standing close to the sink, where the colander is awaiting the spaghetti, and have your tongs ready to toss the ingredients together.

Good-quality dried spaghetti should cook in under 10 minutes, so start tasting after 8 minutes. These days it seems to be smart in Italy to serve pasta not just *al dente* (tender but still firm to the bite) but nearly raw, something frankly unpleasant. Also remember that it will go on cooking after it is drained.

As soon as you are satisfied that the spaghetti is nearly done, quickly (but carefully) remove from the heat and drain in the colander. Before it is completely drained and while there is still a thin coating of water on each strand (the retained moisture is an important contributor to the texture of the sauce), tip it into the bowl and toss thoroughly with the pesto, potatoes, and beans.

Serving

Serve at once in large, warmed individual bowls, with large spoons and forks. Torn basil leaves may be added to garnish. You can serve with added Parmesan, but with so much of it in the pesto it hardly seems necessary.

Sauté of Lambs' Sweetbreads with Peas and Mint

This is a classic spring dish using the sweetbreads of the new season's lamb, at its best in April or May when all the ingredients will be in top condition. Lambs' sweetbreads are much cheaper than those of veal, but just as delicious. Sweetbreads are the thyroid glands of the animal and should never be frozen.

Ingredients (for 4)
1 1/4 cups Lamb Stock (see page 21)
1 1/2 pounds lambs' sweetbreads
1 pound small green peas in the
   pod
salt and pepper
flour, for coating
4 tablespoons butter
12 mint leaves (any type of mint
   other than spearmint)

Utensils
roasting pan
slotted spoon
wooden spoon
saucepan
large sauté pan

Mise en Place
Make the Lamb Stock as described on page 21 or thaw it if made earlier and frozen.

Prepare the sweetbreads: Wash them thoroughly, ideally by leaving them under cold running water for as long as you can (doing this for an hour or two while you are making the stock would be ideal). Put them in the saucepan and cover with cold water. Bring to a boil, lower the heat, and simmer 2 minutes. Immediately drain and refresh in cold water until cool enough to handle. The fat and membrane that hold the lobes together will now be opaque. Pull these off (they come away easily). Put the cleaned and drained lobes in the refrigerator until needed.

Blanch the peas in boiling salted water for 2 minutes, drain, and refresh in cold water.

Holding Point – you are now ready to cook and everything can be held in the refrigerator several hours.

Just before cooking, cut the sweetbreads into bite-size pieces and roll in flour seasoned with salt and pepper.

Cooking
Melt 2 tablespoons of butter in the pan and sauté the sweetbread pieces to brown them lightly.
    Add another 1 tablespoon of butter, together with the peas, mint leaves, and the stock and simmer together 3–4 minutes.
    Finally, swirl in the remaining butter and adjust the seasoning, if necessary.

Serving
Serve at once in hot soup plates, either alone as a first course or with fresh noodles as a main course.

MAIN COURSES

Salmon Cutlet with Herb-Dressed Sorrel

Twenty years ago the Troisgros brothers introduced this dish to the international restaurant-going cognoscenti by serving it very publicly as part of a memorable feast (which also included a truffled soup en croûte *by Bocuse) to French President Valéry Giscard d'Estaing. It was their reworking of a Loire specialty that used whatever river fish were on hand, in combination with creamed sorrel.*

The original recipe and innumerable subsequent derivatives all cook the sorrel in a way that renders it into something horrid like a cow-pat. Having first made a strongly flavored butter and herb sauce as part of the Mise en Place I then cook the salmon on its own. Finely shredded sorrel is dressed with the warm sauce at absolutely the last moment and the salmon is then presented on a mound of this lemony fresh-tasting salad.

Ingredients (for 4)

2 sticks (1 cup) unsalted butter (yes – a whole half pound)
1 shallot
bunch of dill
bunch of flat-leaf parsley
4–5 tarragon leaves
bunch of chives
1 pound sorrel (this is a lot – about a shopping bag full)
1 wild salmon fillet, weighing about 1 pound
about 6 tablespoons flour
salt and pepper
2 glasses (1 1/4 cups) of dry white wine, or 1 glass (2/3 cup) of Noilly Prat
2/3 cup heavy whipping cream
sunflower oil

Mise en Place

Chill the butter until hard, then cut it into 1/4-inch cubes • Peel and coarsely chop the shallot • Remove and discard large stems from the herbs and chop them all coarsely • Remove stems from the sorrel leaves. Place 5 or 6 leaves on top of each other and roll them into a cigar shape (imagine you are in Havana and looking around for a suitable thigh). Cut these across into fine strips • Cut the salmon fillet into 4 slices through the skin and at an angle of 30 degrees, starting toward the tail end • Sprinkle the flour on a plate, season lightly, and mix in to make a seasoned flour.

Cooking

First make the sauce (it can be made in advance): Put the wine or Noilly Prat and the chopped shallot in a large non-aluminum saucepan. Season generously with salt and pepper. Put over high heat and boil rapidly until the wine has almost completely evaporated (as for Beurre Blanc, see page 23).

Add the cream off the heat and return to a medium heat. Stir, then simmer until it becomes syrupy. The reduction does not need undivided attention, but it would be wise not to leave the kitchen. (You can prepare the salmon while the sauce is reducing.)

Pack your blender or food processor with all the herbs and pour in the hot reduced sauce. Put on the lid, cover with a dish cloth, and blend until you have a smooth green purée. Set aside to cool. This whole process of making the sauce will take 20–30 minutes.

Return the sauce to the rinsed-out pan and simmer. Do not boil or overcook or you will lose the beautiful green color. Off the heat, swirl in the small pieces of

Utensils

*large 3-quart non-aluminum
     saucepan for the sorrel*
*blender (or food processor as inferior
     substitute)*
*large nonstick frying pan for the
     salmon*
large bowl

butter, 4 or 5 at a time, gently rotating the pan to melt them in. You can also do this with a small whisk or a wooden spoon. Set in a warm place or over the lowest heat your rangetop can achieve.

Put 2 of the salmon cutlets in the seasoned flour and turn to coat them evenly. Shake off any excess. (The flour amalgamates with the fat from the fish during cooking to form a thin crust.)

Put the frying pan over high heat and add a tiny amount of sunflower oil. Sauté the cutlets, skin-side down, for 2 minutes. Turn them carefully and give them 1 minute on the other side. (If using the thicker cuts, double the cooking times.) Transfer the cooked cutlets to a warmed plate.

Quickly coat and cook the other two cutlets in the same way. (If you are feeling confident, you may like to cook all 4 at once, either in one large pan or in two pans side by side. Alternatively, use a hot broiler, leaving out the flour but following the same cooking times.)

Transfer the sauce to a large bowl and drop the sorrel into it. Toss swiftly. If you have the temperature right the sauce will coat the sorrel leaves completely, leaving no free sauce in the pan. Getting the balance of sorrel to sauce is very important. Essentially you want about 2 tablespoons of sauce (including butter) to a large handful of sorrel per person.

Serving

The sorrel will start to discolor and collapse immediately. Rush for your 4 warm plates and mound the dressed sorrel on them. Place the salmon cutlets on top of each mound and serve at once.

Sliced Sea Bass with Soy and Shredded Vegetables

This dish is based on one served at the celebrated Poons Restaurant on Leicester Street in London's Chinatown. They would be shocked by my addition of butter, which is not terribly Cantonese, but it adds a last luxurious touch to the rather astringent flavor of the soy.

Sea bass is well suited to this treatment, and so are sole, turbot, and halibut. This is one recipe, however, where you cannot substitute cheaper, flakier fish like cod or flounder, because they would just break up.

You will need to use two frying pans, if you want to cook enough for four. However, as the final stages must be seamless and have to be gotten right first time, I suggest here making it a meal for two. Note that I have specified using the frying pan and not a wok, because it is more practical.

Ingredients (for 2)

1 pound sea bass, filleted and any stray bones removed
1 pound washed and trimmed spinach
1 carrot
4 scallions
juice of 1 lemon
2 tablespoons soy sauce
$1/4$-inch piece of fresh gingerroot
1 garlic clove
4 tablespoons butter
2 tablespoons flour
1 tablespoon sunflower oil
1 fat hot red chili pepper, seeded and cut across into thin rings, for garnish (optional)

Utensils

large saucepan
blanching basket
small bowl
flat plate
large nonstick frying pan
tongs
spatula

Mise en Place

First prepare the fish: Slice the sea bass fillets across at an angle of 30 degrees to produce cutlets weighing about 1 ounce •

Prepare the vegetables: Blanch the spinach in a large pan of boiling salted water 30–45 seconds, drain, and refresh in cold water. Drain again and squeeze out the water gently. Fluff up the cooked leaves – the spinach must not be a compressed lump • Cut the carrot and scallions into julienne strips.

Combine the lemon juice and soy sauce in a small bowl. Peel the ginger and grate it into this mixture • Slice the garlic into thin slivers • Cut the chilled butter into cubes about $1/4$-inch across • Put the flour on a plate.

Holding Point – you are now ready to cook and everything can be held in the refrigerator for several hours.

Cooking

Once you've started this stage, you can't stop until you finish. Coat the fish pieces in the flour and shake off any excess. Heat the oil in the pan over high heat.

Place the floured cutlets carefully in the oil in a single layer without any overlapping and immediately turn the heat down to medium.

Cook 1 minute and then turn the cutlets over. Immediately add the spinach, vegetable julienne, the garlic, and the soy mix.

Turn the heat back to high and add the pieces of butter to the liquid areas of the pan. Swirl until it melts and incorporates.

Serving

Serve at once on warmed plates, scattered with some chili rings if you like.

Poached Halibut on the Bone with Hollandaise Sauce

When buying fish to cook on the bone, allow about 1 pound per person. Poaching fish is the simplest of all cooking techniques and if you follow the few basic rules set out below you cannot go wrong.

Ingredients (for 4)

about 2¹/₂ quarts Court-bouillon (see page 21)
2 tablespoons white wine vinegar
1 whole halibut or summer flounder, weighing 3–4 pounds, fins and gills removed but skin left on (ask the fishmonger for all the trimmings except the gills to freeze for fish soup), and fish cut the fish into 5 steaks.

FOR THE HOLLANDAISE SAUCE:
1 shallot
1 tablespoon white mignonette pepper (coarsely crushed white peppercorns, see page 10)
juice of ¹/₂ lemon
1 tablespoon white wine vinegar
3 egg yolks
2 sticks (1 cup) butter
sea salt

Utensils

pan large enough to hold the fish steaks in a single layer (e.g. big Le Creuset casserole)
small saucepan
fine strainer
food processor
bowl set over a large pan of hot water
slotted spoon

Mise en Place

First make the Court-bouillon as described on page 21 and bring it back to a simmer if necessary. Stir in the vinegar.

Cooking

Make the Hollandaise Sauce: Do you really want to do it properly or will you use the food processor? Assuming the latter, try a slight variation on the standard Magimix formula by peeling and mincing the shallot and putting it into a saucepan with the pepper, lemon juice, and vinegar. Boil it down to about 2 teaspoons of liquid and strain this into the food processor. Add the egg yolks and process a few seconds to combine.

Meanwhile melt the butter over low heat. When liquid, turn on the processor and add it in a thin stream through the feeder tube, leaving the solid sediment from the melted butter in the pan. The mixture will be quite thin.

Season with salt, then pour it into a bowl set over hot water and whisk until it thickens. Taste and adjust the seasoning if necessary. Turn the heat all the way down and keep the sauce warm. The water should not be more than hand-hot.

Now poach the fish: Slide it into the simmering court-bouillon with the dark skin sides of the steaks upward and poach gently about 10 minutes. You can tell when it is done because the bones will start to protrude slightly. Drain immediately and remove the carrots from the court-bouillon.

Serving

Serve the fish on a warmed serving plate with the carrots arranged around it and accompanied by boiled new potatoes, offering the Hollandaise in a warmed sauce boat.

Oxtail Stew with Basil Dumplings

Oxtail is a forgiving cut that can be cooked for a very long time before it dries out. Rich, voluptuous, and satisfying, this is the food of reassurance and reaffirmation. With dumplings, I can think of nothing better on a cold day.

These feather-light dumplings are better for being made in a food processor as the less you handle them, the lighter the result. The order in which you process the ingredients is important. Also, you should use as little water as possible to complete the processing.

Ingredients (for 4-6)

2 oxtails, cut into pieces
2 onions
2 celery stalks
2 carrots
2 garlic cloves
flour, for dredging
salt and pepper
sunflower oil, for browning
2 glasses (1 1/4 cups) of robust red
   wine
bouquet garni of bay leaf, parsley
   stems, and a sprig of thyme
2 tablespons Worcestershire sauce
2 tablespoons tomato ketchup
chives or basil leaves, for garnish

FOR THE BASIL DUMPLINGS:
2 cups self-rising flour
1 teaspoon salt
1 teaspoon black pepper
10 basil leaves
2 tablespoons butter or goose fat
3 egg whites

Utensils

fine strainer
food processor
heavy frying pan
large casserole (preferably Le
   Creuset)
large saucepan
flour sifter

Mise en Place

The day before: Soak the oxtail pieces in ice water for 4 hours to extract blood and impurities, then trim off excess fat. Pat dry with paper towels • Chop all the vegetables into small dice and mince the garlic.

Cooking

Working a few pieces at a time, dredge the oxtail in flour seasoned with salt and pepper, and brown in oil in the frying pan. Pack them into the casserole, standing upright in a single layer.

Add a little more oil to the frying pan and brown the diced vegetables, stirring constantly. Transfer to the casserole. Deglaze the frying pan with the red wine, scraping to incorporate all the burnt bits, and pour this over the oxtail and vegetables.

Tie the bouquet garni together and push this down into the center. Add the Worcestershire sauce and ketchup. Pour in just enough water to cover. Season.

Bring to a boil, turn down to a bare simmer, and cook until the meat starts to pull easily away from the bone, 2 hours or more. Remove from the heat and store in a cool place overnight.

The next day: Lift off the fat from the top of the stew. Drain off the sauce, then purée and press it through the strainer.

About 20 minutes before serving, put the oxtail to reheat gently in the strained sauce. Put a large pan of lightly salted water on to heat for the dumplings. (Never cook fresh herb dumplings in with a stew but always separately in salted water.)

Prepare the dumplings: Sift the flour into the food processor, together with the salt and pepper. Add the basil and process until the leaves are finely shredded and the flour has turned a light green. This takes no more than 30 seconds, probably less. Add the fat and process briefly. Within seconds the dough will crumb. Stop processing. Add the egg whites and process. The dough will quickly start to hold together. Stop processing. Have cold water ready to dribble down the feeder tube and process again. Add the water, literally a teaspoon at a time, and work quickly. The dough should start to bind within seconds. Turn off the processor the instant this begins to happen and transfer the dough to a lightly floured surface. If your hands are hot, run cold water on them to cool them, then dry them and gently roll the dough into a cylindrical shape about 10-inches long.

Cut the dough into 12 equal cylinders. (Do not roll into balls as this will make the dumplings heavier.) Poach in the gently simmering water for 15 minutes. Remove with a slotted spoon.

Serving

Serve the oxtail stew in warmed soup plates, with 2 or 3 dumplings per person. Garnish with chives or a few basil leaves torn over.

Filet Mignon with Polenta and Salsa Verde

If one must talk about restaurants having signature dishes, then this has to be one of mine. It remains on the menu by popular demand. The combination of textures and flavors works so well: This is beef at its best, moist and succulent, offset by the crisp polenta croûte, *which also absorbs the juices. The clean, sharp taste of the green sauce provides the perfect complement, making a dish that has depth and balance.*

Ingredients (for 4)

4 filet mignons, weighing 5 ounces each (trimmed beef tenderloin cut from the center)
2 cups instant polenta
4 ounces Parmesan cheese
1 stick ($^1/_2$ cup) unsalted butter
salt and pepper
sunflower oil, for frying and greasing
$^2/_3$ cup beef stock
mignonette pepper (see page 10)
$^1/_3$ cup dry sherry or Madeira wine

FOR THE SALSA VERDE:
2 garlic cloves
large bunch of flat-leaf parsley
bunch of basil or mint leaves
2 tablespoons capers
1 tablespoon Dijon mustard
1 tablespoon wine vinegar
$^2/_3$ cup extra virgin olive oil

Utensils

saucepan for making polenta, preferably nonstick
2 baking sheets
2 heavy frying pans (one for the steaks and the other for the polenta – they need to be large enough to cook all of the two elements at the same time)

Mise en Place

Remove the steaks from the refrigerator well ahead of time to let them come to room temperature • Make the polenta at least 1 hour before you cook the steaks, following the package directions. Grate the Parmesan cheese and lightly oil the baking sheet. Then stir the cheese and half the butter into the polenta and season liberally with salt and pepper. Pour onto the baking sheet. You should have a sheet of polenta about $^1/_2$-inch thick. Let it cool and then refrigerate. When cool and set firm, using a cookie cutter of a size slightly larger than the steaks, cut 4 rounds from the sheet of polenta. Brush these with sunflower oil and lightly oil the pan. Also lightly oil the second baking sheet.

To make the Salsa Verde: MInce the garlic and then put it in a food processor with all the other ingredients except the olive oil. Process until evenly chopped and then add the oil, continuing to process until smooth. Taste and adjust the seasoning, if necessary.

Preheat the oven to its highest setting.

Cooking

Put one of the frying pans on a medium heat and melt half the remaining butter in it with 1 tablespoon of oil. Lightly season the polenta rounds and fry them 1 minute on each side. Then transfer them to the oiled baking sheet. Bake 10 minutes, then remove from the oven, and carefully turn the polenta, using a metal spatula. If it sticks and shows signs of breaking, put it back into the oven and cook for a little longer. As they start to crisp, the polenta rounds will lift around the edges and detach easily. After turning, put them back in the oven and bake 5 minutes longer. The idea is to have the polenta finished just before the steaks are ready.

Cook the steaks: Heat the other frying pan until very hot. Flatten the steaks slightly with the heel of the hand and season with salt and mignonette pepper. Cook over high heat for 3 minutes on each side for rare, 4 minutes for medium. Transfer the cooked steaks to a warm plate, cover, and keep warm.

Pour the beef stock and sherry or Madeira into the pan and stir to deglaze, quickly reducing the liquid to a syrupy consistency. Add the remaining 2 tablespoons butter, a small piece at a time, swirling the pan until it incorporates. This finishes the texture of the sauce and gives it a beautiful gloss.

Almost a condiment, the raw Salsa Verde has beome a very fashionable sauce. It goes well with most grilled meat and poultry.

Serving

Put a crisp polenta *croûte* on each warmed plate and top with a steak. Stir into the sauce any juices that have exuded from the steaks while resting and then spoon this over each steak before spreading the salsa verde on the top.

This dish has everything: subtle yet forceful, perfectly juxtaposed textures and a visual delight. *Faites simple* indeed.

Roast Rack of Lamb with Flageolet Purée

Pairing the new season's spring lamb with flageolets is very French. The meat is roasted pink, with a seared outer crust, and the beans are cooked until they will collapse at the slightest pressure, then puréed with olive oil and lemon juice.

Ingredients (for 4)

1 pound dried flageolets
1 carrot
1 celery stalk
1 onion
6 garlic cloves
1/2-pound unsmoked slab bacon
2 sprigs of rosemary
bay leaf
about 1/2 cup olive oil
2 racks of lamb, ends of bone frenched
salt and pepper
sprig of thyme
several sprigs of flat-leaf parsley
1 lemon

Utensils

large pan for the beans
colander
roasting pan
food processor

Mise en Place

First prepare the beans: Put them to soak overnight in plenty of cold water. Next day, drain them and put in a pan with at least double their volume of water. Bring to a boil over high heat and boil hard 10 minutes (they will throw a creamy white scum). Drain in a colander, rinse in clean water, and return to the pan.

Cook the beans: Chop the carrot, celery, onion, and 4 of the garlic cloves into a brunoise (see page 187) and put into the pot with the beans, the piece of bacon, one of the rosemary sprigs, and the bay leaf. Cover with cold water, allowing a 1-inch head above. Bring to a gentle simmer, stir, and film the surface with olive oil. Cook very gently for 2 hours. Remove from the heat and set aside.

Preheat the oven to its highest setting and brush the roasting pan with oil • Brush the racks of lamb with olive oil. Using a small sharp knife, score the fat in a diamond pattern and rub salt and pepper into the cuts and on both sides of the meat • Slice the remaining garlic cloves across into very thin slivers and strew them in the roasting pan. Scatter half the remaining rosemary leaves and half the thyme over the garlic and sit the lamb racks on the garlic, fat side down. Scatter the remaining rosemary and thyme on top of the meat • Chop the parsley and juice the lemon.

Cooking

Roast the lamb 15 minutes. Then carefully drain the fat from the pan. Turn the racks to bring the fat sides up and continue roasting 10 minutes.

Transfer to a warm place (above the rangetop, for example) and let rest.

Gently reheat the beans, which by now should have absorbed most of their cooking liquid. Purée them in the food processor with the lemon juice and 3 tablespoons of olive oil. Add a little water if necessary to achieve a thick but spoonable consistency. Adjust the seasoning, if necessary.

Then carve the racks into chops.

Serving

Put the bean purée into a warmed serving bowl, drizzle over a couple more tablespoons of olive oil, and garnish with the chopped parsley. Take to the table with a large spoon for people to help themselves and serve the chops on a separate warmed serving platter.

Beijing Crispy Squab with Chinese Seaweed

Squabs are not so much pigeons as plump domesticated doves. If you cannot get any, this recipe also works well with squab chickens or poussins. In either case you will need one bird per person and, since you will be deep-frying, it may be better to make this a dish you cook for two.

You could serve the squabs with pancakes like Peking Duck, but try Chinese "seaweed" instead. Of course, this is not seaweed at all, but finely sliced greens.

This recipe was developed by Juliet Peston, my co-chef at the restaurant for seven years.

Ingredients (for 2)

4 ounces fresh gingeroot
6 scallions
2 squabs
3 tablespoons salt
$1/2$ tablespoon five-spice powder
2 tablespoons Sichuan pepper
sunflower oil, for deep-frying

FOR THE SEAWEED:
2 pounds collard greens
2 teaspoons salt
2 teaspoons sugar

Utensils

heatproof plastic wrap
steamer
deep-fryer, or deep-frying pan or large wok with a heatproof thermometer
spider (see page 16)
anti-splatter mesh screen (optional)
tongs
strong serrated knife
coffee grinder
candy thermometer

Mise en Place

The day before: Cut the ginger and scallions into chunks and stuff them into the body cavities of the birds • Put the salt, five-spice powder, and Sichuan pepper into a coffee grinder and pulverize. Rub the skins of the birds all over with this mixture, then carefully wrap each bird in the heatproof plastic wrap to hold the spices uniformly against the flesh. Refrigerate 24 hours.

An hour before you start cooking, prepare the "seaweed": Remove stems from the collards and wash the leaves. Working with one leaf at a time, roll it up like a cigar and cut this across to make the finest strips you can manage. Spin dry and put to one side on paper towels to absorb any moisture. The drier you can get them, the better.

Cooking

Put the squabs, still wrapped, in the steamer and steam 40 minutes. Then set aside to cool.

In the deep-fryer or frying pan, heat the oil to 350°F. Unwrap the squab and, using a spider (see page 16) or deep-frying basket, carefully put them into the oil, keeping your face well back because the oil will surge up with the moisture and spit ferociously. Put an anti-splatter screen in place if you have one. In any case, beware: This is a dangerous piece of cooking and not for the faint-hearted.

The birds will be floating on one side. After 5 minutes, using tongs, turn each bird onto the opposite side, holding them until they float in that position without rolling back. The oil will splatter again at this point.

After a total frying time of 12 minutes, remove the birds and drain on paper towels. The squab should be a shiny mahogany color with crisp skin.

Bring the oil up to 375°F. Fry the greens a handful at a time about 2 minutes (they will visibly darken) and remove with a spider to drain on lots of paper towels. (They can be made in advance and stored in an airtight box.)

Serving

When cool enough to handle, use a strong serrated knife to saw the birds in half, cutting down from the breastbone ridge. Discard the ginger and scallion.

Toss the seaweed with the salt and sugar. Put a mound of it in the middle of each of 2 warmed plates, then place the halves of the bird on either side and serve at once. Finger food for sure, so finger bowls will be appreciated.

Sauté of Chicken with Morels

Morels are the finest (and most expensive) wild mushrooms you can buy. They have a distinctive shape — like a partly unfolded umbrella — and are usually inky black. Perhaps of all the varieties of wild mushrooms you can buy dried, morels retain more of their vibrant flavor and texture when reconstituted.

A sauté is one of the most frequently used methods of cooking in the professional kitchen because a dish can be prepared to order in about half an hour. It is, in any case, an ideal method for cooking chicken. Use thighs and drumsticks for this dish as they have more flavor and are less prone to drying out.

Ingredients (for 4)

2 ounces dried morels
8 shallots
1 tablespoon sunflower oil
1 stick ($^1/_2$ cup) butter
4 chicken drumsticks (with skin)
4 chicken thighs (with skin)
salt and pepper
1 glass ($^2/_3$ cup) of dry white wine
1 $^1/_4$ cups chicken stock
1 $^1/_4$ cups heavy whipping cream

Utensils

fine strainer
heavy frying pan large enough to hold all the chicken pieces without crowding (or use two)
brush

Mise en Place

Put the morels in the strainer and rinse them briefly under cold running water. Then soak them in warm water for half an hour. Take them out of the liquid and put to one side. Pass the liquid through a fine strainer (a tea strainer is ideal). This has excellent flavor and will form an integral part of the sauce • Peel and slice the shallots very thinly and put with the morels.

Cooking

Put the sunflower oil and half the butter in the frying pan and melt over low heat.

Season the chicken pieces with salt and pepper, rubbing well into the skin. Put the pieces in the pan, skin-side down. Arrange the pieces so they lie flat, but they can be quite tightly packed. Cook without touching them for 25 minutes. Turn over (the skin should be crisp and golden) and cook 10 minute longer. Test that the juices run clear with a skewer, then take the chicken pieces out and reserve in a warm place.

Pour all fat out of the pan but do not wash it. Turn up the heat a little and add 2 tablespoons butter. Sweat the shallots and morels in this about 5 minutes, then turn the heat up further and moisten with the wine. Bring to a boil, then add the stock and the morel soaking liquid. Bubble until it is reduced by half.

Add the cream and simmer until the sauce is thick enough to coat the back of a spoon. Return the chicken pieces to the pan, skin-side up. Lower the heat and warm through for 10 minutes.

Serving

Serve immediately with mashed potatoes or plain boiled Basmati rice.

VEGETABLES

Gratin Dauphinois

Everybody has a variation on the dauphinois *theme. This version was first shown to me by Rowley Leigh who was taught how to cook the universally loved dish by the Roux brothers, so the pedigree is faultless. It is unfashionably rich, expensive, and unhealthy, so very small portions please.*

I don't worry about what sort of potato, though they should be slightly waxy. No cheese is necessary, for the amalgamation of the potatoes and cream produces a cheesy effect. It is vital not to have the oven too hot or the cream will curdle.

I love to eat this with roast lamb, for me a marriage made in heaven.

Ingredients (for 4)
2 pounds potatoes
1 garlic clove
2^1/$_2$ cups heavy whipping cream
^{2}/$_3$ cup milk
^{1}/$_4$ nutmeg
salt and pepper
butter, for greasing

Utensils
mandoline grater (see page 15)
large bowl
heavy saucepan
grater
1 ^{1}/$_2$-to 2-inch deep gratin dish
large spoon or spatula

Mise en Place
Preheat the oven to 275°F and grease the gratin dish generously with butter • Peel and slice the potatoes on the mandoline into a bowl of water. The slices should be about ^{1}/$_4$-inch thick. (Using a food processor to slice the potatoes would remove too much of the starch) • Peel and mince the garlic.

Cooking
Put the cream and milk into a heavy saucepan. Grate the nutmeg into it, season with salt and pepper, and add the minced garlic. Place over medium heat.

Drain the potato slices and return them to the bowl. When the cream mixture is hot, pour it over the potato slices and turn to coat thoroughly and evenly. Adjust the seasoning, if necessary.

Transfer to the prepared gratin dish and pack down firmly with the back of a large spoon or spatula. The mixture should be very liquid and the dish should not be full to the top.

Bake 1 hour. If the surface is not golden and bubbling at the end of this time, brown the top under the broiler.

Boiled New Potatoes

The Jersey Royal, the first of the crop, deserves its reputation as the Queen of new potatoes. Very expensive and packed neatly in woven wooden drums, their arrival is something we eagerly await – for the flavor is incomparable. Later in the season they are not as good and by June one should switch to other varieties. In the USA any of the many tasty varieties of round red potatoes, such as those from Florida and California, are probably the closest approximation.

In recent times we have seen new potatoes coming from all over the world, like Charlotte, Belle de Fontenay and the enchanting, knobbly Pink Fir Apple. Many of them are exceptional. Experiment and try different varieties. Unless you do, supermarkets will stop stocking them.

With all new potatoes it is important that they have not formed a full skin – it should still be flaking away. Once a skin has formed completely, the potato is past its best – but will be perfectly acceptable when peeled.

Prepare all new potatoes by rubbing them with a scouring pad under running water. They need no clever cooking method and should simply be boiled in plenty of salted water.

Served hot with a pat of butter, or cold with extra virgin olive oil and sea salt, they are one of the finest things I can imagine. The combination of the newest potato and black truffle, however, is extraordinary. If you have made the Ravioli of Leeks and Truffles (see page 150), try a dish of new potatoes tossed with any truffle butter you have left over and frozen for just such an experiment.

Baby Beets and Scallions Stewed in Cream

Many people believe that beets are no more nor less than slices of purple woody root vegetable kept in a jar of acid vinegar. This perception is so deeply imbued that many actually grow to love the sensation of putting something in their mouths that causes involuntary pursing of the lips and a sudden inhalation of air. When offered sweet baby beets that have never been subjected to pickling they become confused, even agitated. Inducing this sensation will give the cook much satisfaction and the guest a happier insight into a great vegetable.

It is not always easy to find baby beets, but it is worth asking your grocer to get some. Dissuade him from boiling them himself and stress that vinegar is not part of your plan. Often beets come pre-packed, in which case they will be larger, probably cooked, and already trimmed and peeled. If this is so, cut them into quarters. Beets bought by the bunch still with their leaves are smaller and much nicer, though inevitably more expensive.

Ingredients (for 4)
1 pound baby beets
1 shallot
1 scallion
2 tablespoons butter
juice of 1 lemon
salt and pepper
about 1 1/4 cups heavy whipping
   cream

Utensils
large saucepan
wide, shallow saucepan to hold the
   beets in a single close-packed
   layer

Mise en Place
Put a large pan of lightly salted water on to heat • If necessary, trim the leaves off the beets, leaving about 1/2 inch of the stems protruding. Cut off the straggly root tip • Mince the shallot and cut the scallion across into rings.

Cooking
Cook the beets in lots of the boiling water until tender, about 30 minutes (remember even young beets can be very woody). Refresh in cold water and peel while still warm.

Melt the butter in the wide shallow saucepan and sweat the shallot in it until translucent. Add the beets, lemon juice, and salt and pepper and turn to mix and coat. Pour around the cream to come halfway up the beets and stew, stirring from time to time, until very hot and the cream has turned an entrancing regal color.

Serving
Transfer to a warmed serving dish, scatter with the scallion rings, and bring to the table immediately.

DESSERTS

Crème Brûlée

This must be one of the most popular desserts in history, but people are always asking me why their crème brûlée does not work; they burn the sugar, the custard curdles, or it separates. Not enough cream or egg yolks? Too much sugar placed under an ordinary broiler? Cooked in too hot an oven? I think the answer lies in organization, cooking the custard on the rangetop and not in the oven, and the judicious use of a small blow-torch. Yes, every kitchen should have one (in fact, nowadays most good hardware stores sell handy inexpensive disposable blow-torches — but do handle them with care).

The combination of cream, eggs, vanilla, and sugar is sublime. Introducing alien ingredients like ginger, honey, or mango is anathema. However, do serve the crèmes brûlées with a bowl of fresh raspberries if you wish.

The quantities in this recipe will fill 6–8 ramekins, which will allow you to have a few spares for testing your blow-torch technique (see below) or simply for later.

Ingredients (for 6-8)

6 egg yolks
5 tablespoons granulated sugar
2 vanilla beans
2 cups heavy whipping cream
6 teaspoons raw brown (Demerara) sugar

Utensils

large bowl
electric mixer
6–8 individual ramekins
roasting pan
large saucepan
wooden spoon
fine strainer
large measure
blow-torch
whisk

Mise en Place

You can make the crèmes up to 3 days ahead: Separate the eggs and put the yolks and granulated sugar into a large bowl. Cut open the vanilla beans on a white plate and remove the seeds. Scrape the seeds into the egg yolks and sugar and beat to a stiff mixture • Have the spotlessly clean ramekins ready in the roasting pan.

Cooking

Put the cream and vanilla beans into a large saucepan and scald over low heat. As soon as it starts to boil, pull it off the heat or it will boil over.

With the mixer on at full speed, pour the scalded cream over the egg yolk and sugar mixture. Be careful — it is very hot and may splash. If using a portable mixer, you will need somebody else to pour for you.

Wash out the pan, put the whole mixture into it, and cook over low heat, whisking. As it starts to get hot, change from the whisk to a wooden spoon and stir very carefully, getting right into the edges of the pan to avoid an unmixed and overcooked custard. As it comes back to a boil and the instant it starts to bubble at the edge, remove from the heat.

Stir quickly and pour through a fine strainer into the measure. Don't dither about at this point or you will end up with very expensive sweet scrambled eggs. Pour immediately into the ramekins, filling them right to the brim because the level will fall. By the way, don't forget to rinse the vanilla beans and add them to your jar of vanilla sugar. Let cool completely.

The caramelized topping is done at the last moment before serving: Sprinkle 1 teaspoon of raw brown sugar on top of each ramekin. Pat it down and then turn upside down to shake off any excess — the sugar topping should be one grain thick. (If you have the consistency of the custard wrong you will certainly find out now)

Briefly play the flame of the blow-torch evenly across the sugar, starting at the edge farthest away from you and working toward you. It should turn a dark, golden brown. If black spots appear, stop immediately. If you like, practice on the spare crèmes brûlées: You will soon get the knack. Don't test for crispness for 4 or 5 minutes, as the sugar is super-hot and will give you a very nasty burn.

Pear and Almond Tart

In its most sophisticated version, this is a Tarte Bourdalue, *which combines frangipanie and* crème pâtissière. *My version is honestly closer to a Bakewell tart, but no less tasty for all that. Without being too rich, the French* ton-pour-ton *almond paste could not be easier to make, and is a perfect complement to the pears.*

We have terrible problems with pears in the restaurant. They need to be at a precise stage of ripeness to hold their shape and texture when poached. Since the pears in this recipe are going to be baked, I can see no reason not to use canned pears. Once you have crossed that bridgehead, try making it with canned apricots or peaches. I could name you a Michelin three-star restaurant that does the same thing, so no need to feel guilty.

This is another tart that uses the processor-produced frozen Pâte Sucrée Pastry Shell described on page 25. If you have already made one of these and have it on hand in the refrigerator or freezer you can whip up a brilliant dessert in minutes. Using this basic, sweet tart shell and the almond cream, you can ring all kinds of changes. For example, try draining frozen raspberry pieces, covering the bottom of the tart with them, and then smothering them in a layer of almond cream.

Ingredients (for 6-8)

1 ready-to-bake *Pâte Sucrée Pastry Shell (see page 25) still in its mold*
1 *pound canned pear halves in syrup*
1 *tablespoon slivered almonds*
confectioners' sugar, to dust

FOR THE TON-POUR-TON (ALMOND CREAM PASTE):
4 *tablespoons butter*
5 *tablespoons sugar*
6 *tablespoons almonds*
6 *tablespoons flour*
1 *egg*
1 *teaspoon rum*

Utensils

food processor
strainer
baking sheet

Mise en Place

First make the almond cream paste: Whizz the butter, sugar, almonds, and flour in a food processor, then add the egg and rum and whizz again to combine. Spoon this mixture into the pastry shell, spreading it out in a fairly even layer. It should not come more than halfway up the side of the shell.

Drain the pear halves in the strainer to get rid of the syrup in which they have been canned. Arrange them on top of the tart in a radial pattern, pushing them gently into the paste. Trim a final pear half and position it in the center. Chill 30 minutes • Toward the end of this time, preheat a baking sheet in the oven set to 375°F.

Cooking

Set the tart on the baking sheet in the middle of the oven and bake until the pastry begins to shrink away from the edge of the mold and go brown, about 25 minutes. The almond cream will have risen almost to engulf the pears.

Scatter over some slivered almonds and dust with confectioners' sugar. Turn down the oven to 300°F and bake 30 minutes longer.

Serving

Serve warm with whipped cream, or crème fraîche.

Lemon Curd Tart

Lemon curd on toast has always been loved by British children, and homemade lemon curd in tarts pleases sophisticated adults in much the same way. The mixture of sharpness and sweetness combined with the satisfying crunch of sweet, short pastry make a dessert that is easy and quick to prepare but has delicacy enough to end the most elegant meal.

For an even sharper and more flavorful variation, try replacing half the lemons with six limes.

Ingredients (for 4-6)

FOR THE PROCESSOR
SWEET SHORT PASTRY:
7 tablespoons chilled unsalted
   butter
1 egg yolk
3 tablespoons ice water
1 $^2/_3$ cups flour
2 $^1/_2$ tablespoons sugar
pinch of salt

FOR THE LEMON FILLING:
6 lemons (more if the lemons are
   small, and only 5 if they are extra
   large and juicy)
6 large eggs
1 cup sugar
2 tablespoons unsalted butter

Utensils

bowl
food processor
plastic wrap
8-inch tart mold
foil
dried beans (for weighting)
grater
whisk
heavy pan

Mise en Place

First prepare the pastry: Take the butter straight from the refrigerator and cut into $^1/_2$-inch dice. Beat the egg-yolk and ice water together. Sift the flour. Put all the pastry ingredients except the egg-yolk mixture into a food processor and work until you have a mixture with a consistency like crumbs. With the machine still running, add the egg and water mix through the feed tube and stop processing the instant the pastry balls. Remove, wrap in plastic wrap and refrigerate for at least half an hour or overnight.

Preheat the oven to 375°F.

Prepare the pastry shell: Roll out the chilled pastry on a floured surface and use it to line an 8-inch tart mold. (The pastry will be very fragile and may break; the high fat content, however, means you can repair it by pressing pieces of pastry trimmings into any cracks or gaps.) Prick the bottom of the pastry shell, line with foil, and pour in dried beans to weight it down.

Cooking

Bake the tart shell "blind", until is golden brown, 15-20 minutes. Take out of the oven and remove the foil and beans. If the bottom is still soggy in the middle, return it to the oven briefly to finish cooking (be careful: At this point the edges can burn very quickly).

While the pastry shell is baking, prepare the filling: Grate the lemons lightly to remove the zest and reserve. Juice the lemons, then whisk the juice in a bowl with the eggs and sugar to combine.

Put the butter and lemon zest in a heavy pan, add the eggs and sugar, and cook over low heat, stirring constantly, until you have a thick custard. This will take about 15 minutes.

The curd needs no further cooking. Let it cool slightly and then pour or spoon into the pastry shell. Refrigerate until ready to serve.

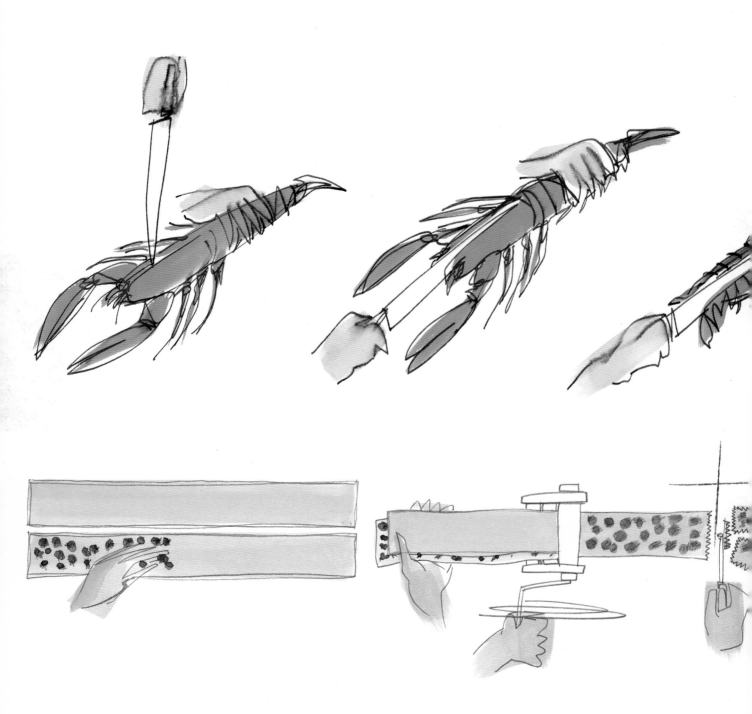

Summer

Summer, a celebration of a world in growth. Vegetables are at their best and asparagus is simply grilled. Choose from light terrines, vivid borscht, and the magic of fresh pesto in minestrone, or revel in the delicate parsley ravioli bathed in intensely flavored jewel-bright chicken broth. Aïoli strikes a triumphant Provençal chord and desserts emphasize the freshness of seasonal fruit.

First Courses
Chilled Borscht with Baby Vegetables
Panzanella
Minestrone with Pesto
Platter of Italian-Style Stuffed Vegetables
Grilled Asparagus with Shaved Parmesan
Chicken Broth with Parsley Pasta
Gravlax with Dill-Mustard Sauce and Cucumber Salad
Deep-Fried Squash Flowers
Pressed Skate and Potato Terrine
Pizza Bianca

Main Courses
Cold Poached Salmon Trout with Tzatziki
Aïoli Garni
Chinese-Style Steamed Fish
Seductive Lobster
Grilled Lamb with Couscous Salad
Baron of Rabbit with Home-Dried Tomatoes
Vitello Tonnato
Capon Salad
Orvieto Chicken

Vegetables
Roast New Potatoes with Garlic
Green Beans
New Season's Carrots
Blanched Spinach Salad

Desserts
Berry Sorbet Jr.
Peach Tea Ice Cream
Sauternes and Olive Oil Cake
Summer Pudding

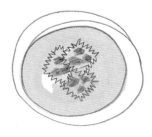

FIRST COURSES

Chilled Borscht with Baby Vegetables

This is a spectacularly pretty dish that tastes as good as it looks. I have tried making it without jellied consommé, but with no success. Others may find vegetarian gelling agents like agar agar work for them, but they do not work for me. I also think the flavor of beef consommé works particularly well with beets.

I have railed against fetal as opposed to baby vegetables elsewhere, but this is one occasion when you can let your purse strings go, and your imagination run riot, as you buy as many pristine tiny vegetables as you can lay your hands on: zucchini, cauliflower florets, carrots, green beans, snow peas or sugar snaps. You are looking for variety rather than quantity. Supermarkets sell baby vegetables in small packs. Buy only one of each, excluding those imported ears of baby corn, which taste of nothing and are really pointless.

Serve with crème fraîche into which you have grated horseradish or stirred a little harissa, the fiery North-African pepper sauce.

Mise en Place
Prepare the beets: If they are uncooked, boil them in lots of lightly salted water until tender (which can take anything from 30 minutes to 1 hour, depending on how large they are). Drain, refresh, and peel while still warm, reserving the peelings. If the beets are large, cut them into neat chunks about the size of the baby vegetables.

Prepare the other vegetables: Trim and peel them as appropriate. Blanch the vegetables separately in lots of boiling salted water and refresh in cold water (see page 26 for times and a detailed description of blanching vegetables).

If using, peel and grate the horseradish. Stir this or the harissa into the crème fraîche (harissa is very spicy, so go carefully).

Cooking
Put the beet peelings (with carrot greens if you have bought untrimmed carrots) into a saucepan with the consommé. Simmer these together 15 minutes – the consommé will take on a deep purple color from the trimmings. Pass through a strainer and put to cool, discarding the tops and trimmings. Adjust the seasoning when cold. (If using canned consommé, it will already be quite salty.)

Mix the blanched vegetables together and put into a soup tureen or, for maximum effect, arrange in individual bowls. Add the beets last to prevent them discoloring the rest of the vegetables, and spoon over the consommé.

Refrigerate until set, at least 2 hours.

Serving
Spoon some of the flavored crème fraîche over the tureen or individual bowls and garnish with chervil leaves or chopped chives.

Ingredients (for 4)
1 bunch of baby beets or 2 medium beets
1 1/2-2 pounds baby vegetables (or more if you like)
about 2 1/2 cups canned beef or chicken consommé
salt and pepper
chervil leaves or chopped chives, for garnish

TO SERVE:
horseradish or harissa to taste
1 1/4 cups crème fraîche

Utensils
large saucepan
blanching basket
grater
strainer
potato peeler

Panzanella

This is a Tuscan bread and vegetable salad. I had known about the dish for a number of years, but had eaten some unpalatable versions and was generally put off by the notion of eating soggy bread. Then I tried making it in Umbria using very stale bread and it was delicious. Returning to London, filled with enthusiasm, I attempted to re-create the dish in the restaurant using English bread and found it soggy again. I then tried it using bread crumbs made from stale bread slices baked with olive oil to crisp them.

While different from the original, this works extremely well. What you have here is all the freshness and vitality of a gazpacho, but in a salad form. For a delicious variation on the theme, use mint instead of basil.

Ingredients (for 4)

8–10 slices from a stale crusty French baguette, cut across
about 6 tablespoons extra virgin olive oil
salt and pepper
4 ripe tomatoes
1 small cucumber (pickling size)
1 medium or 2 small red onion(s)
1 celery stalk (from the inside of the head)
1 carrot
bunch of basil
2 tablespoons red wine vinegar

Utensils

baking sheet
large serving bowl (see Mise en Place)
food processor

Mise en Place

Preheat the oven to its highest setting. Trim any dark crust off the bread and arrange the slices on a baking sheet. Sprinkle lightly with olive oil and salt.

Prepare the vegetables: Dice the tomatoes roughly without peeling or seeding them. Peel the cucumber and cut into dice about half the size of the tomato dice. Repeat this procedure with the onion(s). Peel and dice the celery and the carrot to the same size. Pick over the basil and tear the leaves from the stems. Put all the chopped vegetables into a large serving bowl at least twice the size of all the ingredients.

Cooking

Bake the bread in the oven until golden brown. It will take no more than 10 minutes. Be careful not to burn it; if you can smell it the slices are ready for the garbage can.

Remove and let cool until the bread can be handled. Then put into a food processor and chop until you have coarse crumbs – do not over-process. Set aside.

Tear the basil leaves into pieces by hand and add to the vegetables in the bowl. Season lightly and stir in the vinegar. Add the bread crumbs and toss thoroughly. Refrigerate until chilled, which will take about 2 hours.

Just before serving, adjust the seasoning if necessary (remember the bread crumbs already have salt on them). Pour over olive oil – the precise amount depends on your preference, but it is possible to put too much and spoil the balance of the dish.

Serving

Toss thoroughly and serve in chilled soup plates.

Minestrone with Pesto

Not to put too fine a point on it, I despise soupe au pistou *and love minestrone. The Provençal dish is inferior in every way to the Italian and misses the point of the basil sauce completely by cooking it into the soup, when it should be stirred in at the table at the last moment to provide a unique burst of flavor.*

There is no absolute recipe for minestrone, but it should contain beans and I like to include a soup pasta like ditali *(slightly larger than the tiny and more commonly available* ditalini, *which I think is just too small as I like the bits of pasta to be about the same size as the beans). Many Italians insist that it is cooked using a Parma ham bone or ham scraps, but there is no reason why the minestrone should not be entirely vegetarian. Most recipes include tomato, though I prefer to leave it out. Otherwise it can be made from a variable mixture of vegetables that may include carrots, potatoes, leeks, green beans, spinach, green peas, cauliflower, onions, broccoli, and zucchini.*

Ingredients (for 8)

1 cup dried borlotti or cannellini beans (canned will do)
about 3 pounds mixed vegetables (e.g. ¹/₂ pound each zucchini, onions, green beans, carrots, and broccoli, plus 2 celery stalks, and 2 garlic cloves)
¹/₂ pound soup pasta, such as ditali
¹/₂ cup olive oil
ham bone or 4ounces Parma ham scraps (optional)
salt and pepper
¹/₂ cup Pesto (see page 23), to serve

Utensils

large saucepan
bowl
blanching basket

Mise en Place

Prepare the dried beans, if using: Soak them overnight in cold water. Then drain and put them in a large pan of water. Bring to a boil and boil vigorously 10 minutes. Drain, cover with fresh water, and bring back to a boil. Simmer about 1 ¹/₂ hours. Do not salt the water at any stage. (If you do not have time, canned borlotti beans make an acceptable substitute, though they must be well rinsed in cold running water before being put into the soup.)

Prepare the vegetables: Cut the zucchini, onions, and green beans into ¹/₄-inch pieces, the carrots into thin rounds, and the celery and garlic into thin cross-cut slices. Separate the florets from the broccoli stems, cutting the stems into small dice. Blanch the green beans and broccoli florets in boiling salted water for 3 minutes and refresh in cold water.

Cook the soup pasta in plenty of rapidly boiling salted water about 5 minutes. Drain, refresh in cold water, and drain again. Put into a bowl, add 1 tablespoon of olive oil, and turn to coat each piece.

Cooking

Put the remaining olive oil into a large saucepan and sweat the carrots, onions, garlic, and celery in it for 5 minutes, stirring from time to time.

Add the zucchini and broccoli stems, together with the ham bone or scraps, if using. Barely cover with cold water and bring to a boil. Turn down the heat and simmer until the vegetables are just tender.

Add the drained borlotti beans. Taste, then season with salt and pepper and cook 5 minutes longer. Stir in the broccoli florets and green beans and simmer for a final 5 minutes.

Minestrone is not so much a soup as a meal. All it needs is good bread and a robust red wine to go with it.

Remove from the heat, let cool, and then refrigerate or store in a cool place overnight. This is essential so the flavors can develop and amalgamate.

When ready to serve, reheat gently. Stir in the half-cooked pasta and simmer until the pasta is tender, about 5 minutes.

Serving
Serve in the largest warmed soup bowls you have, passing the pesto separately for people to help themselves.

Platter of Italian-Style Stuffed Vegetables

This is a rather prosaic title for a dish of great vivacity and charm. It makes a meatless main course, or the individual elements can be served on their own as antipasti. *Serve all the vegetables warm or at room temperature. Arrange them on a large platter and bring to the table for people to help themselves.*

Stuffed Onions

This is Anna Del Conte's recipe for Scodelle di cipolle ripiene *(doesn't that sound so much more delicious?) from* Secrets from an Italian Kitchen. *She has kindly allowed me to quote it in return for our recipe for the Peppers with Mozzarella and Anchovy, which she is including in her latest book.*

Mise en Place

Prepare the onions: Peel and plunge them into boiling salted water. Cook until the outer leaves are soft but still slightly crunchy, about 15 minutes. Refresh in cold water, drain, and let cool. When the onions are cool, cut them in half across the middle. Pull out the centers to make eight cups with the four outer leaves, reserving the other removed leaves. If you are left with a hole in the base, place another leaf in the bottom to seal it.

Preheat the oven to 400° and oil a baking dish just big enough to hold the 8 onion cups. Sit them in the dish • Chop the anchovies, capers, chili, oregano, and garlic and mix in a bowl. Flake in the tuna • In another bowl, soak the bread in the milk for 5 minutes. Squeeze it dry and break it up with a fork.

Cooking

Heat a spoonful of oil in a sauté pan. Chop the onion leaves removed from the centers and sauté them in the oil for a few minutes, taking care not to brown them. Add the bread, stir, and continue to sauté for a couple of minutes before stirring in the tuna mixture.

Spoon this mixture into the onion cups, filling to just above the rim. Sprinkle with bread crumbs, drizzle a little more oil over the tops of the onions, and carefully pour a few tablespoons of water into the bottom of the dish to prevent burning and sticking. Bake until the top is golden, about 30 minutes.

Zucchini Gondolas

Mise en Place

Prepare the zucchini: Halve them lengthwise and scoop out the flesh with a teaspoon, to make little dug-out canoes (what Cajun chefs call *pirogues*). This being an Italian dish, however, perhaps gondolas are more appropriate. Reserve the pulp.

Preheat the oven to 400°F • Mince the onion and garlic • Strip the thyme leaves and chop • Grate the Parmesan cheese.

Ingredients (for 4)

4 onions
5 tablespoons extra virgin olive oil
4 canned anchovy fillets in oil,
    drained
1 tablespoon capers
1 small dried hot chili pepper,
    seeded
2 teaspoons dried oregano
    (preferably freeze-dried if
    available)
1 garlic clove
6-7 ounces canned tuna in oil,
    drained
2 slices of white bread
²/₃ cup milk
2 tablespoons dry bread crumbs
salt and pepper

Utensils

saucepan
colander
baking dish just large enough to
    hold the onion halves in one layer
2 bowls
sauté pan

Ingredients (for 4-6)

6 medium-sized zucchini
1 onion
1 large garlic clove
1 small sprig of thyme
1 ounce Parmesan cheese
3 tablespoons olive oil
1 heaped tablespoon fresh white
    bread crumbs

Utensils

shallow baking dish or pan just large enough to hold the zucchini in one layer
sauté pan

Ingredients (for 4)

about 5 tablespoons extra virgin olive oil
black pepper
basil leaves, for garnish

FOR THE PEPPERS WITH MOZZARELLA AND ANCHOVY:
2 red bell peppers
1 garlic clove
1/2 pound buffalo Mozzarella cheese
8 canned anchovies in oil, drained

FOR THE PIEDMONTESE PEPPERS WITH PESTO:
2 yellow bell peppers
4 small plum or 12 cherry tomatoes
4 teaspoons Pesto (see page 23)

Utensils

2 baking dishes (see right)
pastry brush

Cooking

Sweat the onion, garlic, and reserved zucchini flesh in 1 tablespoon of olive oil in the sauté pan, until the onion is soft and translucent. Put into a food processor with the bread crumbs and cheese and process until you have a smooth paste. Add the thyme leaves and another tablespoon of olive oil and process briefly to mix in evenly.

Fill the zucchini shells with the mixture and arrange in the dish or pan so they are all sitting upright. Dribble the remaining olive oil over their tops and carefully pour 1 tablespoon of water into the bottom of the dish, avoiding the zucchini (the steam generated will help the cooking process and reduce the risk of burning).

Bake until the gondolas have wilted slightly and browned, about 30 minutes.

Duo of Stuffed Peppers

Mise en Place

Preheat the oven to 350°F • Carefully cut each pepper in half, first cutting through the stem so that each half has the stem attached. Before cutting, look at how the pepper is shaped because you want the two halves to sit like boats. Clean the insides of the peppers of all pith and seeds. Any seeds that stick tenaciously can be removed by upending the half pepper and tapping it sharply on a work surface. Arrange the red pepper halves in a baking dish in which they just fit snugly so that they will hold each other upright. (Play around until they all sit securely.) Repeat with the yellow pepper halves in the other dish.

To prepare the Peppers with Mozzarella and Anchovy: Peel and mince the garlic. Sprinkle it evenly into the red pepper halves and add a good tablespoon of olive oil to each. Brush the edges and stems with more oil. Grind over some pepper.

To prepare the Piedmontese Peppers with Pesto: If using plum tomatoes, peel them by immersing in boiling water for 30 seconds, refreshing in cold water, and then peeling them with a small sharp knife. Spoon the pesto into the bottom of each pepper half. Place 1 plum tomato or 3 cherry tomatoes on top and trickle over a tablespoon of olive oil. Brush the edges and stems of the peppers with more oil and grind over some black pepper.

Cooking

Bake the peppers about 45 minutes. By that time they should have wilted and started to char around the edges. Oil will spill into the baking dishes, so check from time to time that they are not frying and burning. If you feel this is happening, add a tablespoon of water to the baking dish.

Turn up the oven to 425°F and remove the peppers. Spoon the oil and juices from the dishes back into the peppers. Set the Piedmontese Peppers aside to cool at this point.

Slice the Mozzarella and place a slice in each of the red pepper halves. Arrange the anchovies criss-cross on each slice. Spoon over any remaining pan juices and return to the oven. When the cheese has melted and is bubbling they are ready .

Serving

If serving this dish on its own, serve each person one of each type of pepper. Use plain white plates for maximum visual impact and strew with torn basil leaves. Good bread is essential to mop up the juices, which are the real joy of this simple dish.

Grilled Asparagus with Shaved Parmesan

In Britain, we think of asparagus with a glowing national pride that has always puzzled me since, in my experience, most of what is produced here should be thrown away or used for soup. We ought to have the best asparagus in the world, but most of what we can buy in markets is withered, woody, and past its best. Indeed, almost any other country's asparagus is superior to ours, though I do not include here the fat white French spears from Argenteuil, which I dislike. To my taste, the slender green asparagus is the best for grilling. Buy it toward the end of the season in June, when it is at its peak.

When buying asparagus, look for a bright green color and hardly any woody stem. As soon as the stems look withered, you have old dried-out asparagus that is not worth eating. With the exception of slender young spears, all asparagus needs peeling. Peelings from the stem can be used to make a good stock base for Risotto with Asparagus (see page 40).

Ingredients (for 4)

2 pounds asparagus
5 tablespoons olive oil
salt and pepper
juice of 1 lemon, or 1 tablespoon balsamic vinegar
4 ounces Reggiano Parmesan cheese, to serve

Utensils

ridged grill pan
large bowl
small bowl
tongs
potato peeler

Mise en Place
Preheat a ridged grill pan • Trim and peel the asparagus stalks and wash them. Pat dry and toss in 1 tablespoon of the olive oil together with a light sprinkling of salt • In a small bowl, mix the lemon juice or balsamic vinegar with the remaining olive oil and season this vinaigrette dressing to taste.

Cooking
Simplicity itself: Place the asparagus on the hot pan until it starts to wilt. Using tongs, turn the spears and grill the other sides briefly. The ridges will mark the spears. You want them to brown them slightly, but not burn them.

Serving
Transfer to a warmed serving dish and dress with the vinaigrette. Using the potato peeler, shave over curls of Parmesan. Serve immediately while the asparagus is still warm.

Chicken Broth with Parsley Pasta

Chicken poached in broth is one of the purest dishes in the canon of cooking. Poached chicken is the Poule au Pot of Henri of Navarre as well as the heart of a Scottish cock-a-leekie. Here the dish is given an Italian flavor by the addition of parsley-stuffed ravioli.

Chicken cooked in barely simmering water will emerge plump, moist, and tender and makes a great base for a wide range of dishes like Capon Salad (see page 93). In times past, the chicken for the pot would have been a tough old farmyard cock, too full of muscle and sinew to cook in any other way. Consequently it would have taken several hours to produce a texture that was remotely edible. No matter how long you cook one of these birds you never reach that ultimate point of melting tenderness, but you do get an unmatchable flavor in the broth. Such birds are hard to come by, though your butcher should be able to get hold of a stewing hen — an elderly chicken that has been laying eggs all its life — but my experience of such hens is that they need to be cooked for several hours, only to fall apart at the critical moment when they are becoming tender.

You may find a true capon, which is a castrated rooster (sorry), or you can use a capon-style bird. The genuine article has rather dense flesh and is ridiculously expensive. The assumption here is that you will be working with good-quality, free-range chickens that take much less time to cook but will still give a brilliant result. If you use one of the larger capon-style birds, obviously one is the equivalent of two smaller chickens.

You will have lots of chicken left over, which you can use in the Capon Salad or in any recipe calling for cold poached chicken.

Ingredients
(for 8–10)

1 capon or capon-style bird, or 2 4-pound free-range chickens, plus as many chicken carcasses and giblets as your butcher will give you and will fit into your largest pan
2 large carrots
2 large onions
2 celery stalks
handful of parsley stems
2 bay leaves
salt and pepper

FOR THE PARSLEY PASTA:
1 quantity Rich Pasta Dough (see page 25)
50 flat parsley leaves

Mise en Place
Put the chickens in a very large pan. If you have been able to get some carcasses, chop each into 6 or 8 pieces using a heavy cleaver and arrange around the birds. Cover with cold water • Trim the carrots. Peel and coarsely chop them • Coarsely chop the onions and celery • Carefully pull the leaves off the parsley.

Cooking
Place the pan on the highest heat you can manage and bring to a boil. As the water reaches boiling point, scum will rise to the surface. Resist the temptation to skim too soon because the foam will thicken, then skim thoroughly. Lower the temperature as soon as it comes to a rolling boil to achieve the barest simmer. This is the point where an occasional bubble will come to the surface, a murmuring simmer — almost a tremble. A fast boil will extract material from the bones that will make the broth cloudy, boiling impurities back into the stock. If this happens you will need to get into the tedium of clarifying the broth with egg whites. To encourage extraction of scum after the first skimming, throw in a handful of ice cubes. Skim once more, then add the vegetables and bay leaves. (There is a school of thought that includes the vegetables from the outset.)

Continue to simmer about 1 hour, skimming at regular intervals. The word "about" is used advisedly, as birds of different sizes will take different cooking times.

heavy cleaver
2 large saucepans (one very large)
spider (see page 16) or long-
  pronged carving fork
fine strainer
pasta machine
pastry wheel or pasta cutter

A smaller chicken may be done in half an hour, and if you overcook them the birds will fall apart. So judge very carefully by size.

While the chicken(s) are cooking, make the Rich Pasta Dough as described on page 25 and let it rest during the subsequent simmering.

Remove the chickens carefully, leaving the carcasses and vegetables in the broth. There is a special implement for this called a spider (see page 16), but if you do not have one (and few people do) use a long-pronged carving fork and something that will slide under the birds to provide a platform to lift with. You may need somebody else to help if the birds are large, as they are fragile at this point and can break apart if you are not gentle.

Continue to simmer the broth, bones, and vegetables for 1 hour more and then pour through a fine strainer into a bowl. Pour the strained liquid back into the pan and return to a high heat. Scum will again come to the surface in prodigious quantities as the fat and albumen coalesce, and it is vital to skim this off carefully before it amalgamates with the stock and clouds the broth. The shimmering clarity of the end product depends on rigorous skimming. Do not leave the pot at this point because a moment's loss of concentration and all your care will have been for nothing as the scum and fat will boil back into the liquid. After carefully removing all the scum that surfaces, boil vigorously and reduce the liquid by half to concentrate the flavor. Taste and season at this point.

Holding Point – at this stage all the ingredients may be kept in the refrigerator for a day or two.

Roll out one-quarter of the pasta dough in the pasta machine, according to manufacturer's instructions and until it is as thin as you can make it. After the final rolling, lay the sheet on a flat working surface. Position the parsley leaves at regular intervals on one half of the sheet of dough, leaving space around all the edges and between each leaf to be able to seal the ravioli edges. Brush the pastry around the edges and in between the parsley leaves with water, then fold the sheet over and pass it through the pasta machine. Using a pastry wheel or pasta cutter, cut the sheet into individual ravioli. (When cooked, you will be able to see the parsley through the pasta, looking like a fine piece of engraving.)

Put a large pan of salted water on to heat for the pasta. Cook the ravioli in the rapidly boiling water until just beginning to become tender, but not quite all the way there. Refresh in cold water and drain in a colander. Shred two chicken breast halves from the poached birds (or one from a capon). Reheat the ravioli in the simmering broth.

Serving

Put 8 hot ravioli in each soup bowl, ladle over the broth, and strew with pieces of shredded chicken.

Gravlax with Dill-Mustard Sauce and Cucumber Salad

Ingredients (for 6)

1 salmon, weighing about 8-10 pounds (as 2 whole fillets, untrimmed and unskinned, this will yield 5-6 pounds of fillet)

FOR THE CURE:
2 large bunches of dill
1 heaped cup Maldon sea salt
2 cups sugar
3 tablespoons freshly ground black pepper

FOR THE CUCUMBER SALAD:
1 large or 3 small English cucumbers (I prefer the smaller as they have better flavor)
$2/3$ cups Maldon sea salt
$2^{1}/2$ cups sugar
2 cups good white wine vinegar or Japanese rice vinegar

FOR THE DILL-MUSTARD SAUCE:
2 tablespoons Dijon mustard
bunch of dill
2 tablespoons olive oil
2 tablespoons heavy whipping cream

This means "buried salmon", an unappealing way of describing a now universally loved dish that is quintessentially Scandinavian. Indeed, all four nations claim it as their own. Being Danish by association (married to one) I favor their claim.

This is a dish that introduces dill to people who previously thought of it just as part of a Jewish pickle jar. If fresh dill is unavailable you can achieve fairly good results with lots of the freeze-dried herb. In Denmark, gravlax is usually served with an over-sweet, mild mustard relish. I serve it with sweet pickled cucumbers and a rather more abrasive sauce to counteract the silky texture and taste of the salmon. Never try and make this with too small a piece of fish as the cure does not work. You will just end up with an over-salted and pretty inedible piece of salmon.

The slicing and serving sound rather complicated but are not, in fact, difficult. You can practice on the first fillet and demonstrate your mastery of the technique on the second, remembering all the while that farmed salmon is now one of the cheapest protein sources available. One fillet will do for six people. The rest will make great second helpings or sandwiches.

Scandinavians eat more salt than anybody except perhaps the Japanese, so consider your second course carefully. No more salt — something gentle and soothing. In any case, gravlax is so rich it is really a meal in its own right. Bread with it and cheese and fruit afterwards. Ça suffit, or however you say that in Danish.

Preparation

To prepare the salmon: Begin a minimum of 5 days in advance — a week is better. Suggestions from elsewhere that this time can be reduced to as little as 2 days should be ignored. It takes at least 5 days for the harmony of pickle and salmon to develop.

Coarsely chop the dill and mix thoroughly in a bowl with the salt, sugar, and pepper.

Lay out a sheet of foil that is at least 3 times the width of a salmon fillet. Distribute one-quarter of the curing mix over approximately the area a single fillet will occupy, leaving the first 6 inches of the foil clear for folding over.

Place one fillet, skin-side down, on the bed of curing mixture and cover with about two-thirds of the remaining mixture. Put the second fillet on top, skin-side up, to make a sandwich. Scatter the remaining curing mixture over the skin.

Now wrap it up: Fold over the clear end of the foil, then bring the sides of the sheet together. Bring the long side over and tuck the sides and ends of foil under. Carefully turn over and adjust to make a neat package.

Put the package on the tray and place in the refrigerator with the other tray on top. Put everything else in the refrigerator you have had to remove to make room for it back on top of that tray to weight it down.

Turn the salmon package daily for 5–7 days. It will exude a salty sugar syrup, which is to be expected, but make sure the tray you use on the bottom has high enough sides to avoid pickling everything else in the refrigerator. If you pickle for the full 7 days, then eat within 3 days.

Utensils

bowl
electrician's pliers or strong tweezers
widest sheet of aluminum foil from the biggest pack you can buy
high-sided metal tray large enough to hold the salmon wrapped in foil and which will fit in your refrigerator
second tray to sit on top
potato peeler
mandoline grater (see page 15)
small saucepan
large strainer
food processor
2 canning jars
flexible slicing knife (desirable but not essential)

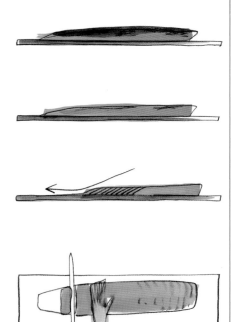

To prepare the Cucumber Salad (again several days ahead): Using a potato peeler, half peel the cucumber, taking off alternating strips along its length to produce a striped effect. Chop the ends off and discard. Using the mandoline, cut it into slices about $1/10$-inch thick and put them in a bowl. Scatter the sea salt and all but 1 teaspoon of the sugar over the cucumber slices and mix thoroughly. (Hands are best for this job.) Let cure 2 hours.

Meanwhile, make the salad dressing: Heat the vinegar in a pan to just below boiling point. Add the reserved sugar, stirring to prevent it solidifying. Then add a teaspoon of salt, stir again, and set aside to cool.

After the cucumber has cured 2 hours, tip it into the strainer and let it drain with the strainer resting over the now empty bowl. Considerable amounts of water will be drawn from the cucumber.

After another hour, discard the liquid that has drained into the bowl and tip the cucumber back into the bowl. Fill the bowl with cold water and leave 5 minutes. Drain and then fill again with cold water. Leave another 5 minutes. Drain in the strainer and taste the cucumber for saltiness. If too salty, then repeat the procedure a third time.

Half fill a canning jar with the salad dressing (there should be plenty leftover). Gently squeeze moisture out of the cucumber and pack loosely into the jar. Seal the top and shake gently to coat the slices with the sweet dressing. This is an excellent pickle and keeps for weeks in the refrigerator if unopened. Once opened, however, it deteriorates rapidly and should be used within 2 days.

To make the Dill-Mustard Sauce: Put the mustard and dill (without stems) in a food processor with 2 tablespoons of the cucumber dressing and whizz it up. With the machine still running, pour in the oil slowly through the feed tube to form a light emulsion. Stop processing. Pour in the cream and churn briefly to incorporate. Transfer to a canning jar. (For real mustard enthusiasts, like me, add another tablespoon of mustard at the beginning.)

On the day of serving: Unwrap the salmon and rinse it gently to wash off all the cure. Lay the fillet with the head end in the direction of your preferred hand and the skin side down. There is a line of bones called "pin bones" that are located from the head end of the fillet running centrally to about halfway along. Using pliers or tweezers, grip them individually and pull them out, easing them away at an angle toward your preferred side. If the fishmonger has left any rib bones, remove them in the same way.

Tidy the edges of the fillet, cutting away the outer strip that contains bones and fins. Don't cut too much away, but these edges will be over-cured anyway and are therefore no great loss. Starting at the tail end, about 6 inches along the fillet, cut at a 30 degree angle away from you toward the tail. The first 2 slices, being from the thinner tail end, will be over-salty and a little dry so don't serve them (eat them yourself rinsed down with a glass of something suitable). Gravlax is traditionally cut thicker than smoked salmon, which makes it that much easier to deal with.

Serving

Put 3 large slices on each plate along with a spoonful of drained cucumber salad and a spoonful of mustard sauce. A sprig of fresh dill sets it off.

Deep-fried Squash Flowers

Ingredients (for 4)

24 summer squash flowers
salt and pepper
sunflower oil, for deep-frying (the
    exact amount will depend on the
    size of pan you use)
flour, for coating

FOR THE TRADITIONAL
ITALIAN BATTER:
2 cups flour, sifted
2 extra large eggs
a little olive oil
1 1/4 cups iced lager

FOR THE TEMPURA BATTER:
1 large egg
1 cup ice water
3/4 cup flour, sifted
1/2 teaspoon baking soda

Utensils

bowl
deep heavy pan or wok for deep-
    frying
candy thermometer
bowl
tongs

Deep-frying is much misunderstood and generally maligned. The British have traditionally eaten fish and chips which, when done well, make one of the few dishes of which we can be proud. However, the quality of our national dish increasingly leaves much to be desired, while deep-frying has generally suffered a thoroughly bad press.

The comparatively recent introduction of electric deep-fryers to domestic kitchens on a large scale has done nothing to improve matters. Those we have tested simply do not achieve the necessary high temperature to seal battered food, delivering quite unacceptable and greasy results. The minimum temperature needed is 350°F, but 375°F is better because the introduction of cold wet food into the cooking oil has a sudden and profound impact on its temperature. If you have one of these fryers, check the temperature with a thermometer and you will almost certainly be in for a nasty surprise. We have tried three models, but none of them came within 15 degrees of the required sealing temperature.

To cook this dish you need a deep heavy pan (or wok) that you fill to just below half full. Use a suitable thermometer to gauge the temperature. When you have eaten perfect tempura or lightly battered squash flowers like these, you will never think again of deep-frying as a heavy-handed technique.

This is not an ideal dish to try and serve for a formal dinner party, but something to give friends who are happy to eat in the kitchen. Cook the flowers a batch at a time and don't overcrowd the pan. Remember also to leave time between batches for the temperature of the oil to recover and leave the thermometer in the oil at all times.

I prefer a lightly mixed batter more akin to tempura. The one given here is from Madhur Jaffrey's Eastern Vegetarian Cooking and produces excellent results. The more traditional batter is what you will find in Italy. Try both and see which you prefer.

Mise en Place

If using the traditional batter, make it ahead of time: Put the flour in the bowl with a pinch of salt and pepper. Break in the eggs, add 1/2 tablespoon of olive oil, and mix. Using a whisk, beat in the cold lager in a steady steam until you have a smooth creamy consistency. Let rest in the refrigerator 20 minutes.

Heat the oil in the pan or wok to 375°F, using a thermometer to be precise. Have ready a warm serving plate (or basket) lined with paper towels and warmed individual plates. Also, make sure your guests are sitting close by, ready to eat the flowers immediately. Put the flour for dusting on a shallow plate.

While the oil is heating make the tempura batter, if using (it requires no resting and must be used as soon as it is made): Break the egg into the bowl and whisk. Then whisk in the ice water. Add all the flour and baking soda in one go. Turn 4 or 5 times with a fork. There should be lumps and little bits of flour not mixed in. This will deliver a much lighter end result.

Cooking

Dust the flowers lightly with flour, then dip them in batter and fry them until golden brown. Turn carefully using tongs (they will be very buoyant and not always easy to turn). They won't take long to cook – perhaps 90 seconds on each side.

Immediately remove and drain very briefly on paper towels.

Pressed Skate and Potato Terrine

Terrines tend to be rather formulaic, and the heavy liver-based variations have rather gone out of favor. They are marvelous with bread for an al fresco lunch, but perhaps rather overpowering and filling for a first course. Pressed terrines are much lighter in effect and, having potato in it, this terrine does not need the counterbalance of bread. Skate works particularly well in this type of dish.

A note of caution: When buying skate, smell it to check that there is no whiff of ammonia. I know that many scholarly food writers say different on this matter, going on about skate's urea metabolism and how the fish should smell of ammonia when it first comes out of the water and that this should then die away. All I know from years of buying and cooking it, however, is that if there is any whiff of ammonia it only gets much worse.

Ingredients (for 6-8)

4 pounds skate wings on the bone (about 4)
5 cups Court-bouillon (see page 21)
2 pounds peeled, boiled potatoes
8–10 small mild gherkins
2 tablespoons flat-leaf parsley
2 teaspoons capers (salted better than brined)
3 tablespoons Dijon mustard
a little olive oil
4 shallots

Utensils

large saucepan for poaching the skate
2 terrine molds
plastic wrap
food processor
serrated knife
cake server

Mise en Place

Prepare the fish: Poach the skate wings in the Court-bouillon until the flesh pulls easily away from the gelatinous bones, about 15 minutes. Drain. (The meat will come away from the bones in untidy strips, but this really does not matter.)

Line the mold with plastic wrap, leaving enough hanging over the sides to fold over the top to cover • Thinly slice the fish and potatoes • Put all the other ingredients in a food processor and chop to combine.

Preparation

Line the bottom of the terrine mold with a layer of potato slices, then pack the mold with alternating layers of skate, the gherkin mixture, and sliced potato until full. You may not need all the gherkin mixture, as the layers of skate and potato should dominate. (Leftover mixture goes well with cold meats.)

Fold the plastic wrap over the top and weight it. The ideal thing to weight it is another mold of identical size with three medium-sized cans of food inside it. If you can't do that, cut a piece of cardboard to fit inside the top and wrap in foil before placing the cans on top. Refrigerate overnight.

Unmold the terrine by pulling out the wrapped package. Unwrap and cut into 1-inch slices using a serrated knife. This can be a tricky business as the terrine may be very prone to breaking up, so it is a good idea to hold a cake server against the end of the terrine as you cut it.

Serving

Serve with a light vinaigrette and with blanched green beans or Blanched Spinach Salad (see page 97).

Pizza Bianca

The very best pizzas are made in wood-fired brick ovens, where the intense heat and the aromatic smoke produce conditions that cannot be matched in ordinary electric or gas-fired ovens. The pizzas are pushed deep into the hottest part of the oven on wooden paddles, the dough exploding into life as it hits the red-hot brick to cook in 2 or 3 minutes, not something most of us can duplicate. However, this not to say that you can't make good pizzas or focaccia *(olive oil bread) at home.*

At the Orvieto cooking school in Umbria, where I teach each summer, I had a lesson in pizza-making from a man who had been cooking pizzas all his life. What impressed me was the simplicity of the dough, which had very little oil in it, and the fact that his tomato topping was commercially produced "passata" used straight from the jar. He cooked them in an outdoor wood-fired oven and the results were sensational, the crust pliant but crisp underneath, the best I have ever tasted.

The chef Wolfgang Puck pioneered new-wave pizza in Los Angeles some ten years ago, with combination toppings of things like smoked salmon and cream cheese. Overnight he turned America's staple into something fashionable and expensive. The imitators moved fast on the heels of the innovator, and Californian restaurants vied with one another to create chic and unusual toppings, many of them frankly bizarre.

I prefer the most basic versions, notably the original Neapolitan pizza margharita of cheese, tomato, and basil. Here we use only the very best buffalo Mozzarella, with the tomato peeled and diced and served with basil leaves as a side salad.

Ingredients (for 4)

(TO MAKE TWO 10-INCH PIZZAS)
3 cups bread flour
1 teaspoon salt
1/2 teaspoon sugar
1 1/2 -2 1/4 teaspoons quick rise dry yeast
about 7 tablespoons extra virgin olive oil
1 1/4 - 1 1/2 cups warm water
1/2 pound buffalo Mozzarella cheese

FOR THE TOMATO SALAD:
6 ripe plum tomatoes
1 tablespoon balsamic vinegar
4–5 tablespoons extra virgin olive oil
salt and pepper
12 basil leaves
few pitted black olives (optional)

Utensils

food processor with metal blade
bowl
2 pizza stones or pans

Mise en Place

Make the dough: Sift the flour into the food processor, together with the salt, sugar, and yeast. Turn on at full speed and add 2 tablespoons of the oil through the feed tube, followed by half the warm water in a thin stream. The dough will now have the consistency of bread crumbs. Add the rest of the water a spoonful at a time until the dough forms a ball and becomes slightly sticky. Continue to process for 5 minutes. If you have inadvertently added too much water and the dough sticks to the sides, shake in more flour a spoonful at a time until it forms into a ball.

Transfer the dough to a lightly floured surface and knead by hand for 2 or 3 minutes. Brush a bowl with a little olive oil, put in the dough in a ball, and brush all over with a little more oil. Cover with a cloth and put to rise in a warm place until it has doubled in bulk. This should take about 1 hour.

Half an hour before you want to cook the pizzas, preheat the oven to its highest setting. If using a pizza stone, put it near the top of the oven • Drain the Mozzarella and cut it into 1/2-inch dice.

Prepare the pizzas: Punch down the dough and divide into two pieces. Working on a heavily floured surface, flatten these into rounds using your fingers and working from the center outward. If using pizza pans, press the dough out in them. Brush with a little oil and arrange pieces of mozzarella over each with space in between and leaving a clear border around the outside. Drizzle a tablespoon of olive oil over each. Do not leave to rise a second time, but use at once.

Cooking

Ideally you want to be able to slide the pizzas onto the hot stones. This is not easy, and you may achieve better results using pizza pans. (Experiment without toppings to see which technique works best for you. The cost will be negligible.)

Bake until the cheese has melted and is bubbling hot, 10-15 minutes.

While they are baking, cut the tomatoes into quarters or eighths. Make a vinaigrette by mixing the vinegar with the olive oil and seasoning. Toss the tomatoes in it. Tear the basil leaves and mix in with the olives, if using.

Serving

Serve the pizza cut in wedges, with the tomato salad on one side of the plate.

MAIN COURSES

Cold Poached Salmon Trout with Tzatziki

Salmon or steelhead trout is a fish without peer. It is related to the freshwater rainbow trout, but at some point exchanged the constricting habitat of the rivers for the open sea. Like the salmon, though, it returns to fresh water to spawn.

Its flesh is pink, but not as red as salmon. Like the lobster, it is so delicious it needs no fancy cooking, no trappings, and is best served with the minimum of distractions. The fish is best poached whole and served cold with some sympathetic side dishes.

Mayonnaise and new potatoes go well with salmon trout. I also like it with tzatziki, the Middle-Eastern cucumber salad spiked with mint and a little garlic. I stress a small amount of garlic — too much and it would be disconcertingly vehement.

Ingredients (for 4-6)

about 3 cups Court-bouillon (see page 21)
1 whole steelhead trout or Arctic char, weighing about 3-5 pounds, cleaned and gills cut out
2 tablespoons white wine vinegar

FOR THE TZATZIKI:
1 garlic clove
1 straight English cucumber
6 mint leaves
2 1/2 cups plain yogurt
salt and pepper

Utensils

fish kettle
saucepan
blanching basket to match the saucepan

Mise en Place

Make the Court-bouillon as described on page 21 and let it cool completely.

Cooking

Put the fish in the kettle and pour over the cold court-bouillon. Stir in the vinegar and just enough cold water to cover. Bring it slowly to a boil. Let it bubble a couple of times, then put on the lid and remove from the heat. Let the fish cool completely in the liquid.

Make the tzatziki while the fish is cooling: Put a pan of salted water to heat. Smash the garlic clove and mince it. Trim the cucumber, then dice it. Mince the mint leaves.

Put the diced cucumber in the blanching basket and dip it in the boiling salted water to wilt it slightly, about 15 seconds. Refresh and drain. Pat dry with paper towels and put into a serving bowl. Add the chopped mint, garlic, and yogurt and season generously with pepper. Mix and taste, adding salt to taste.

Remove the fish from the court-bouillon, and place it on an oval serving plate. Remove the skin from the top surface.

Serving

People do some grotesque things to whole cold fish. My pet dislike is the caterer's cucumber fish scales . . . yuck! Leave something this beautiful alone.

Simply serve with warm boiled new potatoes and the tzatziki. Nothing else is needed except cold dry white wine.

Aïoli Garni

Food and drink are often made memorable and desirable by association. On occasions, without the proper context, it is difficult to think what the excitement is all about. A glass of retsina, drunk with the one you love under the shadow of a vine and outside an enchanting Greek taverna, with the secret bay gleaming in the background, is one thing. Drinking it alone and broke while watching television on a winter's night is another altogether.

Aïoli is one of many French gustatory sacred cows that are at the heart of regional food fantasies. The kik ha fars of Brittany, Nice's soupe au pistou, brandade de morue from the Languedoc – these are the stuff of which dreams are made. All too often, however, our memory distorts and we wonder whether perhaps the snapshot taken through gauze at twilight is a true image, or a nostalgic piece of nonsense, about as jolly in reality as a medieval ploughman's lunch.

Among these distortions, the ritual of aïoli could take center stage. Picture the scene, this summer's Friday or Saturday in Provence. Our camera tracks in slowly, embracing the action in wide shot. Tables set up in the village square, groaning under the weight of huge platters of glistening salt cod, mounds of boiled potatoes, buckets of escargots, vivid vegetables, and shining viscous bowls of golden, garlic mayonnaise. It is Jean de Florette scripted by Peter Mayle.

The atmosphere is festive, a happy family occasion. And, as the afternoon wears on and the rosé goes down, all are suffused with the same glow of contentment. An apple-cheeked grandmother, helped to her chair by an attentive son, looks around her. "Oh la-la. C'est le vrai aïoli, n'est-ce pas?"

Cut to . . . a group of embittered British people sitting outside a café miserably sipping pastis that tastes unaccountably of aniseed balls. A waiter, who is grumpy because Provence is now overrun by ghastly foreigners, is busily slamming down a scraggy piece of gray cod, a bowl of something that looks like lubricant, a few old potatoes, and a bottle of inadequately chilled, thin pink wine. A wife whispers to her husband in tones of disbelief: "Is that it then? Is that aïoli?"

The answer would be, yes it is. As you would have to reply if asked whether sliced white industrial loaf is bread. For aïoli is indeed a movable feast, something to be interpreted up or down the quality scale. It must, of course, have garlic mayonnaise and in France it would always have salt cod and almost always escargots, because Provence is riddled with them. But after that the rules are pretty relaxed. I prefer to serve poached fresh cod rather than the salted form, which is better treated differently (brandade, for example). The vegetables must all be cooked – this is not a platter of crudités.

The crowning glory is, of course, the aïoli itself. Much is made by nearly every food writer I can think of about using a stone pestle and mortar. Richard Olney says "a good aïoli should be mounted slowly, rhythmically, and regularly, the pestle turned always in the same direction (clockwise is easiest for me), and, when finished, should be stiff and heavy with a sweaty surface." He says that using a blender is too violent and destroys the fruit of the olive oil, while making the aïoli lighter than it should be. Much as I love my pestle and mortar (and indeed rarely travel anywhere without them), I find that using an electric mixer makes very acceptable mayonnaise and, far from destroying the fruitiness of the olive oil, the sauce benefits from mixing in at least 50% sunflower oil, for mayonnaise made solely from extra virgin oil is incredibly intense.

Here then is the Little and Whittington method that makes more than enough for 8 people, and maybe 10. This is not, by the by, a dish for small numbers. Aïoli Garni makes a wonderful communal dish for a summer party, and the more elements the

Ingredients
(for 8-10)

2 1/2 quarts Court-bouillon (see page 21)

1 whole cod, weighing about 5 pounds, head removed, and cleaned

3 pounds new potatoes,

1 pound green beans

2 heads of broccoli

1 pound carrots

4 large or 8 small globe artichokes

juice of 1 lemon

8–10 eggs

4 ounces best-quality black olives

FOR THE AÏOLI (GARLIC MAYONNAISE):

4 garlic cloves

2 egg yolks

salt and white pepper

1 1/4 cups extra virgin olive oil

juice of 2 lemons

1 1/4 cups sunflower oil

a little boiled water, let cool to warm

Utensils

electric mixer

fish kettle

very large serving plate

several large saucepans

better. It is only what you make of it. Rosé would be the wine of choice, for this is, after all, a Provençal tradition. People often get drunk at aïoli feasts, all part of the fun. Since it will be summer, and you will hopefully be outside, you could throw leftover aïoli with impunity at anybody who gets too carried away.

Mise en Place

Make the aïoli well ahead: Crush the garlic to a pulp using some suitably heavy implement and put into the bowl of the mixer with the egg yolks. Switch on and beat together with 1 teaspoon of salt and 1 teaspoon of white pepper. (Black pepper leaves visible specks, but if you do not mind this go ahead and use it.) Start to add the olive oil in a thin stream. After you have incorporated half of it, add half the lemon juice. Now beat in half the sunflower oil. If the mayonnaise becomes too thick, add a tablespoon of the warm water. Repeat the process, using the rest of the olive oil, then the remaining lemon juice, and finally the remainder of the sunflower oil. Drip in water if at any stage it gets too thick. The consistency should be heavy, a dipping rather than a pouring thickness. If it should separate, just put a third yolk into another bowl and beat the curdled glop into it, a little at a time, until it holds again. Taste. Add more lemon juice if you think it needs it and more salt and pepper. The garlic, being raw, will continue to gain in strength for several hours, but, then, this is supposed to be an emphatic sauce. Turn into a bowl and store in the refrigerator.

Make the court-bouillon as described on page 21 and let it cool completely.

Prepare the fish: If the fishmonger has not already done so, cut off the head of the fish. (Cut out the gills with scissors and discard, then freeze the head for use in your next fish soup) • Wash and trim all the vegetables.

Cooking

Put the cod in a fish kettle, just cover it with the cold court-bouillon (adding more water if necessary), and bring it slowly to boil. Bubble gently 1 minute, than remove from the heat, and let cool in the liquid. When cold, remove from the liquid and scrape off the skin on the uppermost side. Put on a large serving plate.

While the fish is cooling, cook all the vegetables in boiling salted water until just tender, but still with a good deal of crunch. Drain and let cool. The artichokes should be cooked in a large pan of boiling salted water to which the juice of a lemon has been added. They are done when the outer leaves come away with ease. Refresh briefly in cold water and drain well upside down. Pull away the inside top leaves and remove the inner choke with a teaspoon. Hard-boil the eggs 7 minutes and let them cool in cold water.

Serving

If you have a large enough platter to do so, surround the cod with the cooked vegetables and eggs (I like them still in their shells) arranged decoratively by color in little piles so that each part of the table will have access to all the ingredients. Scatter the whole dish with the olives and put the aïoli in 2 or 3 bowls around the table.

Chinese-Style Steamed Fish

It was in London's Chinatown that I first ate steamed fish and discovered that many of the restaurants there sold whole cooked sea bass as loss leaders at a price that was about the same as you could buy it at the fishmonger, sometimes less.

Steaming is a great technique for many different fish, as long as they are cooked whole and on the bone. They don't have to be expensive: flounder, for example, is excellent cooked this way, as is whiting. If you want to go up-market, try steaming a true Dover sole.

You can use a range of different pieces of kit for steaming. I like the bamboo baskets you buy cheaply in Chinese markets, but you can also use a custom-made metal steamer or just a large wok with a lid and a rack. You steam the fish on the plate on which you will serve it. Make sure it is large enough for the fish to sit flat on the plate when it is placed in the steamer.

This dish can be for two people, or provide a small amount for four. In a Cantonese meal the fish would be brought at the same time as all the other dishes, but I prefer to eat it on its own. The Chinese also tend to scatter the fish with lots of flavoring ingredients, like dried shrimp and bits of ham, which I find unnecessary.

Ingredients (for 2-4)

1 pound very fresh fish on the bone (skinned and cleaned, but otherwise whole)
1 carrot
2 scallions
1-inch piece of fresh gingerroot
1 garlic clove
1 hot red chili pepper
2 tablespoons sesame oil
2 tablespoons sunflower oil
1/4 cup Kikkoman soy sauce
coriander leaves (cilantro), for garnish

Utensils

steamer (see right)
serving plate of a matching size
bowl
small pan
2 sets of chopsticks

Mise en Place

Set up the steamer with water in the bottom and put it to heat • Make sure the fish is scrupulously clean. If there is any blood in the body cavity, rub this with salt and rinse under cold running water • Cut the carrot, scallions, and peeled ginger into julienne strips, putting them immediately into ice water in a bowl and tossing to mix the strands • Cut the garlic into paper-thin slices. Cut the chili across into thin rings and remove the seeds.

Cooking

Put the sesame and sunflower oils in a small pan to heat gently – be careful, sesame oil has a very low burning point.

Pour a little soy sauce on the serving plate and then arrange half the drained vegetable julienne on it to make a bed for the fish. Place the fish on top, and scatter over the rest of the julienne. Pour over the remaining soy sauce and put to steam. The size of the fish does not affect the cooking time, which will be between 12 and 15 minutes. Test that it is done after 10 minutes by sliding the tip of a knife into the back at the center and pulling upward: The flesh should detach easily. You do not want it undercooked because it will not come off the bone. It is, however, difficult to overcook because steaming is a gentle, forgiving technique and you would probably have to leave the fish for 25 minutes before it was ruined.

Halfway through the steaming, put the garlic and chili to infuse in the warmed oil.

Serving

Remove the fish plate from the steamer, spoon some of the juices in the bottom of the plate over the fish, and wipe a round the edge of the plate for a neat presentation. Pour the now hot and aromatic contents of the saucepan over the fish and scatter some coriander leaves over.

Eat immediately on hot plates using chopsticks. (If the oil cools it will make the dish greasy.)

Seductive Lobster

Most of us regard lobster as a special and expensive treat, but when you find yourself paying an arm and a leg for sea bass then, all of a sudden, the costly crustacean does not seem quite so rich and rare after all. Having said this, you must allow at least 1 pound live weight per person, so it is never going to be bargain basement grub. So what? This makes the perfect seduction supper, and since when was that a cheap date?

When buying lobster, remember that it may have been in a distributor's holding tank several weeks. While on crustacean death row it does not eat, so although looking big and mean on the carapace, it is getting thinner and thinner inside. If your fishmonger sells you a lobster that turns out when cooked to have very little meat in it, then it has been held in a tank for too long and you are entitled to be angry.

Big lobsters are called "breakers," those which have lost claws or legs, "cripples." Not PC at all. Victor Hugo, served a lobster with only one claw, demanded of the waiter why it was so disfigured. The waiter said it had come off worst in a fight in the holding tank. "Take it away and bring me the victor," quipped Victor.

And what of cooking your lobster? Opinions vary as to the most humane form of despatch. Should you put it in cold water and bring it to a boil, when the lobster is supposed to go out painlessly? (The logic of this escapes me.) Or, stab a point through its spinal cord? Or, inject it with morphine? I have considered all the options and discussed crustacean capital punishment with a number of wise lobsters. Their refusal to articulate a preference confirms my view that the best method is to drop them into a lot of fast-boiling heavily salted water and put the lid on quickly while whistling the Marseillaise to cover up any shrieking.

Lobster is one of the most delicious natural foods that needs the minimum of adornment. I eschew lobster thermidor and all such abominations. If ever something should be kept simple, this is it.

Mise en Place

Put a large pan of water to heat, salting heavily (it should be about as salty as the North Sea but not as salty as the Dead Sea). Say good-bye to your lobsters, checking that the rubber bands around their claws are tight so they cannot demonstrate their resentment on the tumbrel en route to Madame Pot.

When the water is bubbling briskly, put the lobsters in and boil 15 minutes. Remove from the heat and let cool in the cooking liquid 15 minutes.

Remove the lobsters from the water using tongs. Snip off the rubber bands and put each lobster on a chopping board with the head toward you. With the tip of a heavy knife, push straight down at the point behind the eyes where there is a little cross and then cut toward you, halving the head. Turn the lobster the other way and bisect the tail. Remove the stomach bag from the head section. This is the only part that is not edible. Crack larger claws using the back of a large cleaver.

Serving

Serve while still warm, with drawn butter (melted butter into which a little hot water has been mixed), Beurre Blanc (see page 23), or extra virgin olive oil, lemon juice, and some Home-Dried Tomatoes (see page 27); or leave to get cold and eat with Mayonnaise (see page 22), cold new potatoes, and a green salad.

Ingredients (for 2-4)

2 2-pound lobsters (for 4, or
  2 1-pound lobsters for 2)
salt

Utensils

large saucepan
tongs
crackers
lobster picks

This lean and succulent cut of lamb is ideal for grilling on a barbecue or ridged grill pan.

Grilled Lamb with Couscous Salad

You could use any one of three cuts for this dish: a leg, boned and butterflied; a rack (in which case it should be roasted rather than grilled); or, my preferred option, the tenderloin cut from the rack. This is a good choice when the lamb has grown up a bit and is no longer quite such a baby (what they mysteriously call "hoggit" in the North of England). The cut consists of the "eye" of the meat that runs from the neck through the loin. Ask for the bones and trimmings if you want to make lamb stock, otherwise don't worry about throwing them away. Much better to do so immediately than bag and freeze to discard at a later date.

The couscous flavored with mint, garlic, lemon juice, and oil is a very Middle-Eastern salad, and a perfect accompaniment to the lamb.

Ingredients (for 4)

2 whole lamb tenderloins (see previous page)
2²/₃ cups instant couscous
2¹/₂ cups boiling water
3 lemons
1¹/₄ cups olive oil
1 red onion
1 red bell pepper
1 yellow bell pepper
bunch of mint
salt and pepper

FOR THE MARINADE:
large sprig of rosemary
small bunch of thyme
2 garlic cloves
2 tablespoons olive oil
¹/₄ cup sunflower oil
1 tablespoon salt
2 teaspoons mignonette pepper (see page 10)

Utensils

2 large bowls (heatproof one for the couscous)
Barbecue or ridged grill pan
tongs

Mise en Place

First prepare the marinade: Pull the leaves off the rosemary and chop them coarsely with the thyme. Cut the garlic into thin slices. Mix the oils, brush the meat all over with them, and put into a dish. Strew with the herbs, garlic, salt, and pepper. Pour over the rest of the oil and refrigerate overnight, or at least 8 hours. If you can, turn it from time to time. Remove from the refrigerator in plenty of time to let it return to room temperature before grilling.

Make the couscous: Put it in a large heatproof bowl and stir while pouring over the boiling water. Go on stirring at least 3 minutes until cool, otherwise the grains will lump together. Juice the lemons and stir the lemon juice into the couscous, followed by the olive oil, continuing to stir gently. All the liquid will be absorbed in due course. Let stand while you chop the onion and peppers into small dice. Incorporate them into the couscous. Coarsely chop the mint leaves and add. Season well with salt and pepper. Refrigerate briefly before serving, but do not chill too long or the oil will solidify.

Preheat the grill pan or light the barbecue well in advance.

Cooking

When ready, sear the drained meat all over before reducing the heat (or moving the meat farther from the coals) and cook, turning frequently, for 15 minutes. It should be pink and juicy in the center. Let it stand 10 minutes, then carve into strips.

Serving

Heap the couscous in the center of a large warmed serving platter and arrange the lamb around it. Spoon and scrape any juices from the carving over the lamb and serve immediately.

Baron of Rabbit with Home-dried Tomatoes

Some people love rabbit, but many remain ambivalent. This could be because of Beatrix Potter. Richard suggested calling this dish Mr. McGregor's Rear Ends of Cottontail and Peter, but accepts this may be a tad anthropomorphic. On that subject, be sure the butcher has removed the heads - skinned, they are enough to put anybody off meat for life. I believe it was just such a head that was used for the horror exiting through John Hurt's diaphragm in Alien.

In the restaurant we tend to cook the saddle of the rabbit – the ribcage to the legs – boned and rolled as neat ballotines, but this is time-consuming and not an easy butchery assignment. I suggest instead that you roast the baron of the rabbit. This means the whole of the rabbit bar the forequarters (i.e. from the rib cage forward), which you use when you make the sauce). If using saddles you will need one per person: Cooking barons will give you enough from two rabbits for four to six people.

Since fresh rabbit is virtually fat-free, it must never be allowed to overcook or it will dry out.

Mise en Place

Well ahead of time, prepare the sauce: Cut the rabbits across at the point where the ribs end, and chop the forequarters into small pieces (See *illustration over page.*) Cut the vegetables into a mirepoix (see page 188). In the large saucepan, brown the bones and mirepoix in 2 tablespoons of the olive oil. Add the vinegar and sugar and toss to coat. Cook until light brown. Pour over almost all the white wine, reserving about 1 glass ($^2/_3$ cup) for deglazing the roasting pan later. Boil hard to reduce until almost all the liquid has gone and it is syrupy. Just cover with cold water, return to a boil, and skim. Turn down the heat and simmer 1 ½ hours. Strain the resulting stock into a bowl, wash out the saucepan, and return the stock to it. Bring back to a boil, skim again, and once more return to a slow simmer to cook until reduced by half. Reserve.

Preheat the oven to 400°F.

Ingredients (for 4-6)

2 farm-raised rabbits (including bones and trimmings for the gravy)
1 carrot
1 onion
1 celery stalk
6 tablespoons olive oil
1 tablespoon balsamic vinegar
½ tablespoon sugar
1 bottle (75cl) of dry white wine
salt and pepper
8 pieces of Home-Dried Tomato (see page 27)
32 black olives
12 basil leaves

Utensils

large saucepan
strainer
bowl
roasting pan large enough to hold
  both barons snugly

Cooking

Put the rabbits on their backs in the roasting pan, dribble generously with olive oil, and season. Roast 15 minutes, then turn over and baste. Dribble on some more olive oil and roast 5–10 minutes longer. Baste again, then turn the rabbits on one side for 5 minutes, and, after a final baste, 5 minutes on the other side. Remove from the oven and let rest 10 minutes.

Carve each rabbit into pieces: Cut them across at the waist. Using a serrated knife, saw off the hind legs. Then cut the saddle in half to give 4 pieces from each rabbit. In the unlikely event of the rabbit not being completely cooked, return the pieces to the pan, roll in the juices, and give them another 5 minutes in the oven.

Transfer to a hot serving plate. Deglaze the roasting pan with the reserved wine and scrape into the sauce. You should have about 1 1/2 cups at this stage. If there is much more, remove some and freeze for use another time.

About 2 minutes before you are ready to serve, stir the tomatoes, olives, and basil into the simmering sauce. Pour over the rabbit just before serving.

Serving

Bring to the table with boiled new potatoes dressed with extra virgin olive oil and salt, or mashed potatoes.

RIGHT Using liberal quantities of olive oil and having a rich gravy, Baron of Rabbit with Home-Dried Tomatoes delivers moist and tender results.

Vitello Tonnato

Fashion in food is a two-edged sword: To be at the cutting edge can be exhilarating, but it is all too easy to contrive for the sake of novelty. Some of the more bizarre combinations favor neither the mixture of produce, nor the palate of the restaurant diner being subjected to innovation for its own sake. This combination of meat and fish sounds odd, but the result is proven and has stood the test of time, though Vitello Tonnato has rather gone out of favor. All the more reason for resurrecting it.

Here the veal is roasted rather than poached and the sauce is made as one process rather than a two-stage affair where mayonnaise is made first. The roast veal could simply be eaten hot with boiled new potatoes and Salsa Verde (see page 50), as this is the classic Italian way of roasting veal. I remember a particularly delicious example eaten at the Agip service station on the autostrada just south of Florence: a thick slice of roasted round served absolutely plain with only a wedge of lemon and the juices that ran out of it. Not the sort of thing one finds along most freeways.

Many people refuse to eat veal because of the way some of it is raised. For those so concerned, whole turkey breast roast can be cooked, glazed, and served with a tuna sauce in just the same way to make Tacchino Tonnato, which is also a much cheaper dish. Using butter instead of olive oil, seal a 2¼-pound turkey roast as described below and then roast in an oven preheated to 375°F with the wine and herbs until firm, 30-40 minutes. Turn and baste from time to time. If the pan dries out, add more wine or a little water. Let cool on a plate and reduce the cooking juices in the pan to about a tablespoon of syrupy brown residue. Pour this over the roast to glaze and then slice and proceed as below.

Ingredients
(for 6-8)

24–36 capers (salt-packed are best)

3½ ounces canned anchovy fillets (those packed in olive oil are nicest – the best anchovies are plain and rose-colored; poor anchovies are dull, gray-tinged, and miserable looking)

2-pound piece of boned veal, rolled and tied neatly (this may sound like rather a lot of meat, but having some leftover for sandwiches is a nice idea)

salt and pepper

2 tablespoons olive oil

about ⅔ cup dry white wine

sprig of rosemary

FOR THE ONE-STEP TUNA SAUCE:

1 lemon

1 garlic clove

sprig of flat-leaf parsley

7 ounces best dolphin-friendly canned tuna, drained

2 large eggs

1 tablespoon Dijon mustard

1 cup sunflower oil

2 cups olive oil (not extra virgin)

Utensils

12- x 8-inch oval Le Creuset (or similar) casserole

food processor

Mise en Place

Preheat the oven to 350°F • Rinse the capers and anchovies if salted and pat dry with paper towels. Split each anchovy fillet along the central line to give two thin strips.

Prepare the sauce ingredients: juice the lemon. Peel and mince the garlic. Pull the parsley leaves from the stems.

Cooking

To roast the veal: Rub it with salt and pepper. Put the casserole over medium-to-high heat, pour in a little olive oil, and seal the veal until a lovely golden brown all over – not blackened.

Add the white wine and rosemary. Roast about 40 minutes. Check from time to time: If the wine evaporates completely, add a little more.

Remove from the oven and finish over high heat on the rangetop, rolling the veal around to gloss the outside with the reduced wine and cooking juices. Let cool completely.

Meanwhile, make the one-step tuna sauce: Put all the ingredients except the oils into the food processor. Leave the eggs whole – there is no need to exclude the whites. Process 30 seconds or until you have a smooth paste. Now add the sunflower oil followed by the olive oil a little at a time, processing constantly, until thickened. Taste for seasoning and adjust, adding more lemon juice if you find the sauce is too bland.

Serving

Cut the veal into thin slices and arrange, slightly overlapping, to cover a suitably sized serving platter. Spoon over the sauce and arrange the anchovies over the top in a lattice pattern, then dot the capers in the centers of the lattice diamonds.

Capon Salad

The combination of succulent poached chicken with a tangy marinade is sublime. This is a classic Renaissance dish from Mantua in Italy's Po Valley, with the sweet and sour flavors so popular in the Quattrocento. All it needs to make a perfect summer main course are some ripe tomatoes and fresh basil, or serve in smaller quantities as a first course. Since capons are hard to come by, you can use a large free-range chicken instead.

Mise en Place

Ideally cook the chicken the day before, as described on page 72, to give it time to cool completely.

Preparation

Preheat the oven to 400°F. Place the pine nuts on a lightly oiled baking sheet and toast them in the oven a few minutes, being careful not to burn them.

Put the wine vinegar in a pan and bring to a simmer. Add the bay leaves, lemon and orange zest, sugar, salt, and pepper. Simmer 15 minutes. Taste for sweetness: If too sour, add a little more sugar. Then add the raisins and toasted pine nuts and set aside.

Pull off any fat and skin from the bird and discard. Roughly shred the meat by pulling apart with your fingers. Put it into a serving bowl and pour over the warm dressing, mixing thoroughly. Let marinate at room temperature for 2–3 hours, then refrigerate overnight. Remove at least 1 hour before you plan to eat.

Serving

Just before bringing to the table, dress with the olive oil and serve with sliced ripe plum tomatoes or Home-Dried Tomatoes and torn basil leaves.

Ingredients (for 4-6)

1 poached capon or large free-range chicken
2 cups pine nuts
1 cup red wine vinegar
2 bay leaves
two 1-inch squares of lemon zest
two 1-inch squares of orange zest
1 heaped tablespoon sugar
2 teaspoons salt
1/2 teaspoon mignonette pepper (see page 10)
2/3 cup raisins
1 cup best-quality extra virgin olive oil, to dress
8 plum tomatoes, sliced, or Home-Dried Tomatoes (see page 27) to serve
handful of basil leaves, torn, to serve

Utensils

baking tray
small saucepan

Orvieto Chicken

This ravishing main-course dish from Umbria needs no accompaniment since the stuffing contains potato and provides a perfect foil to the chicken, which must be free-range and have its giblets. The quality of the local chickens around Orvieto – where I first came across this recipe – was superb, with a flavor that more than matched a French poulet de Bresse.

Ingredients (for 4)

1 free-range chicken, weighing about 4 pounds, with its giblets
1 pound potatoes
1 onion
30 large garlic cloves
1 fennel bulb, preferably with plenty of stem and leaf
1/2 pound good black olives
sprig of rosemary, about 6-inches long
1 lemon
6 tablespoons extra virgin olive oil
salt and pepper
1 glass (2/3 cup) of dry white wine

Utensils

cherry pitter
large heavy frying pan
1 or 2 thin wooden skewers
roasting pan

Mise en Place

Clean the chicken liver by scraping off any green patches and threads. Cut the top off the heart at the point where it turns white and muscular. Clean the gizzard by cutting open and, rinsing away any stones or grit under the tap, then slide a small sharp knife against the tough wrinkly membrane to remove the two dark oysters of meat rather as you would when skinning a fish. Dice this meat, the heart, and the liver.

Prepare the other ingredients: Peel the potatoes and dice them into cubes of about 1/2 inch • Peel and dice the onion • Pull apart the garlic heads until you have 30 cloves. Peel two of them, smash them with the flat of a knife blade, and mince • Dice the fennel • Pit the olives (the ideal tool is a cherry pitter) • Pull the leaves of rosemary from the twig • Juice the lemon.

Preheat the oven to its highest setting.

Cooking

Put 2 tablespoons of olive oil in a sauté pan and sauté the onion with the chopped giblets, until the onion wilts and goes translucent, 5 minutes or so. Do not let it brown. Add the minced garlic, potatoes, and fennel and sauté 10 minutes, until the vegetables are nearly cooked. Season with salt and pepper to taste, mix in the lemon juice, and let cool.

When cool enough to handle, stuff the chicken with the mixture and close with the skewer(s), pushing through the legs and skin around the cavity opening. This works perfectly well: There is no need to sew it shut.

Season the outside of the bird according to taste. We prefer our chickens liberally seasoned, because the sea salt helps crisp the skin.

Arrange the bird resting on one side in a roasting pan and put in the oven. After 20 minutes, turn it onto the other side. After 40 minutes, remove it from the oven (remembering to close the oven door to stop the temperature falling too dramatically) and position it breast up. Strew the garlic cloves, olives, and rosemary evenly around the bird and drizzle with a little olive oil. Add 1 tablespoon of water to the pan and return to the oven to roast 20 minutes longer.

Remove and test doneness by inserting a toothpick or small skewer into the thigh: The juices should run clear, but do not worry if they are slightly pink. Put the bird on a hot serving dish, with the garlic and olives scattered around and let rest in a warm place for 15 minutes. (Leave the oven on so you can put the assembled dish back in if you find the thighs are still pink when you carve the bird.) Letting the chicken rest is vital since this completes the cooking process while all the juices go back into the meat.

Spoon the fat from the roasting pan, tilting the pan and trying to leave any juices behind. Over high heat, tip in the wine with an equal quantity of water. Deglaze the pan, boiling and scraping. This is an excellent method of making a simple gravy,

Serving

Pile the stuffing in the center of the large warmed serving plate. Using a strong serrated knife, carve the bird into eight pieces and place neatly, skin upward, around the stuffing. Pass the gravy in a sauce boat.

VEGETABLES

Roast New Potatoes with Garlic

This recipe uses new potatoes that have grown a little large and have formed a full skin. It is certainly not how to treat the first of the crop, which needs nothing but melted butter and salt.

Ingredients (for 4)

8 large new potatoes in their skins
$1/4$ cup olive oil
8 unpeeled summer garlic cloves
sea salt
rosemary leaves
few drops of balsamic vinegar

Utensils

pot scourer
large saucepan
roasting pan

Mise en Place

Preheat the oven to its highest setting • Scrub the potatoes energetically with a pot scourer • Cut each potato into four.

Cooking

Parboil the potatoes: The best way to do this is to put in a pan of cold salted water and bring to a boil. As a fast boil is reached, remove from the heat and let stand 5 minutes before draining and cooling under cold running water. Drain well again.

Put the oil in a roasting pan and roll the potatoes and garlic in it to coat them evenly. Then arrange the potatoes so they sit with a cut surface on the pan's bottom. Sprinkle with a little sea salt and roast 20 minutes without moving them (this lets a proper crust form on the base and thus avoids sticking).

Remove from the oven and turn the potatoes, then roast 10–15 minutes longer. Add the rosemary leaves for the last few minutes of cooking.

When the potatoes are crisp and brown, remove them from the oven and sprinkle with balsamic vinegar, shaking the roasting pan.

Serving

Add a touch more sea salt and serve at once.

Green Beans

Green beans – notably the tiny haricot vert, which needs no trimming – are one of my favorite vegetables. There is a tendency these days not to cook them enough, which in my view is as wrong as overcooking them.

Always cook them at a fast boil in a lot of lightly salted water and with the lid off the pan as this helps them retain a bright color. The finest green beans may take 5 minutes, the slightly larger ones perhaps 6 or 7. Start tasting after 5 minutes – they should still have some residual crunch but not be raw.

Either serve at once, dressed with a little butter, or refresh in cold water and hold till needed. Reheat by dipping in boiling water for 30 seconds.

Jane Grigson suggested an alternative of serving them with a minced shallot sweated in butter with a minced garlic clove The drained green beans are added with a little chopped parsley and stirred a couple of minutes to warm through. Green beans are also delicious tossed in a light vinaigrette and served warm as a salade tiède.

New Season's Carrots

The fashion for baby vegetables has been taken to an absurd point, where they are used before developing a decent flavor. Vegetable infanticide is not for me, but the first carrots of the summer are a different matter entirely. Nothing looks nicer or tastes better than a fresh bunch of carrots. When buying them, the green tops are a good indicator of how fresh the carrots really are. No matter how small the carrots, I always peel them, for unpeeled carrots taste inevitably of earth.

People who claim to loathe the vegetable are often converted by the following treatment. I have seen customers in the restaurant reluctantly accepting one to try from an enthusiastic fellow diner, whose eagerness to share the taste experience diminishes as the convert devours the lot.

Ingredients (for 4)

1 pound of bunched carrots with
    their green leaves
1 teaspoon salt
$1/2$ teaspoon pepper
1 teaspoon sugar
4 tablespoons butter

Utensils

shallow wide-bottomed pan

Mise en Place

Trim the green stems to within $1/2$ inch of the top. Hold by the remaining stems and peel with a potato peeler, cutting off the straggly root end to make a neat presentation. Then wash thoroughly to rid the stems of earth.

Cooking

Put the carrots in a shallow, wide-bottomed pan and barely cover with cold water (if you have any flat mineral water, use it). Add the salt, pepper, and sugar.

Bring to a boil and boil vigorously until the water has almost evaporated. Check whether the carrots are cooked; if still too crisp, add a little more water and cook until done to your liking.

At this point, and just before the last drops of water have gone, throw in the butter and toss the carrots in it to coat them. (There must be some water in the pan when you add the butter or it will burn and ruin the dish.)

Blanched Spinach Salad

Blanched spinach is a great gift to the cook, for it will stay happily in the refrigerator for a day to be revived in boiling water to serve hot. It is also very good in its own right as a cold salad, simply dressed with olive oil and a tiny squeeze of lemon juice. Not too much, though, as this will discolor the spinach and one of the nicest things about it is the vivid green.

Ingredients (for 4)

2 pounds bulk spinach
about $1/4$ cup extra virgin olive oil
1 tablespoon lemon juice
salt and pepper

Utensils

large saucepan
large bowl of ice water
blanching basket
colander

Mise en Place

Put a large pan of salted water on to heat • Pick over the spinach and discard stems • Fill a large bowl with ice water.

Cooking

Blanch the leaves in the rapidly boiling salted water for 2 minutes. Refresh in the ice water and drain in the colander. Gently squeeze out the water, pressing down with a wooden spoon. Do not ram it down: You don't want a solid lump. Transfer to a bowl and toss to separate the leaves as much as you can. Refrigerate until ready to use.

Serving

Dress the spinach with olive oil, tossing to coat evenly. Squeeze over a little lemon juice and season before taking to the table.

DESSERTS

Berry Sorbet Jr.

The name reflects a fondness for the classic music of Motown. Sorbets are so easy to make with a sorbetière or ice-cream freezer that many people fail to do so, as if ease of execution is synonymous with cheating in the kitchen. You can obtain good results using frozen fruit pulp, but this will never match the astonishingly heady flavor of fresh berries. My personal favorites are raspberry and black currant.

Only make berry sorbets from fruit that is in season, and only make enough to eat within 24 hours. Do not freeze for another day — this simply misses the point.

Ingredients (for 4)
1 pound seasonal berries
1 lemon
3/4–1 cup sugar

Utensils
food processor
strainer
sorbetière or ice-cream machine
wooden spoon
suitable freezerproof container
ice-cream scoop or metal spoon

Mise en Place
Pick over the fruit and juice the lemon.

Preparation
In a food processor, purée the fruit wth the, sugar and lemon juice. Press through a strainer into the sorbetière and churn till frozen. Scoop into an appropriate freezerproof container and put in the freezer. Keep up to 24 hours, no more.

Remove from the freezer 30 minutes before serving. At the same time put to chill some pretty glasses in which to serve it.

Serving
Scoop into balls with a spoon or ice-cream scoop and serve in the chilled glasses.

I once went out after dark to get some mint from the garden of a friend's restaurant to garnish a sorbet. The portion was rapidly returned with the message that, no matter how authentic, the diner would prefer his sorbet without a caterpillar. So, as a general rule, do not decorate this sorbet with mint leaves.

Peach Tea Ice Cream

You can buy peach tea, which gives this ice cream its unique flavor. However, if you cannot find any, use an aromatic and floral China tea such as jasmine.

Ingredients (for 4)
6 ripe peaches
1 teaspoon peach tea
2 tablespoons sugar
1/2 quantity (1 pint) Vanilla Ice Cream (see page 28)

Utensils
saucepan or kettle
bowl
ice-cream machine or sorbetière

Mise en Place
Put 1 1/4 cups of water to heat for the tea • Meanwhile, quarter the peaches. Peel them, detach from the pits, and cut into wedges • When the water is boiling make the tea and add the sugar. Let cool in a bowl until just warm, then infuse the peach wedges in the tea for 1 hour.

Preparation
Make the Vanilla Ice Cream as described on page 28, adding 3 tablespoons of the tea to the custard before transferring it to the ice-cream machine and churning.

When nearing the end of the churning, drain the peaches. As the ice cream starts to freeze, add them and continue to churn until set.

Sauternes and Olive Oil Cake

It is unlikely that you will be using a vintage Château d'Yquem to make this. Fortunately it works well with most sweet wines, including the dreaded Beaumes-de-Venise. The olive oil, however, must be of the very best quality – extra virgin, green, and full of fruit – and will cost as much as a medium-priced Sauternes.

This recipe I have based on an inspired idea of Alice Waters, chef proprietor of Chez Panisse in Berkeley, California. She is one of the paramount masters of modern cooking, and her philosophy and recipes have been among my most profound influences.

Ingredients (for 8-12)

1 cup cake flour, plus more for
    dusting
1/2 lemon
1/2 orange
4 eggs
2/3 cup sugar
2 tablespoons Sauternes or other
    sweet wine
3 tablespoons best-quality extra
    virgin olive oil, plus more for
    greasing
confectioners' sugar, to dust

Utensils

grater
10-inch springform cake pan
parchment paper
pastry brush
electric mixer
rubber spatula
flour sifter

Mise en Place

Measure all the ingredients and sift the flour into a bowl. Grate 1/2 teaspoon of zest each from the lemon and the orange, using the second-finest grating surface.

Preheat the oven to 285°F. Cut a circle of parchment paper to fit the bottom of the cake pan exactly and line the bottom with it. Brush the sides of the pan with olive oil and dust with flour, shaking out the excess.

Preparation

Combine the eggs and sugar in the bowl of the mixer and beat on high speed until it is off-white in color and stiff. Add the orange and lemon zest. Turn the mixer to low and pour in the flour in a steady stream to combine with the egg and sugar mixture. Quickly add the wine and the olive oil. Switch off as soon as you have poured in the oil (it will not be fully incorporated).

Remove the mixer bowl and, with the spatula, stir gently, starting from the center at the bottom and working outward and upward while rotating the bowl one quarter-turn. Repeat three more times (which means the bowl will have been turned full circle). This is called "folding" and is the best way of ensuring all the elements are thoroughly mixed without losing lightness by being heavy-handed.

Working quickly, pour this batter into the pan, using the spatula to scrape the last of it from the bowl. If the batter collapses when you are folding in the flour, go ahead and bake anyway – it will be a little heavy, but will still have all the flavors.

Cooking

Put immediately into the center of the oven and bake 25 minutes. Do not open the door for at least 15 minutes. After 20 minutes, insert a small clean knife into the center of the cake (I stress clean because I have on occasion tested with a garlic-tainted knife, which does nothing to improve the flavor). If it comes out clean the cake is done, so remove it; if the batter clings to the knife, bake 5 minutes longer, by which time it should be cooked – but there is no harm in testing again.

Let cool in the pan on a wire rack, removing from the pan as soon as you can handle it. It is unlikely to stick because you have oiled the pan. If it does, it will be immediately apparent when you undo the spring clip. Refasten and run a small clean sharp knife around and it will unmold easily. Leave the paper on the base and return to the rack to cool completely.

Serving

Lightly dust the cake with confectioners' sugar and cut into wedges. Serve with seasonal fruit, such as peach segments, or Compote of Winter Fruits (see page 185).

Summer Pudding

A classic taste of late summer, this is one of the few dishes that uses sliced white bread to advantage. I don't know anybody who does not love a summer pudding, which is one of the few English desserts admired by French and Italians alike. You should only make it when berries are both abundant and cheap, and note that a proper summer pudding should never include strawberries. Remember also that it has to be made at least the day before it is needed and is better for 2 or 3 days in the refrigerator.

Ingredients (for 4)

1 slightly stale loaf good-quality
  sliced white bread
1/2 pound red currants
1/2 pound black currants
1/2 pound white currants
1-1 1/4 cups sugar
1/2 pound raspberries
1/2 pound blackberries

Utensils

large saucepan
8-inch diameter flat-bottomed mold,
  or soufflé dish
jelly roll pan
plate or round wooden board that
  just fits inside the top of the
  mold, or soufflé dish
metal spatula

Mise en Place

Remove the crusts from the slices of bread.

Cooking

Put all the currants in a pan with the sugar and bring to a bare simmer over low heat. Cook 10 minutes, until you have a very liquid mixture. Remove from the heat, stir in the raspberries and blackberries, and let cool.

Line the mold with the bread, cutting the slices in half for the sides and into triangles for the bottom.

Spoon in the cooled fruit mixture to fill the mold right to the top. If you do not have enough fruit, then add more raspberries. Finally, cut more bread triangles to cover the top of the bowl (which will be the base when unmolded).

Set the bowl in the jelly roll pan and put the plate or round board on top. Weight this down with about 4 pounds of cans and refrigerate 24 hours, removing from time to time and pouring over any remaining fruit syrup. The bread should not be recognizable as a separate entity by the end of the process, but be amalgamated with the fruit. Should you have any fruit mixture left over at the end of the process, freeze it to use as a coulis for another dish.

Next day, remove the pudding from the refrigerator and take off the plate or board. Slip a metal spatula round the inside of the mold, being careful not to puncture the outer surface. Put a serving plate on top and, holding the mold tight to the plate, invert. Tap the base sharply and lift away the mold to reveal the summer pudding, standing proud and brilliantly colored.

Serving

If you can, serve with Devon clotted cream or with crème fraîche.

Autumn

Autumn, a transitional time when the soil yields wild mushrooms and a profusion of vegetables in the rich months that precede the austerity of winter. Game birds are paired with braised cabbage and *pancetta*, an eclectic mix of French method, and Italian flavoring – the best of all possible worlds. Now orchards give us apples at their best – a moment to savor the famous Tarte Tatin.

First courses
Caldo Verde
Cream of Mussel Soup with Saffron
Pappardelle with Cèpes
Salt and Pepper Squid
Spaghetti Salsa Rossa with Clams
Danish Omelet
Wild Mushroom Tart
Cantonese Salad of Braised Beef Shank

Main Courses
Grilled Sea Bass with Parsley Salad
Partridge with Braised Cabbage and Pancetta
Sole Florentine
Japanese-Style Pork Belly with Dancing Bonito
Osso Buco with Risotto Milanese
Calves' Liver with Melted Onions and Sage
Salmis of Grouse
Wrapped Breast of Chicken with Wild Mushrooms
Turbot Steak with Cèpes

Vegetables
Hasselback Potatoes
Broccoli with Anchovies
Ratatouille
Turkish Braised Vegetables

Desserts
Roast Figs with Honey Ice Cream
Chocolate Brownies with Fudge Sauce
Tarte Tatin
Chocolate Mousse Cake

FIRST COURSES

Caldo Verde

Caldo Verde *is one of the essential tastes of Portugal. Anybody who thinks good food has to be difficult to make should try this most basic of soups, which – despite its absolute simplicity – is delicious and is another of those comforting dishes to warm the heart.*

The quantities given make a lot of soup and – with good bread – it can be a substantial main course in its own right. It also keeps well and is just as nice, if not better, reheated. The soup is also delicious without any sausage, if you prefer.

Ingredients (for 8-10)

2 pounds potatoes
2 garlic cloves
1/2 pound smoked chorizo sausage or zampone
1 pound collard greens or Savoy cabbage
1 1/2 quarts light chicken broth or water
salt and pepper
6 tablespoons extra virgin olive oil, to serve
1 tablespoon coriander leaves (cilantro), to serve

Utensils

large pot
potato masher or whisk

Mise en Place

Peel the potatoes and, if they are large, cut them into smallish pieces • Peel and coarsely chop the garlic • Cut the sausage across into 1/4-inch slices • Pull away the outer leaves from the greens or cabbage. Remove stems and shred the leaves as finely as you can. The best way to do this is to roll the leaves into tubes as if making a cigar, then cut these across. In Lisbon, the soup is so much a part of everyday life that market stalls sell big plastic bags of ready-shredded cabbage. There is also a hand-cranked machine like a giant pencil sharpener you can buy to do the job for you.

Cooking

Put the potatoes and garlic into the pot with the broth or water and bring to a boil. Lower to a simmer and cook 15 minutes, then season.

Mash in the pot to a fairly smooth purée. Add the slices of sausage and the shredded cabbage and simmer about 5 minutes longer, until warmed through. Taste and adjust seasoning if necessary.

Serving

Ladle into large warmed soup bowls. Pour a tablespoon or so of olive oil in rings on top of each serving. If using coriander, tear a few leaves and scatter over each portion before serving or pass separately at the table.

Cream of Mussel Soup with Saffron

Mussels, if British, used to be big and old and covered in barnacles, or — if you were lucky — imported bouchots brought over from Normandy. Pollution of our native beds and the heavy commercial development of farmed mussels in Holland mean that most of what you can buy today is Dutch. They will have been efficiently cleaned and be of a uniform size, but are not as tasty as the French or British mussels of old. Since shellfish poisoning is potentially fatal, it is perhaps preferable to be philosophical about this slight loss of flavor.

Ingredients (for 4)

2 1/4 pounds mussels
1 large leek
1 celery stalk or piece of celeriac
   (celery root)
1 garlic clove
1 bottle of dry white wine
1 1/4 cups heavy whipping cream
pepper
12 saffron threads

Utensils

lidded pot (large enough to hold all
   the mussels in a single layer)
colander
large bowl
strainer
second saucepan

Mise en Place

Prepare the mussels: With a small sharp knife, beard the mussels and then scrub the shells. Sharply tap any that are open: If they are alive they will close — discard any that do not. Don't leave the mussels in water too long as this leaches out the sea salt and makes them tasteless. The best way to keep mussels once washed is to rinse them and put them into a pot covered with damp seaweed, then put a lid on top to prevent evaporation. Your fishmonger may have some seaweed if you ask for it.

Chop the vegetables into a fine julienne • Slice the garlic clove.

Cooking

Put the mussels in the pot, pour over the white wine, and cover with the lid. Place over a high flame and bring to a boil. Shake the pot vigorously a couple of times to redistribute the mussels and ensure even cooking. They are done when they open. Discard those few that stubbornly remain closed.

Pour the contents of the pot into the colander placed over a bowl to catch the wine and mussel liquor. Pour the liquor through a fine strainer into another pan and put most of it to warm on low heat. Put some of the liquid in a large clean bowl and shuck the mussels into this.

Throw the julienne and garlic into the liquid in the saucepan, add the cream, and bring to a boil. Lower the heat, season with a little pepper, put in the shucked mussels and saffron threads, and simmer gently until hot.

Serving

Serve in large warmed soup bowls. You may prefer to serve the mussels in their shells. If so, be even more scrupulous when cleaning the shells.

Pappardelle with Cèpes

Pappardelle come from Tuscany and are broad hand-cut noodles traditionally served con lepre, *with a rich and gamy hare sauce. I make them using my Rich Pasta Dough (see page 25) and like them better with fresh cèpes (porcini) or with leftover* coq au vin, *the chicken shredded but with the usual garnish of bacon and baby onions and mushrooms. You can also use a meat sauce from a* daube *of beef.*

If fresh cèpes are not available – or are just too expensive – then you can use a mixture of dried cèpes and sliced common mushrooms to good effect. Whatever sauce you use, make sure there is at least that times the amount of pappardelle *as there is sauce – pasta dishes must never become stews with noodles.*

Ingredients (for 4)

10 ounces fresh cèpes, or 2 ounces dried cèpes and 7 ounces common mushrooms
$2/3$ quantity Rich Pasta Dough (see page 25)
semolina flour or farina, for dusting
1 garlic clove
small bunch of chives
1 tablespoon extra virgin olive oil
2 tablespoons butter
salt and pepper
1 cup heavy whipping cream
large chunk of Reggiano Parmesan cheese, to serve

Utensils

large bowl
pasta machine
pastry wheel, pasta cutter, or small sharp knife
large saucepan
large heavy-based frying pan
colander
grater

Mise en Place

Prepare the mushrooms: For fresh cèpes in common mushrooms, detach the stems and cut off and discard the earthy ends. Wipe the caps with a damp cloth, but do not wash or immerse in water – which they absorb like sponges. Peel the stems, but not the caps, and slice both thinly • To prepare dried mushrooms: Soak them in 1 1/4 cups of warm water for half an hour. Then drain and rinse to get rid of tenacious grit. (The soaking liquid can be strained and used in a stock.)

Prepare the pasta: Make the pasta dough as described on page 25. Divide the dough into four pieces and roll each through the pasta machine, following the manufacturer's instructions, finishing on the narrowest setting. Using a pastry wheel, pasta cutter, or a small sharp knife, cut the dough into wide strips about 4-inches long by 1-inch wide. They should not be absolutely uniform – you want them to look homemade. Pile the noodles loosely on a surface that has been lightly dusted with semolina flour. If you are not using the pappardelle immediately, arrange them on a wire rack to dry. Heat a large pan of lightly salted water to boil the pasta.

Peel, smash, and mince the garlic • Snip or cut the chives into 1/4-inch lengths.

Cooking

Put the oil and butter in the frying pan over medium heat and sauté the mushrooms in it until brown, about 5 minutes. Add the garlic, season well, and stir in the cream. Lower the heat and let simmer and thicken over low heat for a few minutes until the sauce coats the back of a spoon.

When the pan of water is boiling rapidly, add the pasta. Bring the water back to a fast boil and cook the pasta 2 minutes.

Using the colander, immediately drain the pasta. Add to the sauce in the frying pan and toss to coat evenly, then simmer gently 1 minute.

Serving

Transfer to a warm serving bowl, scatter with the chives, and serve at once. Pass the block of cheese with the grater at the table.

Salt and Pepper Squid

Despite its slowly increasing popularity, squid is still not something you find very often at a private dinner or lunch. Is it that people fear a slimy tentacle, or the nightmare of preparation? The keen cook should not allow prejudice to exclude this delicious and quick-cooking option from the menu. Indeed, once you have found how easy squid is, you will make it an everyday fish, as commonplace as sole.

This method of cooking is essentially Sichuan, but while the spicing is mouth-tingling, surprisingly it does not overwhelm the squid. Instead it complements the rich flesh to perfection.

I suggest you cook this in two batches and give your guests seconds rather than overload the oil, as it is vital that the exterior crisps. This technique doesn't suit over-large squid; those weighing $1/4$-$1/2$ pound are ideal. This also ensures that you get lots of tentacles — these are the tastiest bits.

Ingredients (for 4)

1 pound cleaned squid (if you can't get your fishmonger to do it for you, see *Squid Roll Sashimi* on page 37 for details of preparing squid)
3 tablespoons salt, finely ground
$1/2$ tablespoon five-spice powder
2 teaspoons Sichuan pepper
$1 2/3$ cups flour
sunflower oil, for deep-frying
coriander (cilantro) leaves, for garnish (optional)

Utensils

coffee grinder
flour sifter
shallow bowl
deep-fryer or deep pan or large wok
candy thermometer
frying basket or spider (see page 16)
4 pairs of chopsticks

Mise en Place

If necessary, prepare the squid as described on page 37. Cut it into bite-sized pieces • Put the salt, five-spice powder, and pepper in a coffee grinder and whizz briefly to combine. Then mix evenly with the sifted flour in a shallow bowl • Heat the oil in a deep pan or wok to 365°F.

Cooking

Roll the squid in the spiced flour, shaking off any excess. The squid will be moist enough to take the flour coating without needing to dip it into beaten egg first.

Deep-fry in the hot oil for 2 minutes (any longer and the squid will toughen). When cooked, drain on lots of paper towels.

Serving

Serve immediately while still piping hot and eat with chopsticks. You could scatter over a few coriander leaves as a garnish, if desired.

Spaghetti Salsa Rossa with Clams

Usually a simple accompaniment for boiled or grilled meats, salsa rossa combined with clams makes a great pasta sauce. Like salsa verde it keeps well in a screw-top jar in the refrigerator up to a month. Canned baby clams (vongole in Italian) are one of the best canned products I know. You could use fresh clams, but I promise you the canned variety are great, and sometimes it is nice to know that all you have to do is reach for the can opener. With a salsa rossa ready in the refrigerator and spaghetti and canned clams in the cabinet, you have everything you need for an impromptu supper. See page 41 for a more detailed treatment of the cooking of spaghetti.

Ingredients (for 4)
³/4 pound best-quality dried spaghetti
salt and pepper

FOR THE SALSA ROSSA:
2 red bell peppers
1 small hot red chili pepper
4 onions
2 garlic cloves
¹/4 cup extra virgin olive oil
16-ounce can Italian plum tomatoes (or purée)
10 ounces canned baby clams

Utensils
large saucepan
sauté pan
food processor
saucepan
colander
tongs

Mise en Place
Put a large pan of salted water to heat for the pasta.

Prepare the sauce ingredients: Preheat the broiler. Cut the bell peppers in half, scrape out the seeds, and broil the outsides until they blister. Scrape off the skin and dice the flesh • Split, seed, and chop the chili pepper • Peel and chop the onions and garlic.

Cooking
Heat the olive oil in a sauté pan and gently sauté the onions and garlic until soft and translucent. Add the chopped bell peppers and the chili and continue frying gently for 10 minutes, stirring from time to time. Do not brown.

Add the tomatoes with the juice from the can, turn up the heat a little, and cook a final 10 minutes.

Transfer the contents of the pan to the food processor and purée. The salsa rossa can now be held in a jar in the refrigerator up to 2 weeks (film the top with olive oil to help it keep).

When the water is boiling rapidly, cook the pasta.

Put just enough of the salsa rossa (I like to use no more than about 2 generous tablespoons per person) into another pan and warm it through. After 5 minutes, add the clams with their liquid to the sauce. Turn up the heat and let bubble gently.

Taste the spaghetti after 8 minutes. When cooked al dente (tender but still firm to the bite), rush to the colander, drain quickly, and return to the pan while a little water still clings to the strands. Spoon the sauce over the pasta and toss to coat.

Serving
Serve immediately in warmed bowls. Do not serve Parmesan cheese with this dish.

Danish Omelet

The correct name for this lovely dish is "Danish Egg Cake," but for some reason people say they are put off by it. This is a shame, because it is seriously delicious and one of the first things I look forward to eating when each year I visit Faborg, the small town in which my wife grew up. It is also one of the few Danish dishes that does not involve the use of herring and, much as I adore herring, you can have too much of a good thing.

There are eight or nine restaurants in Faborg — none of them, it must be said, Michelin rated — but my favorite egg cake is served at a lovely old pub called Tre Krona, where I like to eat it washed down with a lot of good Danish beer. Traditionally it is served with rugbrod, a bread in my view more akin to floor tiles than anything I want to eat, so I say, "Hold the rugbrod, more beer on the side." Bliss.

Egg cake may be cooked as individual omelets or in a large serving, in which case the pan is brought to the table and people help themselves to thick wedges.

The Danes use a local bacon that they call speck, which it is not, being closer to ordinary bacon. You can use either smoked or unsmoked. The tomato in the dish must be raw. There is something about a sweet raw tomato that goes brilliantly with an omelet. You might also like to try the egg cake with a topping of strips of smoked eel mixed in with the bacon, to produce a happy marriage of flavors and textures.

Ingredients (per person)

4 thick slices of bacon
1 tomato (or 3 cherry tomatoes)
1 tablespoon sunflower oil
3 eggs
salt and pepper
1 tablespoon heavy whipping cream (optional and certainly not traditional)
1 tablespoon butter
handful of chives
1 ounces smoked eel fillet (optional)

Utensils

roasting pan
roasting rack
omelette pan or heavy frying pan with an ovenproof handle for a larger omelette (a paella pan would also work well)
pastry brush
bowl
whisk
metal spatula

Mise en Place

First prepare the bacon: Preheat the oven to 400°F. Arranged the bacon slices on a rack in a roasting pan in the oven and cook until they just begin to crisp. Remove from the oven and reserve. (This is a very good way of cooking bacon for other dishes — much better than frying and easier than broiling.)

Reduce the oven temperature to 325°F • If not using cherry tomatoes, cut the tomato into wedges and reserve • Brush the omelet pan with a little sunflower oil • Beat the eggs in the bowl with a little salt and pepper and the cream, if using, until just amalgamated. Do not over-beat.

Cooking

The cooking technique is somewhere between that of making a classic omelet and stirring scrambled eggs, since what you want to achieve is a layered effect of lightly browned egg and moist creamy egg.

Put the pan over medium heat, add the butter, and swirl it around. Tip in the beaten eggs before the butter is completely melted. The eggs will start to set at once. Using a metal spatula, push the egg away from the edges. Leave 60 seconds, then repeat the process. Turn down the heat and cook very gently until the base is set and lightly browned, 3-4 minutes.

If the cake is very large and still liquid, stir the surface and put it into the cooler oven to finish cooking about 4 minutes, though remember that it will anyway continue to cook in the pan when taken off the heat. This is a case of practice makes perfect. After you have made it three or four times with a certain number of eggs, you will know precisely how to achieve the perfect balance between under- and over-cooking.

While the eggs are cooking, return the bacon to the oven to warm through.

Serving

Arrange the tomatoes around the edge of the pan. Cut the bacon into ¼-inch pieces and use them to cover the top of the cake. Scatter with chopped chives and chopped eel fillet, if using.

Wild Mushroom Tart

This recipe was stolen from Simon Hopkinson at Bibendum in London, who does an extraordinary version using fresh cèpes only.

Ingredients (for 4)
1 pound assorted fresh wild
mushrooms, such as chanterelles,
black trumpets, and cèpes
9 tablespoons unsalted butter
2 garlic cloves
handful of flat-leaf parsley
salt and pepper
1 pound ready-rolled puff pastry,
thawed if frozen
chopped chives, for garnish
(optional)

Utensils
bowl
2 baking sheets

Mise en Place
First prepare the mushrooms: Detach the stems if necessary, and cut off and discard the earthy ends. Wipe the caps with a damp cloth, but do not wash or immerse in water – which they absorb like sponges. Peel the stems, but not the caps. If very large, slice into pieces.

Make the garlic butter: Cut the butter into small pieces. Peel, crush, and mince the garlic. Remove the parsley leaves from their stems and coarsely chop the leaves. In a bowl, mix the butter, garlic, and parsley with a generous amount of salt and pepper. Mash them together with a fork to mix. (A food processor tends to over-chop the parsley, producing a vivid green paste.)

Preheat the oven to its highest setting.

Prepare the pastry: For each person take one sheet of puff pastry rolled out to a thickness of $1/8$ inch and cut into a 6-inch diameter circle (use a plate as a template). Lay out on the baking sheets (do not oil the sheets).

Make the tarts: Divide the wiped mushrooms into equal amounts. Take a handful of the mushrooms and press in your hands to make a compact ball. Mound in the center of each pastry circle, leaving a clear border of pastry about 1-inch wide • With the blunt side of a small kitchen knife, crimp the base of the pastry circles at $1/4$-inch intervals all around. This will push the pastry up around the edge and will encourage the pastry to lift around the edge as it bakes, to form a neat case around the mushroom filling • Put a 2-tablespoon lump of garlic butter on top of each mushroom mound.

Holding Point - at this stage you can freeze the tarts until needed (up to 12 hours). Then bake from frozen, but add 2 minutes to the cooking time.

Cooking

Put the tarts in the oven (if any mushrooms spill onto the pastry border, take care to push them back into the middle). Check them after they have been in the oven 5 minutes. If the pastry has ballooned in the middle, prick with a sharp knife or skewer to deflate.

Bake until the pastry has risen and browned and the mushrooms have collapsed, about 15 minutes in total. The mushrooms will exude water and juices which add a delicious flavor to the pastry base while making it a little soggy. This is perfectly acceptable as long as you serve at once – the tarts are not nice lukewarm or cold.

Serving

Serve immediately on warmed plates, scattered with a few chives if you like.

Cantonese Salad of Braised Beef Shank

I was introduced to this dish by a visiting chef from Hong Kong, who produced an over-elaborate banquet of which I found this dish the most memorable (never having been an enthusiast of the carved-carrot school of presentation so loved by the Chinese).

The Chinese do not share our concern with serving meat hot. On the contrary, many dishes like crispy roast pork and Cantonese duck would be ruined by reheating and are supposed to be eaten at room temperature. This is worth remembering when eating in a Chinese restaurant, where it is generally assumed that ignorant gwailo will complain if their roast meats are not hot and it is therefore a wise precaution to say "cold meat" loudly several times to avoid a microwaved mess being brought steaming to the table. For a spectacular argument, try sending this back.

The size of the cut of meat specified may seem rather large for 4 people, but you simply can't cook a small piece of meat in this way. However, these quantities provide lots of second helpings and sandwiches.

Of all Chinese spices, star anise is the most distinctive and powerful, so it should always be treated with respect.

Mise en Place

The day before: Put the stock ingredients into the saucepan and bring to a boil. Lower the heat and simmer half an hour. Then immerse the beef in the simmering stock and return to a boil. Skim, then simmer gently 2½–3 hours. Remove from the heat and let cool in the stock.

The next day: Remove the beef from the pan and drain. With a very sharp knife cut it into the thinnest slices you can, slicing downward through the round.

Prepare the other ingredients: Using a potato peeler, cut strips of skin off the cucumber lengthwise to produce a striped effect. Cut the cucumber in half lengthwise, scoop out the seeds, and slice it into julienne • Wash and trim the scallions and slice these into julienne • Mix the sesame oil with the tiniest amount of chili oil • Cut the lemons into wedges.

Serving

Arrange the beef slices overlapping on a large serving platter. Scatter the two juliennes on top. Strain a little of the soy stock around the edge of the fanned meat slices. Sprinkle with the oil mixture.

Arrange lemon wedges around the meat for people to squeeze over the dish at the table.

Ingredients (for 4)

about 2½ quarts Soy Master Stock (see page 20)
1 beef foreshank, weighing 2–3 pounds, cut about 2 inches thick in a round, bone removed and tied into a compact roast
1 cucumber
4 scallions
few drops of sesame oil (best Japanese)
few drops of Chili Oil (see page 11)
2 lemons, to serve

Utensils

large saucepan or casserole
potato peeler
strainer

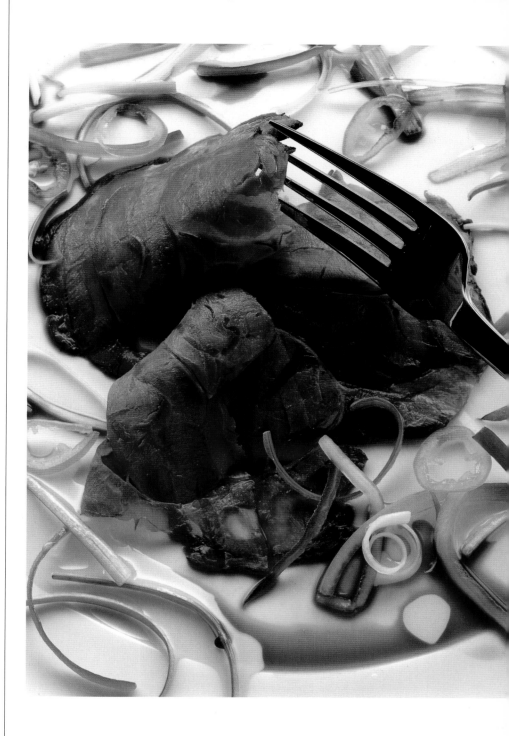

*This treatment of beef shank complements
the gelatinous muscular cut perfectly and is
an unusual cold dish for an autumn lunch,
with its subtle yet aromatic spicing.*

MAIN COURSES

Grilled Sea Bass with Parsley Salad

Simple food does not always mean it is easy to prepare. There are techniques involved with this Japanese style of grilling that you will need to approach with care. Note the word "care" and not "trepidation."

Sea bass has enjoyed a growing vogue in recent years and is one of the few bony fish people in Britain and the US have embraced enthusiastically. Chinese restaurants were the first to popularize it, typically steaming the fish with ginger and scallions.

As you will be paying a lot of money for your sea bass, insist that your fishmonger scales and cleans them for you and trims off the dorsal spikes. (These are, incidentally, poisonous. Get one of those under your skin and it will hurt.) You will need $^3/_4$ pound of whole fish for each person. However, do not attempt to grill a fish larger than 2 pounds in weight because while cooking the thickness of the flesh around the spinal bone the outside will overcook and dry out.

You may like to try the salt-grilling technique with mackerel first as it is a fraction of the cost of sea bass and works just as well.

You can use either a heavy ridged cast iron grill pan, as in the restaurant, or a barbecue, which works perfectly because you don't want the temperature too high. A domestic broiler will also deliver good results as long as you set the pan about 4 inches away from the heat source, or as far as your oven configuration allows. The timing is the same in all cases.

The parsley salad is taken from Gay Bilson of Berowra Waters restaurant in New South Wales. If any dish represents my "melting pot" approach it is this. You will need one really large bunch of flat-leaf parsley – different markets call it different things: Cyprus, Italian, Chinese, Egyptian. Do not try to substitute ordinary curly parsley.

Ingredients (for 4)

*2 whole sea bass, each weighing
     about 1 1/2 pounds*
salt and pepper
very large bunch of flat-leaf parsley
16 black olives
1 shallot, scallion, or red onion
1 garlic clove
*10 salt-packed capers (not those
     ones you buy in jars, which are
     usually disgusting)*
*4 Home-Dried Tomatoes (see page
     27)*
*1 tablespoon good-quality red wine
     vinegar*
*1 1/4 cups extra virgin olive oil (the
     best quality you can get)*
*chunk of Reggiano Parmesan
     cheese, to serve (optional)*
2 lemons

Utensils

*ridged grill pan or barbecue (it must
     be large enough for the fish to be
     contained within the cooking
     area)*
long-pronged carving fork
olive pitter
salad spinner

Mise en Place

Heat the grill pan or light the barbecue charcoal well in advance. If using a grill pan, do not put it on the highest heat.

If the body cavity of the sea bass has any blood in it, clean it by rubbing with salt and then rinsing under cold running water. Using a very sharp knife, cut 2 slashes on each side of the fish down to the bone. This will help the heat distribution and ensure even cooking. Sprinkle the outside of the fish liberally with sea salt. Do not brush the skin with oil.

Pick the parsley leaves off the stems, discarding the stems or reserving them for stock. Wash the parsley and spin it dry.

Pit the olives. Then chop them by hand together with the shallot, garlic, capers, and dried tomatoes. Do not use a processor, which will purée the ingredients (the pieces should have separate definition). Assemble all these in a salad bowl, pour over the vinegar and olive oil, and set aside. Do not add the parsley at this point.

Cooking

Grill the fish on one side about 5 minutes. Leave it alone – however tempted you may be to push it around, don't do it as you will only damage the skin. Wait until you see signs of cooking: the color changing as it cooks and the head and tail starting to lift slightly. If barbecuing, you can tell the degree of doneness by the state of the skin – moisture released inside the fish will cause the skin to balloon slightly. At this point, carefully slide the fork under the fish, working from the tail and pushing along the length of the fish. Lift the fish and turn it over. If you try to turn it by lifting from the middle, the fish will break.

   As the other side of the fish cooks, finish the salad by adding the parsley to the other ingredients. Toss together. You can shave Parmesan cheese over the salad if you like the idea. Try the combination and see whether you prefer it with or without.

Serving

If you have individual fish for each person, then send them to the table on separate plates: Place a handful of the salad beside each fish and a half lemon on the other side. If you are working with larger fish, present them on a serving platter for people to help themselves.

Partridge with Braised Cabbage and Pancetta

Gray partridge is the British native feral bird and immeasurably better than the commercially reared and released French, or red-legged, variety. I find the French are generally not at their best with game dishes, often cooking the animal when it is too fresh. We British have some of the best game in the world, but it is often spoiled by over-hanging and undercooking. If the French are often guilty of under-hanging, the British aristocracy's continuing love affair with rotten game beggars belief and should be ranked alongside Bombay Duck as a national culinary perversion. You can buy frozen partridge from some specialty meat and poultry markets in the US. Or, substitute other game birds that weigh about 3/4 pound each.

Ingredients (for 4)

2 carrots
2 celery stalks
1 large onion
2 heads of Savoy cabbage
1/2 pound pancetta or unsmoked
   slab bacon
4 ounces (1/2 cup) duck fat or 1 stick
   unsalted butter
4 dressed gray partridges, tied and
   barded
salt and pepper
6 juniper berries
1 1/4 cups game stock or Chicken
   Stock (see page 19)

Utensils

salad spinner
smallish roasting pan just large
   enough to hold the birds
casserole dish large enough to hold
   the cabbage
foil

Mise en Place

Preheat the oven to its highest setting • Peel and dice the carrots, celery, and onion finely into a brunoise (see page 187) • Cut the cabbage in half, cut out the base stem, and coarsely shred the leaves. Wash them and spin dry • Cut the pancetta stem, into lardon strips (see page 187) but do not blanch.

Cooking

Melt a little of the duck fat or butter in the roasting pan and roll the partridges in this to coat. Season generously with salt and pepper and roast on their sides for 7–8 minutes. Turn to roast on the other side for the same time. Remove from the oven and let cool (leaving the oven on if intending to finish rather than hold).

Melt the remaining fat in the large casserole and sauté the pancetta lardons over a medium flame for 3 minutes, stirring constantly. Add the vegetable brunoise and continue to sauté until the vegetables start to color, about 3 minutes. Add the cabbage but do not stir. Turn the heat down low and press the cabbage down into the pot. It will be very full to begin with, but the cabbage will shrink down as it steams over the pancetta and brunoise mixture.

Cover and cook 5 minutes. Stir, cover again, and cook 5 minutes longer. Add the juniper berries and ground black pepper but no salt (because the pancetta is already imparting its salt to the dish).

Push the partridges into the cabbage, breast-sides up, so they are half buried. Pour the stock over the cabbage. Grease a piece of foil with duck fat or butter and cover the birds loosely so the breasts do not burn.

Holding Point – the dish can be held for several hours at this point.

Put to heat in the oven 15 minutes to complete the cooking process.

Serving

Serve a bird per person on its own bed of cabbage. Large hot plates, please. No need for any further sauce as the cabbage will be moist enough. Finger bowls will indicate to your guests that they should use their hands to finish every morsel of the partridge.

Sole Florentine

This is adapted from an old-fashioned dish of classic French cuisine, which refers to anything seated on spinach as à la florentine. At its worst, the description on a menu means overcooked fillets of sole on stringy spinach with a floury béchamel and a gratin involving cheap cheese. Here the dish owes more to Italy than France, for it includes uncooked Parmesan cheese to finish it. In a sense the classic recipe has been disassembled and the constituent elements put back together in a lighter and fresher way.

Buy large fish and work on the basis of $3/4$ pound of whole fish per person. Have your fishmonger skin and fillet the sole for you, making sure you get the bones and trimmings for the sauce.

This is a dish that requires careful planning and swift execution, but is in no way difficult. Avoid doing it for a formal dinner party. Instead, this an ideal supper dish for friends who can be sitting and waiting. The sauce can be used with other fish and, surprisingly, freezes well.

Ingredients (for 4)

$1\,^1/_2$ pounds fresh spinach
1 lemon
3 pounds Dover soles (see above),
 skinned and filleted
1 stick ($^1/_2$ cup) butter
salt and pepper
2 ounces Reggiano Parmesan
 cheese, to serve

FOR THE SAUCE:
bones and trimmings from the soles,
 head discarded
1 carrot
1 small leek
1 celery stalk
2 tablespoons butter
1 glass ($^2/_3$ cup) of dry white wine
1 $^1/_4$ cups heavy whipping cream
1 bay leaf

Mise en Place

First make the sauce: Cut the sole bones and trimmings with scissors into 1-inch pieces. Rinse and drain. Peel the carrot and dice it. Trim the leek and cut it into rounds; chop the celery stalk • In a small saucepan, melt the butter over low heat. Add the vegetables and bones and trimmings and sweat together, stirring constantly, for 2 minutes. Do not allow to color. Add the white wine and turn the heat up to medium. Simmer 5 minutes. Add the cream and simmer until the cream is syrupy, about 15 minutes. Add the bay leaf for only the last 3 minutes of cooking, otherwise its flavor will be too intrusive • Strain the sauce into a bowl, wash the saucepan, and return the sauce to it. Taste and season accordingly. If the sauce is not of a coating consistency, return to medium heat and simmer until it coats the back of the stirring spoon. Remove from the heat and let to cool.

Preheat the oven to its highest setting • Wash and pick over the spinach, then spin it as dry as possible (this is essential) • Juice the lemon.

Prepare the fish: Cut the sole fillets lengthwise into 3-inch oblongs about $1\,^1/_2$ inches wide. Brush the baking pan with about 1 tablespoon of water and arrange the pieces of sole in it, leaving small gaps between the pieces. Dot each piece with a little of the butter and season lightly.

Utensils

small saucepan
strainer
salad spinner
nonstick shallow baking pan or
    sheet
large heavy frying pan
colander
potato peeler (if shaving Parmesan)
    or grater

Cooking

Put the sauce in its pan over very low heat as it burns easily.

Place the pan of sole in the oven. You now have about 5 minutes to cook the spinach before the fish is ready.

Put a large heavy frying pan on high heat. Add half the remaining butter and immediately add the spinach. The pan will seem over-full, but the spinach will start to wilt immediately. Toss and turn the spinach as it cooks very quickly. You are trying to cook at a pace that allows the water to evaporate as it cooks. Season at the end – it takes plenty of seasoning.

If the spinach has gone watery in the pan, then tilt the pan and press excess moisture out as you do not want any green-tinted water swilling about on the plates. If very watery, drain in a strainer, pressing lightly. This whole process should take no more than 2 minutes. It is really the best way I know to cook spinach.

Rush to the oven and peer at the sole. When cooked, the small pieces of fillet will have shrunk quite alarmingly and exuded quite a lot of water, which will be mingled with the melted butter in the pan.

Retain all the juices in the baking pan and add these to the sauce, as they have lots of flavor. Turn up the heat under the sauce and whisk in the remaining butter in small pieces, together with a few drops of lemon juice. Take off the heat to prevent the sauce separating.

Serving

Transfer the spinach to the center of four very large warmed dinner plates. Place the sole on the beds of spinach: There should be about 5 pieces per person. Spoon the sauce over the sole (do not drown – 2 or 3 tablespoons per serving will be enough). Sprinkle with grated Parmesan or shave curls of the cheese over and serve at once.

Japanese-Style Pork Belly with Dancing Bonito

We tend to think of Japanese food as being elegant and formal, but they have a whole tradition of earthy peasant food, which is now starting to be seen in the West. Here, the pork is simmered for a long time until meltingly tender, its fattiness cut with generous additions of Colman's mustard.

I always used to use Japanese mustard for this dish until I discovered that the Japanese import mustard from England only to do something mysterious to it before putting it in small tubes and exporting it back to us at an inflated price. The result is delicious, but in my view it does not justify the mark-up.

You will need to pay a visit to a Japanese grocer to get some of the ingredients, but they all keep for ages so it will be an investment for many dishes to come. Unsmoked side pork can be found in Asian markets.

Ingredients (for 4)

2$\frac{1}{2}$- pound piece of fat fresh pork belly (side pork)
2$\frac{1}{2}$ quarts Soy Master Stock (see page 20)
2-inch piece of fresh gingerroot
2 pounds seasonal greens or bok choy
2 tablespoons Colman's English mustard powder
2 scallions
2 tablespoons bonito flakes

Utensils

2 large pans
small bowl
colander
blanching basket
medium saucepan
serving dish with lid

Mise en Place

Prepare the pork: Cut it into 16 chunks, put them into a large pot of cold water, and bring to a boil. Lower the heat and simmer 20 minutes. Drain in a colander, discarding the water. Put the pork back into the pan and pour over the stock liquid. The chunks need to be covered and to achieve this you may have to add about the same amount again of water.

Peel and slice the gingerroot and add it to the pot • Wash the greens and trim off the stems.

Cooking

Bring the stock to a boil, then lower the heat and simmer about 2 hours, by which time the pork should be moist and tender. It is very important to cook it as slowly as possible to prevent the meat becoming dry and fibrous.

When ready, carefully transfer the meat to a plate and let it cool. As soon as you can handle the meat, remove the skin and any bones.

Bring the stock back to a boil and skim. Leave it simmering on the rangetop.

When ready to serve, warm the pork gently in $\frac{1}{2}$ cup or so of the stock. (After you have finished, let the stock cool, then strain it into a suitable container and refrigerate. It will keep pretty much indefinitely and can be used again and again with the addition of a fresh piece of ginger each time.)

While the pork is cooking, mix the mustard powder with an equal amount of water in a small bowl, and finely slice the scallions.

Blanch the greens in boiling salted water for 2 minutes and refresh in cold water. Squeeze out excess moisture, but do not compress the leaves too much.

Just before serving, gently reheat the greens in a few spoonfuls of the stock in a separate pan.

Serving

Mound the greens in a warmed serving dish. Arrange the pork chunks on top with a dab of mustard on each. Scatter over the sliced scallions, followed by the bonito. Quickly put on the lid and bring immediately to the table. When you take off the lid the bonito flakes will have been moved by the moist heat to dance in the air.

Osso Buco with Risotto Milanese

The Milanese are the undisputed masters of veal cooking and this is one of their greatest dishes. Most recipes for the classic osso buco use tomatoes, but I prefer the veal shanks cooked bianco. It is important to get your butcher to cut the individual pieces thickly enough for marrow retention, as the meat cooks and pulls away from the bone. Many recipes also call for a mirepoix (see page 188) in the first stage of cooking which is then strained out and discarded, a finer brunoise (see page 187) being substituted to finish the dish. This seems to me unnecessary.

Risotto Milanese is the archetypal risotto, golden from saffron and flavored with fine chicken broth. It is the most simple and pure in effect, for there is nothing to distract from the rice. It is therefore, ironically, the most difficult to achieve perfectly. This is the risotto over which the ultimate luxury is to shave white truffles, but it is also the only risotto to be served as an accompaniment, traditionally as here with osso buco. Some Italian recipes also call for the addition of beef or veal marrow, but this seems to me an unnecessary extra richness. See page 27 for my fuller treatment of the cooking of risotto.

Ingredients (for 4)

4 ossi buchi (this is what to ask for, and don't let them sell you any pieces of veal shank that are less than 2 inches wide)
3 tablespoons flour
salt and pepper
2 large carrots
1 celery heart
1 large onion
2 tablespoons sunflower oil
1 quart very dry white wine
bay leaf

FOR THE RISOTTO MILANESE:
1 large onion
3 ounces Reggiano Parmesan cheese
1 quart Chicken Stock (see page 19)
6 tablespoons butter
1 1/2 cups Arborio or other Italian risotto rice
1/2 glass (1/3 cup) of dry white wine
12–16 saffron threads
salt and pepper

Mise en Place

Shake the veal pieces, one at a time, in a plastic bag with the flour seasoned with salt and pepper • Mince all the vegetables, including the onion for the risotto. Grate the Parmesan for the risotto.

Cooking

Put the sunflower oil in the frying pan over medium heat and brown the veal lightly, two pieces at a time. When the pieces are brown all over, transfer them to a colander set over a bowl to drain.

Then lightly sauté the vegetables (remembering to reserve the onion for the risotto) – they should not brown. Transfer to the casserole dish, distributing them evenly. Set the drained veal on top of the vegetables and season. Pour over the wine just to cover the shanks. If it does not quite cover them, then add some water. The larger the pot you are using, the more liquid you will need. This is why it is always a good idea to use a vessel in which the contents will just fit.

Bring to a boil, skim, and lower the heat to a bare simmer. Put in the bay leaf and cook gently until the meat starts to loosen from the bones, 1 1/2–2 hours. This is the point where you begin to worry about getting them out intact, but until it has been reached the ossi buchi are not done.

When cooked, carefully lift the shanks out of the sauce and lay them on a tray to rest. Keep warm, if serving immediately. Strain the sauce into a clean pan and put the vegetables with the meat. Heat the gravy and skim well just as it comes to a boil. Taste and, if it lacks body, reduce it at a simmer about 15 minutes to concentrate it.

Holding Point – the osso buco can be cooled and then held in the refrigerator to be reheated gently later while you make the risotto.

FOR THE GREMOLATA:
1/2 garlic clove
handful of flat-leaf parsley
zest of 1 large or 2 small lemons,
*   taken with a citrus zester*

Utensils
large plastic bag
grater
large frying pan
colander
bowl
casserole dish or heavy pan in which
*   the ossi buchi will fit snugly*
heavy-bottomed large pan with
*   sloping edges where the bottom*
*   meets the sides (the cast-iron Le*
*   Creuset casserole dish, is perfect)*
ladle (holding about 3/4 cup)

To make the risotto: In a saucepan, bring the chicken stock to a boil and turn down to a simmer.

Melt half the butter in a deep heavy-bottomed pan with sloping sides over medium heat, then sauté the onion until translucent. Add the rice and continue to sauté, stirring to coat with the butter and onion mixture and being careful not to brown by using too high a heat. It is at this point that you should hear the rice "clicking" against the side of the pan as you stir. Add the wine and boil 1 minute, stirring all the time.

Add a ladleful of simmering stock and stir until it is absorbed. As soon as it is, add another ladleful and continue to repeat this process until the stock is nearly finished. Throughout the cooking of the rice, you must stir constantly, being sure to push the spoon firmly – but not roughly – against the sides and bottom of the pan to prevent any rice from sticking.

After 15 minutes, add the saffron threads and the remaining stock. Taste: The rice should be al dente, i.e. tender but firm to the bite and not chalky. If insufficiently cooked, add boiling water a half ladleful at a time until it is.

When you are satisfied that the risotto is cooked, draw the pan off the heat and stir in the remaining butter and the Parmesan. Season, if necessary. Cover and let stand 2–3 minutes. Stir once more just before serving.

While the risotto is cooking, gently reheat the veal if necessary in the gravy. While the risotto is standing, make the gremolata: Mince the garlic, flat-leaf parsley, and lemon zest and mix them together.

Serving
Put a mound of risotto on each of 4 warmed large soup plates and place a veal shank beside it. Ladle the sauce around the meat and sprinkle the gremolata sparingly over it.

Calves' Liver with Melted Onions and Sage

Veal liver is one of the most subtle and expensive variety meats you can buy, and that subtlety is all-important for this sauté. Seared calves' liver, still pink and juicy in the middle, is vastly superior to any other animal's liver. Lambs' liver, for example, just will not do.

The first time you cook this dish, I suggest you do so for two rather than four people – in which case halve the quantities. There will seem to be a lot of onions when you first start out, but they cook down to a fraction of their original bulk as the water evaporates from them.

Ingredients (for 4)

1 pound calves' liver, cut into 4 thin slices
¼ cup flour
salt and pepper
1 tablespoon sunflower oil
4 tablespoons butter
4 large sage leaves
5 tablespoons dry white wine, or 2 tablespoons balsamic or sherry vinegar
2 tablespoons Chicken Stock (see page 19)

FOR THE MELTED ONIONS:
8 large yellow onions
6 tablespoons butter
bay leaf
2 tablespoons white wine vinegar
1 tablespoon sugar

Utensils

heavy casserole with lid
sauté pan large enough to hold all the liver (or 2 sauté pans)
metal spatula

Mise en Place

At least 2 hours ahead, prepare the Melted Onions: Slice the onions into thin rings. Melt 4 tablespoons of the butter in the casserole over low heat. Stir in the onions and bay leaf. It is important not to let the butter brown – you are making a white compote, not caramelized onions, which is a different dish altogether.

Put on the lid and cook, covered, over very low heat for 30 minutes, by which time the onions will have started to collapse. Remove the lid and stir thoroughly. Cover again and continue to cook 1 hour more.

Remove the bay leaf and add the vinegar and sugar. Season with salt and pepper. Stir and turn up the heat to medium. Cook to evaporate the liquid, stirring while you do so. Stop cooking before the onions take on color. Keep warm for immediate use, or store in a closed container in the refrigerator up to 1 week.

Prepare the liver: Carefully remove any tubes or threads from the liver. Put the flour on a plate and season well. Coat the pieces of liver in the seasoned flour and shake off any excess.

Cooking

Heat the sauté pan over medium heat. Put the sunflower oil in the pan with half the butter and gently lay the slices of liver in this. Cook 2 minutes, then turn. Scatter over the sage leaves and cook 1 minute more.

Serving

Arrange beds of the warm melted onions on 4 warmed plates, place the cooked liver slices on top, and keep warm.

Turn up the heat under the pan and deglaze it with the wine or vinegar, scraping and stirring. Add the of chicken stock and bubble before swirling in the remaining butter to finish the sauce. Pour over the liver and serve immediately.

The Calves' Liver with Melted Onions and Sage is served here with Hasselback Potatoes, see page 132.

Salmis of Grouse

Salmis is an easy method of dealing with game, which allows prior preparation and pretty much guarantees moist results by combining roasting with stewing. It is an excellent way of cooking birds that have very little natural fat in their meat, and the recipe includes the basic method of making a good gravy or jus.

While this recipe specifies grouse, it works just as well with pheasant, partridge, or squab pigeon, though you need to adjust the cooking times accordingly. The preliminary roasting should only half-cook the bird.

It may seem like a complex recipe, but it is actually very straightforward and its two-stage nature makes it an ideal dinner-party dish, since all the preparation and early cooking of the birds and the gravy may be done the day ahead.

Ingredients (for 4)

4 grouse
salt and pepper
8 thick slices of bacon
1 1/2 sticks (3/4 cups) butter
1 onion
1 carrot
2 celery stalks
2 teaspoons sugar
2 tablespoons red wine vinegar
1/2 bottle (about 1 1/2 cups) of red wine
2 or 3 tablespoons port or Madeira wine (optional)
8 juniper berries
1 teaspoon cracked black pepper
Chicken Stock (see page 19 – optional)
1–2 teaspoons potato flour (optional)

Utensils

roasting pan or shallow casserole in which the birds fit snugly
string for barding
chopper or meat cleaver
chopping board
large bowl
strainer
saucepan

Mise en Place

Preheat the oven to its highest setting.

Prepare the birds: Wipe their insides clean with a damp cloth to remove any bitter fluids. Season copiously inside and out, rubbing the salt and pepper into the skins. Using 2 pieces of string on each bird, tie the bacon neatly to cover the breasts. (I prefer bacon to the barding pork fatback usually used by game dealers and tying the barding material yourself means you can season underneath it.)

Cooking

Place the roasting pan or casserole over medium heat and melt all but 4 tablespoons of the butter in it. Brown the grouse all over in this about 3 minutes. Given you have selected a pan or casserole in which the birds fit snugly, and assuming you are cooking 4 birds, brown them 2 at a time, using half the butter for the first 2 and the remainder for the second pair.

Then arrange all 4 birds in the pan with their breast-sides up and roast 10 minutes. Remove from the oven and let cool completely.

When cool, take the grouse out of the casserole and put this on the rangetop without washing it. Make a mirepoix (see page 188) of the onion, carrot, and celery and put to sweat and brown over low heat in the pan, stirring from time to time.

Cut the strings and remove the bacon from the grouse. Discard the string but reserve the bacon. Pull the legs away from the body and cut through the joint to detach. Put these into a bowl. Cut down on both sides of the breastbone to detach the breast meat. (The breasts are deep and you want to follow the contour of the ribcage with the knife all the way down to the point where it is attached to the stump of the wing. Cut through the joint to give you a neat breast half with the wing bone still attached.) Put this breast meat with the legs. As you work blood and juices will run out; scrape these into the bowl as you go along.

You should now have 8 breast halves, 8 legs, 4 carcasses, the meat juices, and 8 pieces of bacon in the bowl. Transfer all the meat to a tray, putting the pieces of meat skin-side up. Cut the bacon into lardons and scatter over the top. Reserve the meat juices in the bowl.

Chop the carcasses into small pieces with a cleaver and add to the mirepoix. Turn up the heat to medium and brown, stirring and scraping, before pouring in the buttery meat juices from the bowl. Add the sugar and vinegar and cook briskly, stirring constantly with a wooden spoon, until caramelized.

Add the red wine, port or Madeira if using, the juniper berries, and cracked pepper. Turn the heat to high and bubble briskly until almost all the liquid has evaporated (you must not leave the dish at this point), stirring until you have achieved a syrupy consistency.

Pour over just enough water nearly to cover the bones. (If you have chicken stock, use it instead but it is not vital.) Simmer until reduced by half, then add cold water to cover the bones again. Reduce again, this time skimming off any scum or fat that rises to the surface. By the time the volume has reduced by half, the bones will have collapsed while the gravy will be dark and rich and full of flavor. Remove from the heat and let cool.

When cool, pass through a strainer into a clean pan, pressing on the bones to extract all moisture. Discard the bones.

Holding Point – ideally all this can be done the day before.

When ready to serve: Bring the gravy to a boil and skim. If the resulting liquid is not syrupy enough, whisk in a teaspoon or two of potato flour dissolved in a tablespoon of water to thicken.

Put the gravy into the casserole and bring to a bare simmer over low heat. At this point, add the legs and lardons of bacon and warm through 2 minutes. Now place the breasts gently in the liquid, skin-side up.

Add the remaining 4 tablespoons butter in small pieces and simmer until melted, shaking the pan with a rotating motion to speed the process. By the time the butter is incorporated the breasts will be just warmed through and ready to take to the table. On no account let the gravy boil at this stage or you will toughen the grouse.

Serving
Serve with plain boiled potatoes as a foil for the rich and glossy sauce.

Wrapped Breast of Chicken with Wild Mushrooms

With elements of both a dish cooked en papillote *and a* saltimbocca, *I believe this is a genuinely original dish – something a chef can rarely say. It is another signature dish of the restaurant.*

Mise en Place
Well ahead: Put the dried mushrooms to soak in warm water half an hour.

Preheat the oven to its highest setting and put $2^{1}/_{2}$ quarts of salted water to heat • Generously butter a roasting pan that is just big enough to hold the four packages • Peel and mince the shallots, then distribute them evenly over the bottom of the dish • Butter four 8-inch squares of foil.

Ingredients (for 4)

2 ounces dried morels
1 ounces dried cèpes (or porcini)
2 sticks (1 cup) butter
2 shallots
8 large leaves of seasonal greens or
   Savoy cabbage (outer leaves only)
8 thin slices of pancetta or 4 of
   prosciutto
1 1/4 cups Chicken Stock (see page
   19)
1 glass (2/3 cup) of dry white wine
4 large chicken suprêmes (see page
   19)
salt and pepper

Utensils

large bowl
roasting pan just big enough to hold
   the 4 packages
foil
2 saucepans
fine strainer or cheesecloth
bowl

Prepare the leaves: Blanch them in boiling salted water 3 minutes and refresh in cold water. Drain thoroughly and cut out the tough bottom part of the stem from each leaf.

Assemble the packages: Spread 2 of the green leaves on each foil square to cover. Place 2 slices of pancetta slightly overlapping or 1 slice of prosciutto to cover as much of the greens as possible. Then place a 1-tablespoon piece of butter in the middle and put a chicken suprême on it. Grind black pepper to season, but add no salt as the ham is salty and the salt taste intensifies when hot. Carefully fold the greens and ham around the suprême, then roll the foil around (*as illustrated below*).

Cooking

Strain the soaking liquid from the reconstituted mushrooms into a saucepan through a fine strainer or cheesecloth. Add the chicken stock and white wine and boil to reduce to 2 1/2 cups of liquid.

Scatter the reconstituted mushrooms over the shallots in the roasting pan. Arrange the four packages in the pan and pour the hot stock over them. Bake 30 minutes.

Remove from the oven and transfer the packages to a hot dish. Let rest in a warm place for 10 minutes while you make the sauce.

Put the roasting pan on the rangetop, bring the contents to a rolling boil, and reduce to about 2/3 cup. Adjust the seasoning, then whisk in the remaining butter a piece at a time until amalgamated. Remove from the heat and transfer to a measure for pouring.

Serving

Unwrap the chicken from the foil and carve each suprême into 3 pieces. Pour the sauce on 4 heated plates and arrange the slices, overlapping, in the center of each. Serve immediately.

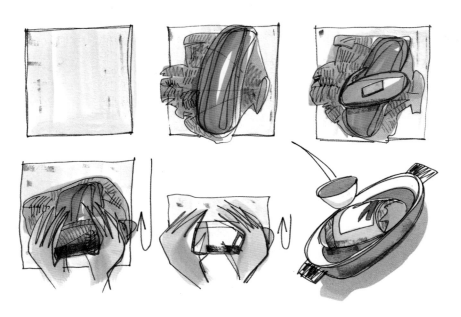

Turbot Steak with Cèpes

This is a special dish for the brief time when fresh cèpes are available. It does not work with dried mushrooms, so don't be tempted to substitute them. If you cannot get fresh cèpes then it is better to use large open-capped common mushrooms.

You can use the same cooking method with halibut and cod, though the latter is more delicate and demands greater care. Note that when roasting fish you do not want the pieces touching or they will stew. Also, the heavier the pan you use the better — indeed, a heavy frying pan with an ovenproof handle is ideal.

Ingredients (for 4)

6 tablespoons butter
2 pounds fresh cèpes
1/2 lemon
small handful of flat-leaf parsley
1 garlic clove
salt and pepper
1/4 cup flour
4 turbot steaks, each weighing about 1/2 pound
about 3 tablespoons sunflower oil

Utensils

roasting pan large enough to hold the steaks with space between them or a heavy ovenproof frying pan
bowl
juicer
metal spatula

Mise en Place

Preheat the oven to its highest setting, the hotter the better • Put the butter somewhere warm to soften, for example in a bowl above the oven.

Prepare the mushrooms: Wipe them gently with a damp cloth, then separate the caps from the stems. Discard any stems that are wormy. Trim the stems, discarding the earthy base, and peel them as sparingly as possible with a potato peeler. Slice the caps and stems into 1/4-inch pieces.

Prepare the garlic butter: Juice the lemon. Mince the parsley and the garlic. Work the garlic, parsley, lemon juice, and some salt and pepper into the softened butter with a fork.

Season the flour and coat the fish steaks, shaking off any excess.

Cooking

Brush the bottom of the roasting pan with the sunflower oil to prevent the fish sticking and lay the steaks in gently, dark side down. Drizzle the top of the steaks with more oil and put into the oven to roast 10 minutes.

Remove the fish from the oven and carefully turn the steaks over, using a spatula and trying not to disturb the crust. Return to the oven to roast 10 minutes longer.

Meanwhile, sauté the cèpes in 1 tablespoon of sunflower oil over medium heat. When they begin to wilt, add the garlic butter and toss the mushrooms in it as it melts.

Serving

Put the cèpes on a hot serving dish. Remove the turbot from the oven and set the steaks carefully on the mushrooms.

VEGETABLES

Hasselback Potatoes

This is a different way of roasting potatoes that originated in the Stockholm restaurant of the same name, though the original version does not use olive oil. Why cutting the potatoes in this way should make such a difference to the texture and flavor is hard to say, but try them once and you may end up preferring them to traditional roast potatoes.

In my kitchen, working with the fierce heat of industrial ovens, we have to pour stock around the potatoes to keep them from burning and sticking. In a domestic oven the olive oil and butter mixture is sufficient for this purpose.

The addition of several unpeeled garlic cloves to the roasting juices gives a subtle depth to the flavor. These cloves are delicious in their own right, sweet and nutty without being overpowering.

Hasselback's restaurant actually sells special wooden trays on which to sit the potatoes in order to limit the depth of cut so that aren't get cut all the way through. You can use a metal skewer for the same purpose, pushing it through the base of the potato along its length, then cutting down to it. Obviously, remove the skewer before cooking.

Ingredients (for 4)

4 baking potatoes, weighing about
    1 1/2–2 pounds in total
12 unpeeled garlic cloves
3 tablespoons olive oil
6 tablespoons of butter
salt and pepper

Utensils

Hasselback board or metal skewer
    (optional)
saucepan with lid
gratin dish (just large enough to hold
    the potatoes snugly)
bulb baster

Mise en Place

Preheat the oven to 400°F and butter the gratin dish.

Prepare the potatoes: Peel them and cut them across, downward, at a slight angle at 1/4-inch intervals, being careful not to cut all the way through (use a skewer as described above if unsure). Put in a pan of very cold water, cover, and let stand 10 minutes.

Cooking

Scatter the garlic in the prepared gratin dish. Then arrange the drained potatoes on top, cut-sides up. Pour over the olive oil and dot with the butter. Season with salt and pepper.

Roast 1 hour. After 30 minutes, baste every 10 minutes until done. The potatoes will brown on top and crisp, fanning apart along the cut lines. Do not attempt to move the potatoes while they are cooking.

Serving

Serve from the gratin dish at the table.

Broccoli with Anchovies

The textures and flavors of broccoli and anchovies combine perfectly, and the addition of really crisp bread crumbs gives an added crunch that is very pleasing. In the restaurant I use leftover olive oil croutons made the day before to accompany fish soup, simply whizzing them in the food processor for a few seconds.

Ingredients (for 4)

*½ French baguette (stale will do if
 not too hard)
1 ¼ cups olive oil
1 ½ pounds broccoli
1 large hot red chili pepper
2 ounces canned anchovies in oil,
 drained
few drops of lemon juice (optional)*

Utensils

*baking sheet
food processor
heavy frying pan
large saucepan
large bowl
small saucepan
colander*

Mise en Place

Preheat the oven to 400°F. Slice the bread into ¼-inch rounds, then brush generously with olive oil and put on a baking sheet in the oven. Check every few minutes, as they tend to burn the instant you turn your back. When crisp and golden, remove the bread and let cool. Using a food processor, make the bread into crumbs. These will keep in a jar in the refrigerator a few days before souring and going off.

Prepare the broccoli: First put a large pan of lightly salted water on to heat – you need very little salt in the cooking water as the florets retain salt and intensify the seasoning. I once had a review that said everything was lovely except the broccoli, which tasted as if it had been cooked in sea water. Point taken! • Split the broccoli into florets, cut out the woody stems, and discard. You can find caterpillar infestation, so watch out. Wash and let soak in a bowl of cold water. This will freshen the vegetable.

Make the anchovy sauce: Split the chili and seed it, then dice it microscopically. Put the remaining olive oil into the small pan with the diced chili and anchovies and heat, stirring occasionally. Simmer a few minutes, then add the bread crumbs off the heat. Stir from time to time while the sauce is cooling or it will set like cement. Taste, adding a squeeze of lemon juice if you find it too rich. The only problem with lemon juice is that it can discolor the broccoli.

Cooking

Cook the broccoli in the boiling water. It will not need very many minutes – it really should be quite crisp and will be disgusting if overdone. Drain in the colander.

Serving

Arrange the broccoli on a warmed serving dish and pour over the anchovy sauce.

Ratatouille

A Provençal vegetable stew best served at room temperature, ratatouille should be a very basic preparation and not over-refined. Bad variations (vegetables diced too small, too much tomato, using dried herbs, and so on) often debase one of the finest combinations of Mediterranean flavors.

It is very important to use the best extra virgin olive oil and to cook all the different vegetables separately, combining them only at the last moment. The eggplants and

Ingredients (for 4)

2 onions
3 garlic cloves
3 large eggplants
6 zucchini (or 12 baby zucchini)
3 bell peppers (1 red and 2 yellow
  — never use green for ratatouille)
2 plum tomatoes
sprig of rosemary
sprig of thyme
1 1/4 cups extra virgin olive oil
salt and pepper
8 basil leaves

zucchini must be very fresh — when they have spent too long on the shelf they go bitter. Some texts advise salting them to remove bitterness, but experience suggests that all this delivers is old, salty, and bitter vegetables.

Making a first class ratatouille takes time — there are no short cuts. It is vital not to fry the ingredients quickly, but to stew them gently and avoid overcooking. The ratatouille improves after a day's rest to let the flavors amalgamate.

Alternatively, ratatouille while still hot is delicious mixed with an equal quantity of fusili or macaroni (or any other robust dried pasta). Simply cook the pasta, drain, and toss it with the ratatouille while it is still warm. Dress with torn basil to serve.

Mise en place

Prepare the vegetables, keeping each vegetable separate: Only peel the onions and garlic, but trim the eggplants and zucchini. Remove stems and seeds from the bell peppers. Scald the tomatoes in a bowl of boiling water for 60 seconds, then refresh, peel, and seed. Cut all the vegetables into bite-sized chunks. (If using baby zucchini, leave them whole.)

Strip the rosemary and thyme leaves from their twigs and chop the leaves.

Utensils

small bowl
colander
large bowl
*large heavy pan (a big Le Creuset
    casserole is ideal)*
slotted spoon

*LEFT If you can't wait to to taste your
ratatouille, slice a length of baguette and fill it
with the hot ratatouille. Press down gently to
let the juices soak into the bread, and devour.*

Cooking

Put about 3 tablespoons of olive oil into a large heavy pan, set over medium heat, and cook the onions, stirring. They must not color. As they soften and turn translucent, add the garlic and cook 2 minutes longer. Using a slotted spoon, transfer the contents of the pan to a colander placed over a bowl.

Add another splash of olive oil to the pan, turn up the heat a bit and sauté the peppers. They need to be cooked until slightly brown, not collapsing but with some residual bite. When done, transfer to the colander. Repeat with the eggplants, then finally the zucchini.

Add the chopped herbs to the vegetables. Season and return all the cooked vegetables to the pan, adding any remaining oil and the juices that have drained into the bowl. Stew together 5 minutes, stirring. Remove from the heat and stir in the uncooked diced tomato. This will cook slightly in the hot vegetables.

If possible, let the ratatouille cool and then refrigerate overnight so the flavors can amalgamate. Return to room temperature before serving. Always check the seasoning at room temperature.

This dish can also be warmed gently to be served hot with grilled meat or fish.

Serving

Just before bringing the ratatouille to the table, tear over the basil leaves.

Turkish Braised Vegetables

The idea for this dish came from Claudia Roden's recipe for winter vegetables in olive oil. It works very well in the restaurant as it is equally good hot or cold. Turkish in origin, it manages to lift coarse root vegetables into a surprisingly light and refreshing dish.

Ingredients (for 4)

2 large carrots
2 leeks
2 turnips
1 small head of celeriac (celery root)
1 large potato
1 large onion
4 lemons
large bunch of dill
1 1/cups extra virgin olive oil
salt and pepper

Utensils

large heavy-bottomed pan

Mise en Place

Wash and peel the vegetables. Keeping the vegetables separate, chop them into uniform cubes about 1-inch across • Squeeze the juice from the lemons and reserve • If serving immediately, chop the dill.

Cooking

Put the large heavy pan over low heat and pour in all the oil. Sweat the onion in this 5 minutes, stirring occasionally. Add the carrots and sweat 5 minutes longer, then add the turnips, celeriac, and potato.

Stew 15 minutes more, stirring from time to time. Add the leeks and cook a final 5 minutes. The vegetables should not color. There will be enough water in them to prevent frying at this temperature. The leeks will lose their fresh green color, but this does not matter. Test now to see if everything is cooked, bearing in mind that all the elements should retain a residual bite.

Season generously and add the lemon juice; taste to check for acid balance. Serve at once or transfer to a bowl and let cool.

Serving

Serve hot or at room temperature. If chilled, return to a pan and warm gently in its own juices. Just before bringing to the table, stir in plenty of chopped dill.

DESSERTS

Roast Figs with Honey Ice Cream

I have never been passionate about figs in their raw state and, yes, I have eaten them in Italy, perfectly ripe and straight off the tree. But roast them and combine with honey ice cream and I am a happy convert. Take care that the honey you use is not too herbal — some of them are so heavily scented they are more suited to the bathroom than the kitchen.

Ingredients (for 4)

1 quantity Vanilla Ice Cream (page 28)
²/₃ cup clear honey
16 ripe figs

Utensils

ice-cream machine or sorbetière
baking pan
wooden spoon

Mise en Place

Well ahead, prepare the Vanilla Ice Cream mixture as described on page 28 • Melt the honey in a bowl set over boiling water until liquid • Pour all but a couple of tablespoons of the honey into the ice cream mixture and churn in the ice-cream machine until frozen.

About 20 minutes before serving, preheat the oven to maximum and remove the ice cream from the freezer. It should be soft enough to scoop easily when the figs come out of the oven.

Cooking

Sprinkle a baking pan with a few drops of water to prevent burning and sticking. Arrange the figs in the pan so they do not touch and roast until the skin starts to brown, about 10 minutes.

Remove from the oven. As soon as the figs are cool enough to handle, make two cross-cuts down into each fig to about half the depth. Squeeze them in the middle to open them at the top. Put a teaspoon of the reserved honey into each and return to the oven to roast a final 5 minutes.

Serving

Put a scoop of the ice cream in the middle of each plate and arrange 4 figs around, or put a spoonful of the ice cream in the middle of each fig with the rest of the ice cream in a bowl for people to help themselves at the table.

Chocolate Brownies with Fudge Sauce

The saying "as American as apple pie" could just as easily be made about chocolate brownies. The American love affair with chocolate is well known, and in this rich and luxurious version of these favorite cakes it is easy to understand why. It is incredibly rich, but try giving people very small portions and watch them come back determinedly for more. The quality of the chocolate is critical, and this is one recipe where an electric mixer is essential — it simply will not work with a food processor.

We serve this knock-'em-dead brownie with a big scoop of vanilla ice cream and fudge sauce poured over. Most people can still walk afterward, though with difficulty. The fudge sauce is easy to make. It sounds like something from the children's menu of a fast-food outlet, but don't let this put you off trying it.

Ingredients (for 4-8)

4 ounces best-quality bittersweet
    chocolate
I stick (*¹/₂ cup*) unsalted butter, at
    room temperature
¹/₂ cup sugar
I extra large egg + I extra yolk
I teaspoon vanilla extract
6 tablespoons flour
2 tablespoons unsweetened cocoa
    powder
¹/₄ teaspoon baking powder
¹/₄ teaspoon salt
Vanilla Ice Cream (page 28), to
    serve (optional)

FOR THE FUDGE SAUCE:
I cup heavy whipping cream
I*¹/₂* cups sugar
4 tablespoons butter
²/₃ cup light corn syrup
²/₃ cup milk
I teaspoon vanilla extract
8 ounces bittersweat chocolate

Utensils

I0-inch springform cake pan
parchment paper
bowl set over a pan of hot water
electric mixer
flour sifter
skewer
heavy-based saucepan

Mise en Place

First make the brownies: Preheat the oven to 325°F and line the cake pan with a disk of parchment paper • Break the chocolate into pieces and put them to melt in the bowl set over hot water, making sure the base of the bowl does not come into direct contact with the water • Put the butter and sugar in the bowl of the mixer and beat at high speed until a smooth creamed consistency is achieved. This takes a few minutes. Add the whole egg and the yolk together with the vanilla, continuing to beat until smooth. Then incorporate the melted chocolate while still beating. Finally beat in the sifted flour, cocoa, baking powder, and salt • Spoon the batter into the prepared pan.

Cooking

Bake 35 minutes, then test with a skewer, pushing it deep into the center of the cake. It should be moist in the middle, and judging precisely when it is ready is not easy. I prefer it slightly undercooked in the center, really moist and fudgy. Remember, it will continue cooking after you remove it from the oven. The cake will have risen, but will fall soon after you have taken it out. Let it cool in the pan, standing on a rack, at least 5 minutes before unmolding it. Leave on the wire rack to cool further.

Meanwhile, make the fudge sauce (here you are essentially making fudge but not taking it to the point where it sets solid). Cook all the ingredients except the chocolate in a heavy pan over medium heat, stirring constantly, until it turns a pale caramel color. Remove from the heat and beat in the chocolate in pieces. Finish by stirring in *¹/₃* cup of cold water. If it is still too thick, continue adding water a spoonful at a time until you achieve a nice consistency.

Serve immediately or hold in a water-bath. If made ahead and chilled, reheat gently in a bowl set over boiling water.

Serving

Cut the brownie cake in half and then cut each half into 4 wedges (the other half will provide second helpings, or keep for later). Serve the brownies on 4 plates with a scoop of ice cream, if using, on top of each wedge and the sauce poured over.

Tarte Tatin

It is said that Curnonsky, the legendary and oft-quoted gastro-person, made the 167-kilometer journey by train from Paris to Lamotte-Beuvron near Orléans just to eat the apple tarte renversée that we know today as Tarte Tatin. It was cooked for him at the Hotel-Terminus Tatin by the sisters Tatin, who are credited with its invention.

The tart is characterized by the use of halved apples baked in caramel with the pastry lid becoming the base when the cooked tart is inverted to be served still warm. It is one of those dishes that sounds simple and is actually difficult to get right. On average it takes a cook in my kitchen a week of trying before he or she produces a saleable tart.

In the restaurant we use a frying pan rather than a cake pan, and I prefer crisp apples to Le Golden delicious, which the French choose as a matter of national honor. I believe the original recipe uses sweet short pastry, but I like puff and find-ready made frozen puff pastry good enough for domestic interpretations. Anyway, since it will be drenched with sugary juices, the quality of the pastry is not the most significant part of the finished dish.

Ingredients (for 8-12)

1 pound best-quality frozen puff
  pastry
12 sharp, crisp apples
juice of 1 lemon
1/2 cup sugar
4 tablespoons butter

Utensils

large bowl
nonstick heavy frying pan with
  ovenproof handle
stainless steel saucepan (if
  necessary)
plate the same size as the top of
  the frying pan
serving or dinner plate slightly larger
  than the pan
bulb baster

Mise en Place

If using frozen puff pastry, remove it from the freezer in plenty of time.

Preheat the oven to 350°F • Peel and core the apples, turning them in the lemon juice in a bowl to prevent discoloration. Cut them in half, squaring off the ends.

Cooking

Put the sugar in the frying pan over low heat to caramelize. Turn the pan from time to time as the heat never distributes evenly and you want to avoid burning. The color must, however, be a dark nut-brown. If your frying pan is black and you are not sure about the color, make the caramel in a stainless steel pan and pour into the frying pan when it has reached a suitably dark brown. If it burns, you must throw it away and start again or the end result will be horribly bitter; however, if there is only one small burned patch, don't worry about it. When the caramel is ready, remove the pan from the heat.

Dot the surface of the caramel with a little of the butter cut into small pieces and pack the apples tightly on top as follows: Put an entire half apple in the center, cut-side up; cut the remaining apples into quarters and arrange them in a wheel around it. This should use up 8 of the apples. Fill in any gaps with wedges cut from the remaining 4 apples. The apples shrink inward during cooking, so the tighter you pack them, the better. The final arrangement should stand proud of the rim of the pan when viewed from the side.

Dot the top of the apples with the remaining butter and put the pan back on a low heat for 5 minutes to melt the caramel and start the apples cooking.

Roll out the pastry to a thickness of about 1/8 inch. Using as a template a plate with the same circumference as the pan, cut a circle out of the pastry. Fold the circle of pastry in half, then fold in half again to make a quarter. Lay this carefully on the apples and unfold to cover them completely. Tuck the edges of the pastry inside the pan at the edges.

Immediately put the pan into the oven and bake 25 minutes. The apples will be cooked and have expanded, pushing the pastry up. Remove from the oven and let cool 10 minutes. If there appears to be a lot of watery fluid around the edges,

extract some of it using a bulb baster

Now the moment of truth: Cover the top of the pan with your serving plate. Holding the pan by the handle (with a pot holder because it will still be hot), invert so that the pastry base is now against the surface of the plate, with the rim outside the circumference of the pan. Sit the plate on the table, rap the bottom of the pan smartly with a suitable implement, and lift away from the tart.

At this point shout triumphantly as the caramel-glossed Tarte Tatin smiles at you in rustic perfection; or, as may well be the case, burst into tears as overcooked apples cling tenaciously to the toffee in the pan and you contemplate an unattractive mess.

Serving
Serve while still warm.

Chocolate Mousse Cake

This recipe involves two separate classic culinary techniques: the making of chocolate génoise and the preparation of chocolate mousse. The mousse can be eaten as a dessert in its own right (simply spoon into ramekins or small glasses and chill) and the génoise can also be used in any number of gâteaux. My finished product is an adaptation of a sachertorte, but lighter, and the mousse is quite heretical.

In Britain, learning to make a Victoria sponge cake (a type of butter or creamed cake) has always been an essential part of what used to be called domestic science. I am sure this is why people have more difficulty making a génoise. With the widespread use of electric mixers, however, achieving a consistent and light result has become child's play indeed.

It is not intrinsically hard to achieve a light texture, but the technique is very different from that for a butter cake. If you have made the Sauternes and Olive Oil Cake (page 100) successfully then you will not have a problem, for they are very similar in execution. Should your first attempt prove a little dry and heavy, just soak the cake with some suitable alcohol. It will still be delicious.

Génoise cakes are best baked the day before they are needed as they will slice better after a night's rest unmolded, cooled completely, and stored in an air-tight container. They also freeze well.

Ingredients (for 8-12)

FOR THE CHOCOLATE
GÉNOISE:
4 tablesoons unsalted butter, plus
    more for greasing
1 cup cake flour, plus more for
    dusting
5 large eggs
2/3 cup sugar
2/3 cup unsweetened cocoa powder

FOR THE CHOCOLATE
MOUSSE:
1 espresso cup of strong, freshly
    made espresso coffee (or strong
    filter coffee)
2/3 cup sugar
4 ounces best-quality bittersweet or
    semisweet chocolate
1 tablespoons brandy, rum, or
    Scotch
4 tablespoons unsalted butter
4 large eggs

Mise en Place

Make the génoise well ahead (ideally the day before): Preheat the oven to 300°F. Cut the parchment paper to fit the bottom of the cake pan and put it in place. Grease the side of the cake pan carefully with butter, then dust it lightly with flour. Shake out any excess.

Make the génoise: Measure all the ingredients • Put the eggs and sugar in the bowl of the mixer and beat at medium speed until pale and thick. This will take 5–10 minutes and it is very important to incorporate as much air as possible at this stage. Continue to beat until you achieve a "ribbon consistency" (stiff enough to be able to write in it), when the mixture will be an off-white color • Put the butter in a pan over low heat to melt • Sift the flour and cocoa together into a bowl, then add to the egg mixture. Remove the mixer bowl and, with a spatula, stir gently, starting from the center at the bottom and working outward and upward while rotating the bowl one quarter-turn. Repeat three more times (which means the bowl will have been turned full circle). This is called "folding" and is the best way of ensuring all the elements are thoroughly mixed without losing lightness by being heavy-handed. If you over-work the mixture at this point you will end up with a leaden cake • Add the melted butter and incorporate lightly in the same way.

Cooking

Working quickly, pour the batter into the prepared cake pan, using the spatula to scrape the last of it from the mixing bowl. Bake the cake 20–30 minutes, without opening the oven door for at least the first 20 minutes.

Test the cake for doneness by inserting a small, clean sharp knife or skewer into the center: If it comes out clean, then the cake is done. If moist bits of batter adhere to it, bake 5 minutes longer and test again. Test one more time if necessary.

TO ASSEMBLE:

1 espresso cup of strong, freshly made espresso coffee (or strong filter coffee)
1 tablespoon sugar
1 small glass (3 or 4 tablespoons) of brandy, rum, or Scotch
2 tablespoons apricot jam (optional)

Utensils

sheet of parchment paper
10-inch springform cake pan
heavy-duty electric mixer (if using a portable mixer instead, set the bowl over a pan of simmering water)
rubber spatula
flour sifter
3 bowls
saucepan in which one of the bowls will fit exactly (so water can be heated underneath it without the bowl actually touching the water)
spatula

When satisfied it is done, transfer to a wire rack to cool.

As soon as you can handle the pan, unclip it and unmold the cake, which should have doubled in volume during the baking. Let cool.

Make the Chocolate Mousse: Brew the coffee and dissolve 1 tablespoon of sugar in it while still very hot.

Put some water into a saucepan with a bowl of matching size sitting just above the level of the water. It is important it should not be in direct contact with the water. Heat to a simmer, just below boiling point.

Break the chocolate into pieces and put these with the sweetened espresso and alcohol in the bowl set over the hot water to melt. It is vital that the liquid and liquor are put in right at the beginning. If added later, the chocolate will separate. Once the chocolate has melted, stir in the butter to achieve a smooth, glossy mixture. Be gentle.

While the chocolate is melting, separate the eggs and put the egg yolks and remaining sugar in a second bowl. Beat until they achieve a "ribbon consistency".

Wash the beaters and, in a third bowl, beat the egg whites until they form soft peaks. The texture should not be as stiff as for a meringue, but more of a thick, airy foam. Take them too far and the end result will be dry and lifeless.

Using the spatula, scrape the chocolate mixture into the egg yolk and sugar mixture and mix until they are just incorporated.

Now the tricky bit: Using a large spoon, scoop up some egg white and throw it into this chocolate batter. Stir it in quickly. This gives it an initial lightening. Now scrape all of that chocolate mixture onto the egg whites and fold in. Be incisive but gentle, trying to retain as much volume as you can. Inevitably you are going to lose some volume, but do not over-work.

Assembly

Make the second cup of strong espresso coffee, sweeten it with the tablespoon of sugar, and add to it a small glass of the same alcohol you put in the mousse. If you like the idea of some fruit in the cake, heat the apricot jam with 1 tablespoon of water until melted, then press through a strainer and reserve.

Now slice the cake across horizontally into 4 layers (a bread knife is ideal for this purpose).

Reserve the best-looking slice for the top. Do not put anything on this layer, but brush the other slices with the coffee and alcohol mixture.

Return one layer to the pan in which the cake was baked and brush with the apricot jam glaze, if using. Clip the pan shut around it and spoon over one-third of the chocolate mousse. Put the second cake layer on top, and spoon on another one-third of the mousse. Repeat with the third layer, and finish with the reserved layer. Do not put anything on the top. Refrigerate overnight.

Serving

While the cake needs no further embellishment, I like to make a simple stencil and use it to dust the top with a confectioners' sugar pattern. When ready to serve, unmold the cake carefully by sliding a warm metal spatula around the inside of the pan before unclipping it. Leave it on the base.

Winter

Winter, when bracing weather stimulates hearty appetites. A time for feasting, with classic dishes like *bollito misto,* and for the heady luxury of truffles and foie gras. Or simple rustic tastes like *daube* of beef, *confit* of duck, and pork cooked in milk Italian-style, until meltingly tender. Desserts emphasize comfort, with magic combinations like panettone bread and butter pudding or apple, prune, and zabaglione tart.

First Courses
Pasta e Ceci

Risotto Nero

Fish Soup with Rouille

Ravioli of Leeks and Truffles

Salad of White-Cooked Pork with Spicy Sichuan Dressing

Potato Pancakes with Smoked Eel and Bacon

Carpaccio of Beef

Pressed Chicken Terrine

Caesar Salad

Scallops with Thai Spicy Cabbage Salad

Main courses
New England Cod Chowder

Calves' Liver and Beets

Saltimbocca of Red Mullet

Tripe Gratin

Pork Cooked in Milk

Crispy Roast Duck

Confit Sarladaise

Bollito Misto

Daube of Beef

Truffled Poached Chicken

Vegetables
Five-Spice Greens

Turnip, Rutabaga, and Carrot Purée

Rösti

Bubble and Squeak

Desserts
Panettone Bread and Butter Pudding

Panforte and Reggiano Parmesan

Black Currant and Apple Streusel Tart

Ravioli San Giuseppe

Compote of Winter Fruits

Apple, Prune, and Zabaglione Tart

FIRST COURSES

Pasta e Ceci

This is the dish that Elizabeth David said is called "Thunder and Lightning," and if you don't throw away the water in which you have soaked the chickpeas you will discover why. By the way, this is essential practice when soaking all dried beans and peas if the "F" in fiber is not to be writ large (and loud) on the latter part of your meal and to the chagrin of your guests.

The point about this dish is that, while essentially a soup, its texture is closer to a vegetable stew. Take care to cook the chickpeas slowly. I have found that, simmered rather than boiled, chickpeas can take anything up to 4 hours to cook. Be sure to stir from time to time to prevent any sticking or burning. You would do well to use Spanish chickpeas for this dish, for Spain produces some of the best in the world. Another imported ingredient to look out for is Italian passata, or tomato purée.

While you can use fresh hot chili pepper, commercially dried hot pepper flakes are perfect for the dish and allow you to be consistent in your spicing. Unless you use the same kind of fresh chili every time, you will find wild fluctuations in the heat.

I use ditali (mini macaroni for soup) for the pasta, but any small commercial dried pasta like fusili will do. Cooking the pasta to the right texture takes a little practice — it needs to be al dente verging on the dente, as it will continue cooking after you have drained it and stirred it into the chickpeas. You want the pasta nearer half-cooked than cooked when it comes out of the water, so that it will then absorb any remaining liquid as the dish stands and finishes.

I think this dish tastes better if cooked with a ham bone or piece of pancetta. Our local Italian grocer keeps the ends of pancetta, which are too small to slice, and sells them for a fraction of the cost of a whole piece.

It is quite common in Italy for the Parmesan cheese to be stirred into the dish along with the additional olive oil just before it is brought to the table, but I think it is nicer for people to be able to help themselves to suit their personal taste. The golden color of the Parmesan on the top of each serving and the green gloss of the oil make a pleasing visual contrast to the otherwise rather uniform color of the dish.

Ingredients (for 4-6)

2 $\frac{1}{4}$ cups dried chickpeas (garbanzo beans), preferably Spanish
2 onions
2 carrots
1 celery stalk
4 large garlic cloves
sprig of rosemary
ham bone (optional but desirable) or 3 $\frac{1}{2}$ ounces pancetta
1 $\frac{1}{4}$ cup tomato purée
1 $\frac{1}{4}$ cups extra virgin olive oil
1 teaspoon hot pepper flakes
$\frac{1}{2}$ pound ditali or other small dried pasta
salt and pepper
chunk of Reggiano Parmesan cheese, to serve
more best-quality extra virgin oil, to serve

Utensils

large bowl
colander
large heavy-bottomed saucepan
large soup bowls
grater
pouring spout for the olive oil bottle to bring to the table

Mise en Place

Prepare the chickpeas: Soak them in cold water for 12 hours or overnight. Cover with at least 2 inches of water; if they absorb all the water and the top layer of chickpeas is left uncovered, they will split and discolor.

Peel and finely dice the onions and carrots • Trim the celery to remove "strings" and mince • Peel and cut the garlic into thin slices • Strip the leaves from the rosemary twig and chop them • If using pancetta, cut it into matchstick strips and then dice.

Cooking

Drain the chickpeas and rinse them. Place them in a large thick-bottomed pan at least four times their volume, together with the ham bone or pancetta. Cover with at least three times their volume of water. Stir in the vegetables to distribute them evenly. Do not season at this point because the Parmesan cheese you will add later has a lot of salt in it and the ham bone or pancetta will also contribute to the seasoning.

Bring to a boil and carefully skim off the scum that rises to the surface. Add the garlic, tomato purée, the olive oil (this will be completely absorbed by the chickpeas during the last stage of the cooking), the rosemary, and pepper flakes.

Simmer until tender. Precisely how long will depend on the exact volume of the water, how close to boiling the temperature is, and how long the chickpeas have been dried. Start to check after 2 hours, but it may take as long as 4.

When the chickpeas are cooked (they will be floury, but still have definition) remove the ham bone, if used. Turn up the heat and boil rapidly 5 minutes. Add the pasta and continue to boil until half done. Stir, taste, and adjust the seasoning if you think more salt is needed, but be careful because the Parmesan cheese will change things dramatically.

Remove from the heat, cover the pan, and let sit up to 10 minutes. The pasta will finish cooking and should absorb any remaining liquid. Don't worry if it is rather soupy: This is an authentic variation on the theme.

Serving

Serve at the table in large warmed soup bowls. Pass the Parmesan with a grater and the bottle of best-quality extra virgin oil fitted with a pouring spout for people to help themselves.

Risotto Nero

The black risotto of Venice achieves its dark presentation from cuttlefish and their ink, a most effective natural dye. Be warned: It works equally well on clothes, tablecloths, and teeth. This was the ultimate designer dish of the Eighties and is good enough to serve into the next century. If any of your guests find blackened teeth distressing, reassure them that this is a form of radical Venetian chic. For my more detailed treatment of cooking risotto, see page 27.

Your fishmonger may be able to get cuttlefish for you, which should be small, weighing no more than 2–3 ounces each. Large ones are impossibly tough. If your fishmonger can get them, tell him to clean them for you and to reserve the ink sacs. If he says he does not know how, fire him or set about the task yourself, but remember that it is important that the ink sacs are undamaged. Do smell the cuttlefish for freshness before buying.

Mise en Place

If your fishmonger has not done it for you, first prepare the cuttlefish: Lay each

Ingredients (for 4)

4 small cuttlefish (which will make
    about 1 pound cleaned flesh)
$2/3$ cup of dry vermouth
2 quarts mussels
1 small onion
$1/2$ bottle (about $1 1/2$ cups) of dry
    white wine
salt and pepper
3 tablespoons olive oil
$1 1/2$ cups Arborio rice (the correct
    Venetian rice is Carnaroli so if you
    can find it, use it)
flat-leaf parsley, for garnish
fine strips of lemon zest, for garnish
    (optional)

Utensils

large bowl
small bowl
small sharp scissors
large saucepan (big enough to take
    the mussels in a single layer) with
    a tight-fitting lid
colander
medium saucepan
large heavy-sided pan with sloping
    sides where they meet the
    bottom (oval Le Creuset-style
    casserole is perfect)
wooden spoon
ladle (holding about $3/4$ cup)
frying pan
spatula

down with the cuttle side uppermost (you can locate this easily because it is the only firm part of the body sac). Slit the thin membrane covering it and pull it gently out from the head end. This will open the body, exposing the innards and the head, which should be pointing away from you. Hold the base of the body and grasp the head from the tentacle end; pull this gently upward toward you and away from the body. It is vital to take care at this point, or you risk bursting the ink sac • Put the body sac into cold water and then lay the head, tentacles, and innards with the head away from you on your work surface. The ink sac is a small gray elongated, pear-shaped pouch about $3/4$-inch long. Gently lift it up and detach it using small sharp scissors, making sure you cut the attached tube rather than cutting into the body of the sac. Put the ink sac to one side in a separate bowl • Cut the tentacles off at their base just above the head (the beak-like mouth will indicate where you should cut). Add the tentacles to the bowl of body sacs in water and discard the offensive-looking innards. Repeat the dismembering process with the other cuttlefish • Rinse the body sacs and tentacles in running water, massaging with your fingers to remove some of the tough outer membrane • Cut each ring of tentacles into 2 or 3 clumps. Slice the body sacs into 1-inch squares and score these with a small sharp knife on both sides in a neat cross-hatch, taking care not to cut all the way through • Squeeze the ink from the sacs onto the plate, rather like squeezing plastic ketchup sachets. Add a little water to thin, and then pour into the glass of vermouth. Wrap the container tightly and refrigerate.

Scrub the mussels thoroughly and discard any that are open and do not close when tapped • Mince the onion.

Cooking

Put the mussels into a pan large enough to hold them in a single layer and which has a tight-fitting lid. Pour the white wine over, cover, and cook over high heat, shaking. Within 2 minutes, they will have opened. Drain in a colander set in another pan. Discard those few mussels that stubbornly refuse to open. Cover the open mussels in the colander with a damp cloth and reserve.

To the mussel liquor in the saucepan add the ink and vermouth mixture and just enough cold water to make about 1 quart of stock. Bring to a boil. Whisking thoroughly to begin with, let bubble 25 minutes by which time you will have a strong black stock. Season carefully and keep over the heat so that it is simmering gently just below a boil. Be very careful not to spill any of this on anything that matters.

Put 2 tablespoons olive oil in the risotto pan and sauté the minced onion until translucent. Add the unrinsed rice and stir to coat until it is uniformly shining.

Keeping the pan over a high enough heat to have the contents just below a boil all the time, add the stock in ladlefuls and stir it in until it is all absorbed. Continue in this way the rice is just cooked al dente.

At this point stir in the mussels and season. Put on the lid and hold off the heat for 3 minutes. Do not put any Parmesan cheese in this dish.

Meanwhile, in a large frying pan over high heat, sauté the cuttlefish very briskly and briefly in the remaining olive oil. They should just take some color and curl up; this will take no more than 2 minutes (any more and you will have pieces of rubber boot). Stir into the risotto.

Serving

Serve on warmed white plates. Scatter chopped flat-leaf parsley over and – if you like the idea – thin strips of lemon zest.

Fish Soup with Rouille

We have no equivalents here to the puréed fish soups of the French Mediterranean coast. These soupes de poisson provençale *are usually served with* croûtes *of oven-toasted bread spread with* rouille, *a vigorous garlic, saffron, and red bell pepper mayonnaise. This recipe is not far removed from* bourride *and* bouillabaisse, *which are fish stews, sharing many of the same ingredients and aromatic flavorings, such as dried orange peel and fennel. Most Mediterranean recipes call for the fish to be sautéed in olive oil, but I cannot see any benefits to be gained from so doing.*

Throughout this book you will have seen references to freezing white fish heads, bones, and pieces for "your next fish soup." Well, this is it.

Ingredients (for 4)

2 pounds mixed white fish, heads removed, cleaned, and scaled
2 pounds heads, bones, and scraps of white fish
1 small crab, preferably a she-crab
2 onions
$1/2$ fennel bulb
2 garlic cloves
6 tablespoon olive oil
$1/2$ bottle (about $1 1/2$ cups) of dry white wine
about $2 1/2$ cups tomato purée
2-inch piece of orange peel, preferably dried (see page 11)
bouquet garni of bay leaf, thyme, parsley stems, and celery, tied with string
salt and pepper
8 saffron strands

FOR THE ROUILLE:
6 saffron strands
about $1 1/4$ cups Aïoli Garlic Mayonnaise (see page 82)
2 teaspoons (or to taste) cayenne pepper or harissa

Mise en Place

First make the Rouille: Pour 1 tablespoon of boiling water over the saffron strands and let steep 5 minutes. Make the Aïoli Garlic Mayonnaise, but using half the quantities. Add the cayenne or harissa and the saffron liquid at the end. Let stand at room temperature for 1 hour before tasting, only then adjusting the seasoning.

Prepare the fish: Remove gills and fins from the heads, rinse in plenty of cold running water, and reserve.

Prepare the crab: In the restaurant we batter it to death, but more squeamish folk can boil it in salted water for 5 minutes. Remove from the water and cool before breaking into small pieces. Take care to smash the legs and claws as these have good flavor. This is messy, and it is important to save all the juices that are produced. Scrape these and any bits into a bowl.

Prepare the vegetables: Dice the onions, fennel, and garlic.

Cooking

Put the olive oil in a large heavy-bottomed saucepan and place over low heat. Sweat the vegetables in the olive oil. Pour over the white wine and tomato purée. Cover with bones and heads and the crab pieces with their juices and then lay the fish on top. Add the orange peel, bouquet garni, and $2 1/2$ quarts water. Season with salt and pepper. Bring to a boil, then lower the heat to a simmer.

Continue to simmer until the fish is cooked and its flesh flakes easily off the bones, about 30 minutes. Strain the broth into another saucepan, discarding heads, bones, orange peel, and bouquet garni.

Pull off the skin from the fish and flake the flesh away from the bones. Purée the flesh and vegetables in a food processor or put through a food mill.

TO SERVE:

1 French baguette
olive oil
1 cup freshly grated Gruyère cheese

Utensils

2 large saucepans
strainer
food processor or food mill
brush
baking sheet

Preheat the oven to 325°F.

Put a strainer over the fish broth and squeeze the purée through it to release the liquid into the broth. Reserve the pulp.

Cut the baguette into slices and put these on an oiled baking sheet. Brush the tops of the slices with olive oil and bake until dry and lightly browned.

About 10 minutes before serving, bring the broth to a boil and bubble to reduce until it has a good flavor. Lower the heat to a simmer and stir in the reserved fish pulp. Taste for seasoning and put in the saffron strands. Simmer 5 minutes more, then taste and adjust the seasoning if necessary.

Serving

Serve from a warmed tureen, with the croûtes, Rouille, and grated Gruyère all served separately. If any of your guests have never had this classic dish, tell them to ladle broth into their bowl, spread Rouille on a croûte or two, pressing Gruyère on the top, and then float these on the surface.

Ravioli of Leeks and Truffles

This is one of the most perfect pasta dishes I know. It is assumed that you have already made pasta (the recipe for which is on page 25). There is no point in trying to make this without a pasta machine.

Black truffles are expensive, but a little goes a long way in this recipe and you will have made enough truffle butter to freeze for another day (truffles freeze extremely well). Truffle butter also keeps in the freezer and makes a real treat stirred into a risotto, to dress pappardelle, melted into the gravy for a roast chicken or roast beef, or with new potatoes (see page 56). Or, try it spread on small bread rolls as they do in Italy. Use the remaining port stock to enrich any other stock.

You may have some ravioli left over (allowing 4 for a first-course serving). Simply blanch briefly in boiling water, drain, and, when cold, freeze them in a bag.

Ingredients (for 4)

2 sticks (1 cup) butter
2 ounces black truffle
1¼ cups non-vintage port wine
¼ cup Veal or Chicken Stock (see page 19)
handful of flat-leaf parsley
2 large or 4 small leeks
1 quantity Rich Pasta Dough (page 25)
salt and pepper
semolina flour or cornmeal, for dusting

Utensils

small saucepan
2 bowls
pasta machine
large saucepan
frying pan
pastry wheel or pasta cutter
colander
large sauté pan

Mise en Place

Make the truffle butter: Well ahead, take the butter out of the refrigerator to let it soften. Scrub the truffle(s), then put with the port in a small saucepan. Add the stock to the pan and bring to a boil. Then lower the heat and simmer gently 15 minutes. Remove from the heat and let the truffle(s) cool in the liquid • As soon as they are cool enough to handle, remove the truffle(s) from the port stock and peel carefully, taking off as little of the surface as possible. Return the peeled truffle(s) to the port • Put the truffle peelings and parsley leaves on a board and mince all together with a large knife. Season well. Put three-quarters of the butter in a bowl with the minced ingredients and mix thoroughly with a fork.

Wash and trim the leeks; you want some green but not too much. Then cut into thin rounds. Rinse again • Make the Rich Pasta Dough as described on page 25 • Put a large pan of salted water on to heat for cooking the ravioli.

Make the ravioli filling: Drain the leeks and put to sweat in a frying pan over low heat with the remaining butter until you have a well-cooked – but not browned – compote. Transfer to a bowl and slice in the truffle(s) as thinly as you can, reserving the port stock. Season with salt and pepper and mix together with a fork.

Make the ravioli: Clear the kitchen table, attach the pasta machine at the right-hand end (or left-hand if you are left-handed), and dust the table liberally with flour. Divide the pasta dough into 4 pieces and roll each out to the thinnest setting. When the sheet size starts to become unmanageable, simply cut in half • Dot one sheet with teaspoonfuls of the filling (see the illustration on the title page). Brush between the fillings with a little water, then cover with the second sheet, pressing down firmly to seal the pasta sheets together between the filled pouches. You should just be able to run a finger down the grid lines created. Do so to squeeze out any air • Run a pastry wheel or pasta cutter along these lines to cut the sheet into individual ravioli about 2-inches square • Repeat with the other sheets of pasta and the remaining filling • Remove all the dough trimmings, compact them into a ball, and reserve to make into tagliatelle or pappardelle some other day • Check the seal on each ravioli, pressing down firmly around the edges. Then flatten the mound of each ravioli lightly to distribute the filling to the edges. Put the semolina

A spider may be used to remove the ravioli 2 minutes after they bob to the surface.

in a bowl. One at a time, drop each ravioli into the semolina and turn to coat with a light dusting. Arrange neatly on a tray. These last steps of securing the seal, flattening, and coating are critically important. If you do not follow them precisely, the ravioli will fall apart during cooking and move you to tears.

Cooking

Cook the ravioli in rapidly boiling water for a few minutes: They should be cooked about 2 minutes after they float to the surface. Drain in a colander and refresh in cold water, then drain again. They can be held at this point.

In the frying pan (which should be big enough to hold 16 ravioli comfortably) over medium heat, put a large lump of the truffle butter, 1 tablespoon of port stock, and a little pepper. Tip in the ravioli and reheat, shaking the pan to ensure that each of the ravioli is coated with the mixture and is hot.

Serving

Serve at once on a warmed communal serving dish, with a hot soup plate for each person. As you will probably have ravioli left to cook, put some more water on to heat as you sit down, because people may demand second helpings.

Salad of White-Cooked Pork with Spicy Sichuan Dressing

This is an easy dish to make and is a very attractive cold first course. It can be prepared a day ahead and benefits from it. Ask your butcher to bone the pork loin and to leave a thin layer of fat on the meat. The bones can be frozen for stock (pork bones are an essential ingredient in Chinese soup stock).

Ingredients (for 6-10)

3-pound boned pork loin roast, cut from the blade end
salt

FOR THE SPICY SICHUAN DRESSING:
2 garlic cloves
2 large scallions
1 large red hot chili pepper
3 tablespoons Kikkoman soy sauce
1 tablespoon sesame oil
1 1/2 teaspoons Japanese clear rice vinegar
3/4 teaspoon sugar
large handful of coriander (cilantro) leaves

Utensils

saucepan large enough to hold the pork roast
bowl
large attractive serving plate
4 sets of chopsticks

Mise en Place

Prepare the pork a day ahead of serving: Heat a large saucepan two-thirds filled with lightly salted water.

Cooking

When the water is boiling, add the pork, which should just be covered by the liquid (add more water if necessary). Bring back to a boil, lower the heat, skim, and simmer gently 1 hour. Remove from the heat and let the pork cool in the stock.

While the pork is cooking, make the dressing: Peel and mince the garlic. Clean and trim the scallions and cut them into thin rounds. Halve the chili lengthwise and remove the seeds.

Put all the dressing ingredients except the coriander in the mixing bowl and stir. The mixture will be quite spicy so take care the first time you make it that it is not too hot for your palate. You might like to try using half the chili and chili oil to begin with.

Once the pork is cool, drain it, wrap in plastic wrap, and refrigerate it and the dressing overnight.

The next day, about 30 minutes before serving, remove the pork and dressing from the refrigerator. Strip the coriander leaves from the stems, chop, and add to the dressing. Unwrap the pork and slice into rounds as thinly as you can.

Serving

Arrange the slices of pork on the serving plate, overlapping them, starting at the outer edge and moving inward to cover the whole plate. Stir the dressing and drizzle about one-third of it over the pork; serve the rest separately. Eat with chopsticks.

Potato Pancakes with Smoked Eel and Bacon

Georges Blanc has a pretty damned ritzy restaurant in Bourg-en-Bresse, in France, complete with heli-pad and staff with superior attitudes, really the kind of place I loathe. I went there once and had all my negative preconceptions reinforced. I loved just one thing on the menu — these potato pancakes, made apparently from a recipe of the great man's mother. Any large potatoes will work. Indeed, if you have some mashed potatoes left over, these will form the basis of an excellent pancake batter.

Potato pancakes make a perfect foil for any number of rich meat and fish recipes, but in the restaurant I like to serve them with smoked eel, crisp bacon, and crème fraîche or horseradish cream. If you do not have crème fraîche or sour cream, sour some heavy whipping cream by squeezing in lemon juice and letting it stand half an hour.

Ingredients (for 4)

1 pound floury potatoes
3 eggs + 2 egg whites
1/4 cup self-rising flour
2/3 cup milk
1 teaspoon freshly grated nutmeg
salt and pepper
sunflower oil, for greasing
butter, for greasing
chives, for garnish
2/3 cup heavy whipping cream

FOR THE FILLING:
8 thick slices of unsmoked bacon
1/2–3/4 pound smoked eel

FOR THE HORSERADISH CREAM:
2/3 cup sour cream or crème fraîche
horseradish root or wasabi powder (see page 11) to taste

Utensils

saucepan
colander
potato ricer or masher
small saucepan
bowl
roasting pan with rack
blini pans (ideally, or small heavy frying pans or one large frying pan)

Mise en Place

The day before: Put a pan of salted water to heat. Peel the potatoes and cut them up. Then boil them until they are just tender. Drain at once in a colander, return to the hot pan, and mash thoroughly or put through a ricer. Do this dry, i.e. don't add any butter, cream, or milk. Store in a bowl in the refrigerator overnight (don't keep for more than 24 hours, or they will blacken as they oxidize).

Next day: Beat the 3 whole eggs and the flour into the mashed potatoes. Mix the milk and cream in a small pan and scald, i.e. bring to just below a boil. Whisk this into the purée until a thick batter is produced. Grate in the nutmeg and season.

About 30 minutes before you are ready to cook the pancakes, preheat your oven to its highest setting • In a large bowl, beat the extra egg whites until stiff. Then fold these into the batter.

Make the horseradish cream: Put the cream or crème fraîche in a bowl and grate the horseradish into it or add the wasabi. The exact amount will depend on your taste.

Cooking

Arrange the bacon slices for the filling on a rack in a roasting pan and cook in the hot oven till crisp. Turn the oven off and leave the bacon in it, with the door just ajar, to keep it warm.

Make the pancakes: Oil the pan(s) with a mixture of sunflower oil and melted butter, then heat until fairly hot. Using a small ladle or large mixing spoon, put just enough batter into the pan to coat the bottom.

Cook over medium heat until just brown, then turn the pancake with a spatula and cook similarly on the other side. Keep the cooked pancakes warm in the oven while cooking the remaining pancakes in the same way, cleaning out the pan with a wad of paper towels and adding some more oil and butter each time.

If preferred (or if you only have a large pan) you can make 2 large pancakes in a big frying pan, then build a single assembly which you cut into wedges to serve.

Serving

To assemble the dish, place a pancake on each plate, then arrange strips of smoked eel and a piece of crisp bacon on top with a tablespoon of horseradish cream to finish the pile. Set a second pancake on top. Strew with chives.

Carpaccio of Beef

Tataki of tuna, where the fish fillet is seared on the outside, cooled, and then served in slices — the main part being raw, but with the contrasting crust of the outside giving it textural interest — gave me an idea for this recipe. Treated in precisely the same way, beef tenderloin yields the perfect meat to eat cold. There is no sense of it being raw, only succulent and melting. Presented on a salad of arugula dressed with truffled olive oil and with Parmesan cheese curls shaved over, it is aesthetically as captivating as it is good to eat. . . a perfect balance of flavors, colors, and textures.

Truffled olive oil, which is infused with the essence of white truffles (tartufi bianchi), is expensive, but a little goes a long way. It is particularly good with rare cold meat as here, but also makes a lovely dressing for warm new potatoes (see page 56).

Ingredients (for 4)

1-pound beef tenderloin roast, from the tail end
$^2/_3$ cup olive oil
salt
mignonette pepper (see page 10)
$^1/_2$ pound arugula
1 tablespoon truffled olive oil
1 teaspoon balsamic vinegar
4-ounce piece of Reggiano Parmesan cheese

Utensils

heavy ridged grill pan
large bowl
tongs
salad spinner
potato peeler

Mise en Place

If the meat is in the refrigerator, bring it out well in advance of the meal to give it time to come to room temperature • Preheat the grill pan to very hot and have ready a large bowl of ice water • Brush the tenderloin with a little olive oil and rub all over with salt and mignonette pepper.

Cooking

Lay the tenderloin on the grill pan and give it 60 seconds on each side, including standing it on its two broad edges (four sides in all), turning with tongs.

Refresh in the ice water and pat dry with paper towels. Let cool, then refrigerate.

Holding Point – the beef can be kept like this in the refrigerator for several days.

Serving

When ready to eat, remove the meat from the refrigerator. Wash the arugula and spin it dry. Put into a bowl, pour over the truffled oil and balsamic vinegar, and toss to coat each leaf. Mound a pile of gleaming leaves on each plate.

Carve the tenderloin into, say, 12 thickish slices at an angle of 30 degrees. Distribute them equally on top of the arugula.

Using a potato peeler, shave curls of Parmesan cheese over the top.

Pressed Chicken Terrine

Adam Robinson, chef/proprietor of the Brackenbury Restaurant in London, first worked for me at L'Escargot, leaving there to join the kitchen team at Ma Cuisine, the seminal Seventies restaurant that played a pioneering role here in serving simple good food. In its heyday it was not unusual for customers to have to wait three weeks for a table. Adam returned to work with me at 192 Kensington Park Road, where he taught me the principles of this dish. I have slightly modified it over the years, but it remains essentially the same clean-textured, light yet satisfying first course.

You can ring the changes by substituting blanched leek greens for the cabbage leaves. If you do, include layers of leek in the terrine as well as for wrapping. The ultimate variation adds layers of fresh foie gras, exchanging half a chicken breast portion for an equal weight of duck or goose liver cut into thin scallops.

Ingredients (for 6-12)

18 outer leaves of Savoy cabbage or
    seasonal greens
1 1/2 sticks (3/4 cup) butter, chilled in
    the freezer
8 skinless boneless chicken breast
    halves
8 slices of Parma ham
salt and pepper

FOR THE TOMATO
COMPOTE:
6 ripe plum tomatoes
1 tablespoon balsamic or sherry
    vinegar
5 tablespoons extra virgin olive oil

Utensils

meat pounder
2 identical terrine molds (nonstick
    loaf pans are a useful substitute)
plastic wrap
deep roasting pan
foil

Mise en Place

Preheat the oven to 275°F • Remove the stems from the cabbage leaves, then blanch them in a large pan of boiling salted water for 2 minutes, refresh in cold water, and drain • Cut the chilled butter into 12 thin slices.

Cooking

One at a time, put the breast halves between sheets of plastic wrap and pound them to make chicken scallops.

Line one terrine mold with the leaves, overlapping them slightly and making sure you have enough leaf hanging over the rim to cover the top when the dish is filled.

Put one layer of chicken on the bottom, using two of the pounded scallops. Cut and trim to make a snug fit, filling in any gaps with the trimmings. Cover this layer with 2 slices of Parma ham. Grind over some black pepper and lay 3 slices of butter on top.

Repeat this procedure three times, ending with ham and butter on the top. Wrap the leaves over the top to cover. Dot with any remaining butter, then cover with foil. Put into a roasting pan and pour water to come halfway up the sides of the terrine mold. Place in the oven.

After 1 1/4 hours, test for doneness by inserting a skewer or sharp pointed knife into the center of the terrine. When removed, the metal should feel quite hot on the tongue (be careful). If it does not, cook 10 minutes more, then test again. Repeat if necessary. Between testings, sterilize whatever sharp implement you use in some boiling water.

When satisfied that the terrine is fully cooked, remove from the oven and let cool 1 hour. Then weight it to press and firm it up (this makes slicing and serving easier). The best way to do this is to place another terrine mold of precisely the same size on top and then weight it with about 4 pounds. Use cans of food to achieve the weight, but do not use more than this weight or you will cause all the moisture from the terrine to exude, leaving it dry and unpalatable. If you do not have another identical mold, then cut a piece of cardboard to the exact internal dimensions of the mold and wrap it in foil. This can then be placed on the top and weighted.

Leave weighted in a cool place until quite cold. Then remove the weights and refrigerate at least 4 hours before serving, or preferably overnight.

Just before serving make the tomato compote: Peel, seed, and dice the tomatoes. Dress with the vinegar, olive oil, and a little salt and pepper.

Serving
Run a metal spatula gently around the sides of the mold, invert it over a cutting board, then tap and shake gently to remove the terrine. Cut into slices using the sharpest knife possible. Serve with the tomato compote.

Caesar Salad

The Caesar salad is one of those great American inventions that actually comes from Tijuana in Mexico, although admittedly from a hotel that catered for gringos rather than local peons. It was popularized in Chasens restaurant in New York, and now can be found all across the States in all sorts of nasty and synthetic variations on the theme: Industrially produced garlic croutons, for example, which give off a halitotic whiff when opened; jars of instant, "lo-cal" Caesar dressing – the litany of horror and degradation has no end. This is the real thing. Once eaten, you will become a Caesar salad aficionado, curling your lip at poor imitations.

For those who do not like anchovies (and apparently some people don't), omit them from the individual plate. Please note, however, that without anchovies it is not a real Caesar salad.

Ingredients (for 4)
*1 large head of romaine
at least a 2-ounce piece of
    Reggiano Parmesan cheese
4 thin slices of baguette or white
    bread
3 garlic cloves
2 egg yolks
1 teaspoon Worcestershire sauce
pepper
1 tablespoon lemon juice
6 tablespoons extra virgin olive oil
2 ounces canned anchovy fillets in
    oil, drained*

Utensils
*salad spinner
grater
frying pan*

Mise en Place
Discard the outer lettuce leaves and rinse those remaining, then spin dry • Grate the cheese • Cube the bread.

Preparation
In the bottom of large serving bowl, mash the garlic to a pulp, then whisk in the egg yolks, the Worcestershire sauce, and some pepper. Whisk in the lemon juice.

In a thin steady stream, beat in 4 tablespoons of the olive oil. Then add the grated cheese and stir until the sauce is creamy and uniform.

Heat the remaining oil in a frying pan and fry the bread until crisp.

Add the lettuce leaves to the bowl and toss to coat them evenly with dressing.

Serving
Arrange the dressed leaves on individual plates and strew with croutons and anchovies. Pass more Parmesan cheese at the table.

Scallops with Thai Spicy Cabbage Salad

The combination of Thai and Indonesian flavorings produces a fresh-tasting but very spicy salad that is particularly good served at room temperature with grilled scallops. The salad is very easy to make and, because of the high vinegar content, keeps several days in the refrigerator.

Large sea scallops are hard to come by, as most of them are bought by restaurants. Buy 3 medium-sized sea scallops per person. Never buy frozen scallops: They just aren't worth cooking, never mind eating.

More than any other ingredient, Thai fish sauce gives that cuisine its characteristic flavor. It can be obtained from most Asian markets.

Ingredients (for 4)

12 medium-size sea scallops
1 small head of Savoy cabbage
1 red bell pepper
1 onion
2 stalks of lemon grass
2 large red hot chili peppers
1-inch piece of fesh gingerroot
1 carrot
1 garlic clove
$1/2$ pound rice vermicelli
$1/4$ cup rice wine vinegar or white wine vinegar
2 kaffir lime leaves
$1/2$ cup sunflower oil, plus more for brushing
$1/4$ cup Kikkoman soy sauce
1 tablespoon Thai fish sauce
bunch of coriander (cilantro)
1 tablespoon sesame oil, to serve

Utensils

several small bowls
small saucepan
wok
ridged grill pan

Mise en Place

Prepare the scallops: Cut the white flesh in half horizontally.

Prepare the vegetables: Quarter the cabbage and cut out the base stem. Finely shred the leaves • Char the bell pepper over a flame or under a hot broiler. Peel off the blackened skin, remove seeds, and finely shred the flesh • Peel the onion and cut into thin rings • Trim the lemon grass and slice the stalks across into very thin rounds. Then cut these across into fine strips • Cut the chili peppers in half longitudinally, remove seeds, then cut each half into 5 strips. Wash the chopping board and knife thoroughly and then your hands immediately. (You will only need to forget this once and rub your eyes or mouth to realize why this is good practice) • Peel the ginger, cut it into slices and then into fine strips • Do the same thing with the carrot and the garlic.

Put the rice vermicelli in a bowl, pour over boiling water, and let soak according to the package directions. Drain well.

This may seem rather a demanding Mise en Place, but it is typical of stir-frying, where getting everything ready takes a comparatively long time while the actual cooking needs almost no time at all. It is actually helpful to assemble all the different elements in bowls, like one of those questionable TV cooks.

Cooking

Heat the vinegar in the saucepan and simmer the lemon grass, lime leaves, and chili peppers 5 minutes; set aside.

Heat the wok and when hot put in half the sunflower oil. Add the onion, garlic, bell pepper, ginger, and carrot. Toss and stir. Add the cabbage and toss again. Add the noodles and toss, then quickly pour in the vinegar mixture, the rest of the oil, and the soy and fish sauces. Boil, toss, and stir. Tip into a bowl and let cool.

When ready to serve, chop the coriander and stir it into the salad.

Put the grill pan to heat. Brush the scallop halves lightly with a little sunflower oil and sear no more than 30 seconds each side. Longer will toughen them.

Serving

Mound the salad on 4 plates and arrange the scallops on top. Dress each with a few drops of sesame oil.

MAIN COURSES

New England Cod Chowder

With minor variations, this is a typical chowder from Maine. The word "chowder" comes from the old French chaudron, *a large pot in which the fishermen would stew whatever they did not sell for their supper. Precisely when milk was first used in North American chowder, rather than fish broth, is not known, but it was probably in the eighteenth century.*

Here I have used a roux to thicken the cooking liquid, in place of the traditional cracker crumbs. I have also added a glass of dry sherry to give a slight edge to the creamy texture of the dish. The addition of chopped chives as a garnish is not traditional, but they add a light taste counterpoint that enhances more than just the appearance. I also prefer to add the fish in large chunks just before serving, so they come to the table lightly poached. The simplicity of both the ingredients and the cooking technique belies the complexity and subtlety of the finished product.

Any firm-fleshed white fish can be substituted for cod. Variations on the theme soon become obvious. A few peeled and deveined shrimp increase the luxury of the dish, while clams — either fresh or canned — make a sympathetic addition. Mussels, previously cooked as for moules marinière, *are also delicious in the soup.*

Ingredients (for 4)

1 1/2 pounds cod fillets
1 large onion
1 pound potatoes
4 thick slices of unsmoked bacon
2 tablespoons butter or olive oil
1 tablespoon white flour
1 wine glass (2/3 cup) of dry sherry
5 cups whole milk
bay leaf
salt and pepper
small bunch of chives

Utensils

large stew pan (a big Le Creuset pot is ideal)
ladle

Mise en Place

Prepare the fish: Toward the thick end of the fillet you will find some large bones on one side. Cut these out. Skin the fish: Hold the fillet by the tail end and just beyond your fingers cut down gently at an angle of 45 degrees until the edge of the blade is in contact with the skin. Run the knife at the same angle along the skin while retaining a firm grip on the tail end. The flesh will come easily away from the skin, leaving you with a compact fillet. Cut the fillets into portion-sized pieces (I like to keep these fairly chunky rather than bite-sized).

Peel and mince the onion • Peel and dice the potatoes into 1/2-inch cubes • If the bacon is very salty, blanch it 60 seconds in boiling water. Then cut it across into matchstick-sized lardons.

Cooking

Put the large stew pan over medium heat and sauté the bacon lardons in butter or oil until the fat has run out from them and they are nearly crisp.

Add the onion and fry until translucent. Do not let it brown. Add the diced potato and turn until coated and shiny. Sprinkle over the flour and stir. Pour in the sherry, stirring all the time, and after a minute add the milk and bay leaf. Turn down the heat and simmer, stirring from time to time, until the potato is just cooked. It should still be in separate cubes but starting to soften. Taste and add salt and pepper to taste.

Holding Point – the dish can be held at this point in the refrigerator several days. If you do, reheat gently and slowly to serve.

To finish: Remove the bay leaf and add the chunks of fish, pushing them gently beneath the surface. The fish will cook very quickly and is done when the flesh turns an opaque white, about 3 minutes.

Serving
Place a piece of fish in each bowl and ladle over the thickened potato broth. Using scissors, chop over some chives. Serve immediately, with good bread.

Calves' Liver with Beets

This is a typical restaurant dish, involving a brief sauté in a nonstick pan and an equally brief deglazing. The whole thing takes only 5 minutes and is adapted from Michel Guérard's recipe in his book, Cuisine Gourmande, one of the most important cook books of recent years and one from which all the chefs I know have drawn inspiration. The beet imparts a stunning color to the finished dish. Quantities given are for two people.

Mise en Place
Season the flour • Mince the shallot • Thinly slice the peeled beet• Chop the chives.

Cooking
Put the pan over medium heat with half the butter. Put the seasoned flour into a suitable receptacle and dredge the liver in it a slice at a time. A plastic bag is a good way of doing this, as you can shake it gently and achieve an even coating. Hold each piece and spank it gently to remove any excess flour.

As the butter foams, add the liver and sauté 90 seconds on each side. Transfer to warmed plates and keep warm.

Turn up the heat. Add the shallot, beet, and sherry vinegar and cook 1 minute, stirring. Add the stock or bouillon and boil vigorously until it is colored by the beet and is a slightly syrupy consistency. Take off the heat and swirl in the remaining butter. Adjust the seasoning if necessary.

Serving
Pour this sauce over the liver and strew with chopped chives. It is even better with fresh horseradish grated over.

Ingredients (for 2)
¹/₄ cup flour
salt and pepper
1 shallot
1 small cooked beet (see page 57)
bunch of chives
6 tablespoons butter
2 slices of calves' liver, each weighing about 6 ounces
1 tablespoon sherry vinegar
¹/₄ cup veal stock, Chicken Stock (page 19), or canned chicken bouillon
fresh horseradish, for garnish (optional)

Utensils
nonstick frying pan large enough to hold both slices of liver easily

Saltimbocca of Red Mullet

Saltimbocca is usually a veal scallop or cutlet wrapped in Parma ham with sage. The ham and the sage are, however, just as complementary to red fish.

While the Italians usually choose to eat their fish whole and on the bone, this is one dish where I prefer to use fillets. The whole point is to take a mouthful that incorporates all three elements, of fish, Parma ham, and sage — hence fillets are essential.

Red mullet is my first choice — it's a Mediterranean member of the goat fish family, with firm, lean flesh. Red mullet is rarely available in the US. This recipe, however, also works very well with fillets of halibut or other similar fish.

Ingredients (for 4)

4 red mullet, each weighing about 8–10 ounces (smaller fish should be avoided as filleting them is akin to microsurgery)

1 stick ($^1/_2$ cup) chilled unsalted butter

8 large slices of Parma ham (i.e. cut from the center of the ham and sliced very thinly)

1 lemon

$^1/_4$ cup flour

salt and pepper

sunflower oil, for frying

8 large sage leaves

Utensils

strong tweezers or electrician's pliers

heavy frying pan large enough to hold the 8 fillets (you can use two pans or cook in two batches)

metal spatula or pancake turner

Mise en Place

Well ahead: Clean and scale the fish and fillet it. Wash the trimmings and freeze for fish soup. Using strong tweezers or small pliers, remove the small line of pin bones down each fillet and any rib bones • Cut the butter in half, straight from the refrigerator, and set aside one piece. From the other piece, cut four equal pieces that are as thin as possible.

Assemble the saltimbocca: Lay one sheet of Parma ham on your work surface. Put one of the thin slices of butter in the center and lay the first fish fillet on top of the butter, flesh-side down. Carefully wrap the ham to form an envelope around the fillet. Repeat with the remaining fillets and refrigerate until ready to cook. They benefit from a couple of hours in the refrigerator so the flavors can mingle.

Juice the lemon • Season the flour.

Cooking

This is one of those dishes that cooks very quickly. Once you start, you are committed and your guests should be at the table.

Heat the pan(s) over medium heat (you do not want it to be too hot) and pour a thin coating of oil into the pan(s).

Press a sage leaf on each fish package and dredge it in seasoned flour. Put the packages into the pan butter-side down. Cook gently until the ham is crisp underneath, about 3 minutes. Do not be tempted to push them around.

With a metal spatula or pancake turner, carefully turn the packages and fry the other side 2 minutes. Transfer to a warmed serving plate. If you are cooking in two batches, the first batch can be held in a very low oven while you cook the second batch.

Pour out the juices from the pan, but do not wash it. Melt the reserved block of butter in the pan over medium heat. When it begins to color slightly, pour in the lemon juice, add a little salt and pepper (but more pepper than salt because of the saltiness of the ham), and stir.

Pour the foaming mixture over the saltimbocca and serve at once. This is a basic *meunière* technique used in restaurant kitchens and is delicious hot, but goes greasy on cooling.

Serving

Choose a vegetable that goes well with the sauce such as new potatoes, or you might try some plain noodles. In the restaurant this dish is served on a bed of fresh *porcini* (cèpes) as a main course.

Tripe Gratin

Tripe is the stomach lining of a ruminant – a beast that chews the cud and that has no fewer than four stomach compartments. Most of the tripe for sale in markets tody is from beef. The best tripe is called "honeycomb" and you can find it in most supermarkets and butchers, though it is less common than it used to be. When cooked, it produces a rich and unctuous dish.

Tripe is one of those things, like andouillette *sausages, that people either love or hate. The British have traditionally cooked tripe with milk and onions or leeks, but it has never been something that featured on restaurant menus until French bistro influences began to have an impact.*

Ingredients (for 4-6)

3 pounds honeycomb tripe
2 carrots
2 celery stalks
3 onions
2 garlic cloves
bouquet garni of bay leaf and
*   parsley stems*
salt and pepper
1 bottle (75cl) of dry white wine or
*   dry hard cider*
2 tomatoes
1 ounce Reggiano Parmesan cheese

Utensils

large pot
4 or 6 individual gratin dishes
grater
baking sheet or roasting pan large
*   enough to hold the gratin dishes*

Mise en Place

Cut the tripe into 1-inch squares • Peel the vegetables and make a mirepoix (see page 188).

Cooking

Put the tripe and vegetables in a large pot. Add the bouquet garni, season, and cover with the wine or cider. Bring to a boil, then lower the heat and simmer 3 hours.

Let cool a little, but before the tripe sets apportion individual servings in the gratin dishes.

While it cools, preheat the oven to its highest setting. Plunge the tomatoes in boiling water for 30 seconds and refresh in cold water. Peel, seed, and dice them.

Scatter the diced tomatoes over the tripe in the gratin dishes and shake the dishes gently to mix the tomato dice in.

Place the gratin dishes in the oven and bake, about 10 minutes, until bubbling hot. Scatter freshly grated Parmesan over and bake until lightly browned.

Serving

Serve at once with boiled potatoes or good bread.

Pork Cooked in Milk

The idea of cooking meat in milk crops up several times in Italian cooking, notably in that of the Bologna region. The ubiquitous Bolognese sauce, for example, has classic interpretations that use milk rather than stock, supposedly to induce a creamier and smoother texture. In Arrosto di maiale al latte, loin of pork is first marinated overnight in dry white wine and vinegar, then browned before being poached in milk. The milk evaporates during the cooking while the fat melts, leaving the meat wonderfully succulent.

At least, it does if you still have a butcher who can produce decent pork with some fat on it. The trend toward leaner pigs is to be discouraged, for the end results are inevitably dry, tough, and tasteless. They don't produce lean pigs in France or Italy, where heart disease remains at a lower level than in Britain or the US. We await the medical revelation that a spoonful of lard a day keeps the doctor away. Another point to make is that in a balanced menu you will not be eating large portions of meat — perhaps 4–6 ounces per person, no more.

While loin of pork is the traditional cut for this dish, you may also use boned leg. In both cases get your butcher to trim and tie the meat neatly and securely. It is important that the shape of the tied roast is of uniform thickness (i.e. cylindrical) to ensure even cooking. If the roast is rolled so that it tapers at one end you will always have problems of dryness at the thin end. Something to choke a brown dog, as the Australians say.

You cook the pork on the rangetop, so need to use a heavy casserole that has a lid and in which the meat fits without too much space around the sides, because you want the milk to come as far up the meat as possible during the early stages.

Ingredients (for 4-6)

2 1/4-pound boned pork loin roast, or boned leg, neatly tied
1/4 cups white wine
3 tablespoons white wine vinegar
salt and pepper
3 tablespoons olive oil
2 1/2 cups whole milk
6-inch sprig of rosemary

Utensils

non-metallic bowl of a size that ensures the pork will be completely covered by the marinade
enameled casserole with a lid into which the pork will fit without too much space around it
tongs

Mise en Place

The day before: Put the pork to marinate overnight in the non-metallic bowl with the wine and vinegar, ensuring it is completely covered. A cool place is preferable to the refrigerator, but if the weather is hot, it is safer to use the latter.

Cooking

Remove the meat from the marinade (reserve the marinade), pat dry with paper towels, and season with plenty of salt and pepper. Put the olive oil into the casserole and place over medium heat until hot but not burning. Cook the meat in this, using wooden spoons or tongs to turn the roast, until uniformly brown.

Pour the milk around the meat (do this slowly so it doesn't boil over). Add the sprig of rosemary. Put the lid on, but slightly offset to leave a small gap from which the liquid will evaporate during the cooking. Adjust the heat to achieve a gentle simmer and cook 1 1/2 hours, turning the meat from time to time.

With a skewer or the prongs of a sharp carving fork, test the pork in the milk for doneness: The meat should give easily under gentle pressure. It may need another 30 minutes — you decide. The milk may or may not have reduced to a brown residue by this time. Be careful if this occurs before the cooking is finished, because you don't want it to burn. If this happens add a little more milk.

Conversely, if the meat is done but there is still liquid in the pot (and experience suggests there will be), remove the meat and skim carefully to remove the fat that will be sitting on the surface, using a large spoon. Now turn up the heat and boil to reduce, scraping any bits away from the bottom and sides. When you have just the dark brown residue, add 2/3 cup of the marinade and deglaze. There will be curdled lumps, but this is correct and will provide all the sauce you need.

Remove the string from the roast and carve into thickish slices, just under 1/2 inch.

Serving

Serve on hot plates, spooning a little of the sauce over. Plain boiled potatoes and spinach go well with the dish.

Crispy Roast Duck

Here we make the most of two birds, using the legs and giblets to make confit, around which we base the later dish, Confit Sarladaise (see page 169). With the breasts left on the bone you can make a delightfully sophisticated roast that bows toward China and France in flavor and execution.

When buying the ducks, ask your butcher to remove the legs, the backbone from behind the breasts, and the wishbones. Get him to clean the gizzards for you and make sure you get all the rest of the giblets (including the livers) and the necks and carcasses. The necks and carcasses are the basis for the gravy to accompany this dish, and the legs and giblets make the confit.

It is probably best to glaze the duck and make the gravy the day before. If the gravy is refrigerated overnight, this has the added benefit of enabling you to remove the last vestiges of fat, which will have set on the surface.

Ingredients (for 4)

*2 ducks (see previous page), each
   weighing about 5 pounds*
2 tablespoons clear honey

FOR THE GRAVY:
1 onion
1 celery stalk
1 carrot
1 tablespoon sugar
1 tablespoon wine vinegar
black pepper
sprig of rosemary
*1/2 bottle (about 1 1/2 cups) of red
   wine*
4–5 tablespoons unsalted butter

Utensils

bowl
stout paint or pastry brush
fan or hair-dryer (optional)
*flameproof casserole or deep heavy
   roasting pan*
strainer
saucepan
roasting pan with rack

Mise en Place

First glaze the duck (preferably the day ahead): Dissolve the honey in 1/4 cup of water, add a pinch of salt, and bring to a boil. Do not reduce: If the glaze is too syrupy it will burn and become black and bitter during roasting. Paint this glaze over the duck breasts and leave overnight in a cool, airy environment. This effectively "wind dries" the skin. Alternatively, use a fan or hair-dryer on a cold setting for 10–15 minutes to blow-dry the skin.

Preheat the oven to 350°F • Prepare the vegetables for the gravy and cut them into a mirepoix (see page 188) • Chop the duck necks and carcass bones into small pieces.

Cooking

Begin by making the gravy (this whole process takes about an hour, so it is a good idea to carry it out in advance): In a flameproof casserole or deep heavy roasting pan, brown the mirepoix in a little duck fat (or oil). Chop the necks and carcasses and brown thoroughly.

   Sprinkle with the sugar (this is essentially a caramelization process), vinegar, and some pepper, and add the rosemary. Continue to brown, stirring constantly. Do not skimp on the browning, but be careful not to char the bones.

   Add the wine and boil hard to reduce, scraping the pan as you do so, until the liquid has almost all evaporated. Add just enough water almost to cover the bones. Return to a boil and skim. Lower the heat and simmer until reduced by half, about 30 minutes.

   Add a handful of ice cubes and skim again. Strain and return to a clean saucepan. This is the technique whereby the classic *jus* (French for gravy) of the French professional kitchen is achieved, creating the stock and the sauce simultaneously.

   To roast the ducks: Place them breast-side up on a rack in a roasting pan and roast 10 minutes. Lower the temperature to 335°F and continue roasting 30 minutes longer. The skin will crisp and balloon in a spectacular way and go a glossy golden brown.

   Transfer to a warmed serving dish and let rest 5 minutes. The skin will deflate slightly (but remain crisp), so if you want to get your guests excited show it to them as soon as the roast duck comes from the oven.

   Toward the end of the roasting period, reheat the gravy and just before serving swirl in the butter to give the sauce its final consistency and gloss. It should resemble the varnish on a burnished mahogany table.

Carving

Transfer the duck to a carving board (still in the kitchen). With the neck end toward you, locate the breast bone and run a sharp knife along it, pressing down vertically until you meet the ribcage. Prise away the breast, which will detach easily from the bone, and continue to stroke the knife down to separate the meat from the bone, working the knife along the length of the breast until the shoulder joint is exposed.

Press firmly to cut through the joint and you will have a breast half with a small nugget of partially cooked fat under the wing. Discard this piece of fat and transfer the carved meat to a warmed serving plate.

Turn the breast so you are working on the left-hand side again (left-handers reverse the process) and follow the same procedure with the second breast half.

A lot of juice will collect around the breasts, which you pour into the gravy.

Serving

Serve the breasts whole, or sliced, pouring the sauce around. Accompany with lightly buttered potatoes, noodles, or rice as a simple foil to the rich complexity of the duck and gravy.

Confit Sarladaise

Confit *is one of the great farmhouse traditions of southwestern France, in which the salted cut-up bird is poached slowly in duck fat or lard and then traditionally preserved in the solidified fat in earthenware crocks.*

It is easy to make and provides you with a rich and subtle dish ready to serve at short notice. This recipe is a perfect combination, teaming the duck with potatoes crisped in its fat, thus making the best possible use of the preserved duck and the fat in which it was first cooked and then preserved.

Gently simmering fatty meat in fat may alarm cardiologists but, paradoxically, the meat emerges after reheating with less fat than if it were roasted.

Preserving the confit:

(Ideally do this several days ahead, say just before or after roasting the rest of the duck.)

Mise en Place

Peel and mince the garlic • Scatter half the salt into the earthenware dish. Lay the legs skin-side down on the salt, with the giblets around them. (Do not use the liver – freeze it for future use. Sauté in a little butter and eat it on toast or use in a *salade tiède*.) Crumble over the thyme and bay leaf and scatter the garlic around the legs • Put the remaining salt on top of the legs and refrigerate the dish for a day. Turn the legs in the salt (which will have partly liquefied as moisture has been extracted from the meat) and refrigerate another day (2 days in all) • To ensure that the confit will keep successfully, extra-clean hands, utensils, and storage container are essential if you are to avoid bacterial contamination.

Preheat the oven to 275°F.

Cooking

Gently heat the fat in a flameproof casserole on the rangetop. (If you put it straight into the oven it will take 1 ½ hours just to come up to cooking temperature.)

Rinse the duck legs of salt under cold running water and pat dry. A shower attachment on a cold tap is ideal for doing jobs like this. Put the legs into the fat, which should just cover them. Add more fat if it does not, and bring it to a gentle simmer.

Ingredients (for 4)

4 baking potatoes
1 garlic clove
sprig of rosemary
sprig of parsley
pepper
red wine vinegar, to serve

FOR THE CONFIT:
1 garlic clove
6 tablespoons salt
4 duck legs and the giblets from the Crispy Roast Duck recipe (page 167)
bunch of thyme
bay leaf
2 pounds canned goose or duck fat or lard

Utensils

earthenware dish (just large enough to hold the 4 legs and giblets)
flameproof casserole
slotted spoon
skimming ladle
strainer
storage container
4 small nonstick cake pans, or tartlet molds
mandoline (see page 15) or food processor with slicing blade
nonstick baking sheet

Put the dish in the oven and cook 1 1/2 hours, by which time the fat will be completely clear, and the duck brown and showing a lot of bone as the meat rides up like a mini-skirt on a white thigh.

Using a slotted spoon, gently remove the confit (which is very fragile). Using a skimming ladle, strain just enough of the fat into a suitable storage container to coat the bottom. Carefully arrange the confit over it, then add the rest of the fat to cover. Be careful not to add the meat juices that will have collected at the bottom. (Do not, however, throw these away as they are delicious poured over roast potatoes or added to a gravy.)

Covered with fat, the confit will keep several months in the refrigerator, though only if you are scrupulous in taking the basic hygiene precautions mentioned above.

Making Confit Sarladaise:

Mise en Place

A few hours before you want to serve the confit, remove the duck legs from the fat, scraping off any fat that sticks to them. Place the legs on a baking sheet, skin-side down, and leave for an hour to let them return to room temperature • Wash the potatoes, but do not peel them. Then cut them across into thin slices using a mandoline or the slicing blade of a food processor. Rinse and pat dry with paper towels or a clean cloth • Peel and mince the garlic • Strip the rosemary leaves and chop them • Remove the stems from the parsley and chop the leaves.

Cooking

Preheat the oven to 400°F.

Put 4 tablespoons of the softened duck fat in a bowl and add the potato slices, minced garlic, and rosemary. Season with pepper and turn to coat the potatoes evenly.

Brush the cake pans with a little more of the fat, then arrange the potato slices in them in overlapping circles.

Bake until brown and crisp on top, about 30 minutes, when the potato cakes will have shrunk away from the sides of the pans.

About 20 minutes before serving, pour off any fat that has run from the confit, then turn the legs skin side-down. Put in the oven to cook 15 minutes, then turn skin-side up and return to the oven for a final 5 minutes cooking, until the skin is crisp and brown all over.

Take the potato cakes out of the oven 3 minutes before the duck is ready, to let them cool slightly.

Serving

Place a potato cake on each warmed plate. Put a duck leg on each cake and sprinkle with chopped parsley. Offer red wine vinegar at the table for people to sprinkle over the dish.

Bollito Misto

Behind its prosaic "boiled meats" title lies one of the great dishes of the global kitchen, and the Italian variation on the pot au feu theme that I like best. Essentially a dish from Piedmont, it is today a house specialty that people in Italy still go a long way to find.

Restaurants that offer it have special steel serving carts with individual compartments for the beef, veal, tongue, chicken, and zampone or cotechino sausage, which are all carved at the table. As well as the broth that is ladled over, the carved meats are accompanied by boiled root vegetables and a sharp-tasting salsa verde, which cuts the richness of the different meat elements. Sometimes a salsa rossa or red bell pepper sauce is served too, as well as mostarda di Cremona – the sweet but hot mustard fruits that were once only found in Italian grocers, but are now more widely available.

This recipe is a version of the bollito misto we serve in the restaurant, where it takes 3 days to prepare. It is really Marcella Hazan's bollito misto with Little variations and a labor of love, strictly for people who like to eat lots of meat.

However, lengthy preparation does not mean it is difficult to achieve. Your hard work will be amply rewarded with a spectacular lunch or dinner, and excellent cold cuts for days afterward. You will also have several quarts of stock left over, which you can reduce and freeze. The leftover meat can also be served as a soup made from the stock and vegetables, with a little leaf spinach blanched and added at the last moment for color and freshness. Alternatively, you can use the meat in a pressed terrine (see page 77).

The very first time I made the all singing and dancing bollito, I had a new kitchen porter called Pinto who had just started working for me. He was very good news, though at that point he spoke no English… One in the morning, the end of a long shift and all was ready for the next day. I put the huge tray of meat and the vegetables into the refrigerator and looked around for the vast pan of jewel-bright, glistening broth. It was nowhere to be seen, for Pinto – thinking my mystical distillation to be dirty water – had helpfully poured it down the sink. I felt sick and had to sit down. I did not say anything to him. What was there to say, after all? But my face must have told its own story, for the next day Pinto arrived at work looking downcast and pressed a note into my hand from his English girlfriend begging my forgiveness and asking me not to fire him.

The quantities given here provide a feast for about 10 hungry devotees, but will comfortably feed 20. If serving large numbers, increase the vegetables so everybody gets an onion, a carrot, and a leek. This dish really has to be cooked in large quantities and just does not work in scaled-down versions. Plain boiled potatoes also go well with it.

Day 1

Mise en Place
Preheat the oven to 375°F • Peel 3 onions, 3 carrots, and 3 celery stalks and chop them all into $1/2$-inch pieces • Brush the veal or beef bones with oil and put them in a roasting pan with the diced vegetables.

Cooking
Roast the bones for $1 1/2$ hours, turning from time to time and checking that they are not burning.

Ingredients (for 10)

13 onions
10 carrots
13 celery stalks
10 pounds assorted veal or beef bones, sawn into pieces
2 tablespoons sunflower oil
1 calf's foot (ask your butcher to singe the hairs off)
1 bottle (750cl) of red wine
4 bay leaves
salt and pepper
1 cross-cut of beef shank, weighing about 2 pounds, and tied in a neat piece
2 veal shanks, each weighing 1½ pounds, tied into neat pieces
2 pieces sawn off the end of 2 veal shanks
1 pickled ox tongue
1 very large chicken (a 6–8 pound capon-type bird is ideal)
10 medium-sized leeks
1 zampone or cotechino sausage
10 medium-sized boiling potatoes (optional)

TO SERVE:
Salsa Verde (see page 50)
Salsa Rossa (see page 109)

Utensils

roasting pan
very large pot
skimming spoon
2 smaller saucepans
blanching basket

Deglaze the roasting pan with the bottle of red wine, scraping up all the caramelized bits from the bottom, and add to the stock pot.

When the stock boils, skim and turn down the heat. Add the bay leaves and season lightly. Simmer 6 hours, skimming at regular intervals and adding more water as necessary to compensate for evaporation. The bones should always be covered with liquid.

At the end of this time, add the calf's foot tied with a long piece of string that you leave hanging out of the pot (this makes retrieving it easier).

After another 1 hour, retrieve the calf's foot and reserve in the refrigerator. Using a large ladle, strain the stock into a large container. Do not attempt to get out the last few ladlefuls of stock. Just triple-line your garbage pail and tip that liquid with the bones and vegetable detritus into it. Tie securely and put in a garbage can outside, with a lid on if you do not want cats or other creatures to have their *bollito* party first in a messy fashion.

Wash out the stock pot and strain the stock into it through a fine strainer. Put on high heat and bring to a boil. Watch carefully. As it comes to a boil the fat will collect slightly to one side of the pot where it and the impurities will be briefly trapped, building up into a prodigious scum. (I always find this exciting, though Richard says I should be careful about saying so in case any sex therapists are following the recipe.) Remove the scum immediately and pour in 2½ cups of cold water. Repeat the process, then return the finished stock to a rolling boil and remove from the heat. Let cool.

Ventilate the area if possible. You really want a cool environment to avoid any risk of bacterial contamination. If the stock goes bad you will cry.

Day 2

Mise en Place

Tie retrieving strings to the beef and veal • Put the ox tongue to soak in plenty of cold water overnight.

Cooking

Return the stock to a boil, lower the heat immediately to a bare simmer, and add the beef shank and the calf's foot.

Simmer 1 hour, then add the veal shanks and pieces and continue to simmer 30 minutes more. Add the chicken and simmer all the meats together 1½ hours. (That is, a total cooking time of 3 hours.)

Transfer all the pieces of meat to a suitable container. Cool then refrigerate. Pick over the calf's foot at this stage, discarding all the bones. You will be left with several large pieces of gelatinous meat. Refrigerate these with the rest of the meat.

Return the stock to a boil and skim as before. Cool as before.

Day 3

Mise en Place

Wash and trim the leeks • Peel the remaining carrots, celery, and onions, reserving the trimmings.

Bollito dos...

* serve lots of good full-bodied red wine, like Barolo
* serve flake sea salt and different mustards as well as the Salsa Verde, Salsa Rossa, and Mostarda di Cremona

Bollito don'ts...

* make Bollito Misto in the summer, when a high ambient temperature threatens the cooling stock
* invite vegetarians to the feast
* serve a first course
* serve a dessert – just fruit and, perhaps, a piece of Reggiano Parmesan cheese

Cooking

Drain the ox tongue, put it a pan, and cover with cold water. Bring to a boil. Taste: If it is salty, discard the water then replace with fresh water and repeat. Add the vegetable trimmings, return to a boil, and simmer over medium heat about 2 hours. Test by inserting a carving fork into the tongue; if it is easy to withdraw then it is done; if the meat grips the fork it needs more cooking.

While the tongue is cooking make the salsas as described on pages 50 and 109.

Drain the tongue and let cool 10 minutes. Then peel off the rough outer skin. This is easy to do while it is still fairly hot, but very difficult if you let it cool too much.

Divide the leeks into two bundles and tie them with string. Bring the stock to a simmer and poach all the vegetables until done, removing each and refreshing in cold water. Cooking the vegetables in this way will help cut the richness of the stock, which by now will have become intensely meaty.

Poach the sausage, still in its foil wrapper, in simmering water according to the package directions. If you plan to serve boiled potatoes, then peel and cook in the water around the zampone.

Turn the oven on to a low heat and put a large roasting pan to warm in it. Also, warm the largest serving dish you have.

At last the final stage is upon you, and your guests (who should have been advised to starve for a day) will be assembled. Cut the strings off the leeks. Put all the vegetables into a pan and moisten with stock.

Unwrap the zampone from its foil wrapper. Do this over a dish as fat will gush out. Now cut one ¼-inch slice of each meat for each person and assemble in batches so you have the right number of servings. (Don't use the ends from the meats: These can be kept for soup to have another day.)

If necessary, adjust the seasoning of the stock (which should not be boiling, but very hot). Using a blanching basket, dip each batch of meat into the stock . Transfer to the hot roasting pan, moistening the meat with ladlefuls of stock until all the servings are ready. The whole process will only take 5 minutes. Cover with foil and put in the low oven to heat 5 minutes more.

Serving

Drain the vegetables and mound them in the center of the warmed serving dish. Then arrange the sliced meats from the roasting pan around them. Ladle over a little more stock. Fanfare and drums left. Enter all, dancing and singing, right. Serve immediately, with the salsas.

Daube of Beef

Slow-cooked meat dishes that use red wine as both a marinade and a cooking liquid are those most of us remember as an early revelation in our introduction to French food. This is comfort food: rich and satisfying. Food with implied memories of the slowest simmering pots on the stove, the house filling with a delicious and all-permeating aroma, as the constituent elements combine into a glorious amalgam. Thus do the toughest pieces of meat give of their best. Indeed, the last thing you want in a daube is an expensive lean cut, for this will only emerge tough, dry, and disappointing.

You will find many supposedly classic recipes that call for lean cuts barded with pork fat. Why? It does not work as well, involves pointless preparation, and will cost more. Always choose a stewing cut like shank or ox cheek, which layer muscle with connective tissue and some fat. The end result will then be meltingly tender and moist.

Ox cheek is perhaps the best cut of all for a wine-enriched stew. It is the muscle that has worked hardest in the beast's life — chewing the cud — and will take perhaps 4 or 5 hours to cook. Each cheek makes two servings, or certainly at least one-and-a-half.

In the restaurant the cheeks are removed when cooked, wrapped, and chilled. Before serving they are then sliced thickly and heated in the finished sauce.

You are unlikely to find ox cheek in the supermarket, but it is worth asking for it in an Asian market. At the time of writing, restaurants are discovering its advantages, which means it is only a matter of time before the good news percolates via food writers and word of mouth to a wider audience… and as ox cheek becomes more sought after, so inevitably the price will rise.

One word of warning: We tend to have been sold the idea that all stewing cuts need to cook all day long to yield their treasure. This is not always the case. Even shank may be fully cooked after as little as 2 hours, while other stewing cuts (in England known to the meat trade as "clod" and "sticking," which I have always thought would make a great name for a butcher) may cook in 1 1/2 hours If you go on cooking past that point the gelatinous and fat elements will cook out into the braising liquid and the meat will progress from moist tenderness to flaking and unpleasant dryness. It is, therefore, worth testing after about 1 1/2 hours, by removing a piece and cutting a small slice off it to taste. Repeat at regular intervals until you are happy with the result. (In the case of ox cheek this will certainly be several hours!) Then next time you cook that same cut en daube you will have a good idea of how long it should stay on the stove.

If you feel the meat is cooked but that the cooking liquid needs reducing, the meat can be removed with a slotted spoon at this stage and then the liquid boiled to cook it down to the required amount. If you think the texture is too thin and it needs further thickening, then a beurre manié can be used: This is an amalgamation of buttered flour (usually equal parts), which is whisked into simmering liquid in small lumps, instantly thickening the sauce. It is unlikely that you will need this refinement, but the technique is a useful one to have up your sleeve. Unlike flour-thickened sauces, which need a long cooking period to eliminate the taste of flour (like the roux of a velouté, or indeed the seasoned flour with which you coat meat before sealing and browning), sauces thickened with beurre manié can be consumed after a few minutes' cooking. Alternatively, use potato flour as an end-of-cooking thickening agent.

In France, daubes and other slow-cooked dishes are called plats mijotés. These are the essential elements in the cuisine du terroir or cuisine bonne femme: a conscious effort to return to the roots of a country-based food culture, where traditional values predominate and where food reflects the natural rhythms of the seasons. I cannot think of anybody who eats meat who is not captivated by a good daube. It is loved by young and old alike, the culinary ingénue and the food sophisticate. It needs nothing more than mashed potatoes to provide bliss at the table.

Ingredients (for 6-8)

4 ox cheeks or 2¼-pound beef
   shank, boned but left in a large
   cross-cut piece (if using shank,
   ask your butcher for some of the
   beef marrow bones, sawn into
   pieces, and use immediately to
   make stock or freeze for future
   use; alternatively, cut out the
   marrow yourself and freeze for an
   entrecôte bordelaise)
1 large carrot
2 large onions
2 celery stalks
2 garlic cloves
1 bottle (750cl) of full-bodied red
   wine
bouquet garni of 2 pieces of
   tangerine peel, 2 bay leaves,
   some parsley stems, and sprig of
   thyme, all tied with string (you
   can buy dried tangerine peel in
   Asian markets)
1 pound button mushrooms
bunch of flat-leaf parsley
flour, for coating
salt and pepper
2 tablespoons lard or duck fat
7½ cups fonds brun (see page 18),
   or canned beef bouillon mixed
   with water, or just water
½ pound smoked slab bacon
1 pound frozen pearl onions

Utensils

heavy casserole large enough to
   hold all the ingredients
   comfortably (a big Le Creuset pot
   with a lid is ideal)
large frying pan
colander
conical strainer
fine strainer
ladle

Mise en Place

The day before: Trim the ox cheeks of any skin or visible gristle. If using shank, cut it into portion sizes, working along the muscles • Peel the carrot, onions, and celery and prepare a mirepoix (see page 188) • Peel and slice the garlic • Put all these ingredients in a large bowl to marinate in the red wine with the bouquet garni overnight.

The next day: Gently wash the mushrooms • Pull parsley leaves from the stems • Season some flour • Drain the meat and vegetables using the colander over a bowl to reserve the wine. Remove the meat and pat dry with paper towels. Reserve the vegetables and bouquet garni.

Cooking

Melt the lard or other fat in the frying pan and brown the ox cheeks or pieces of beef shank all over 2 at a time, first coating them in the seasoned flour. Put the browned pieces in the casserole. When all the meat is browned and in the casserole, place over very low heat. After 5 minutes, turn the meat and sprinkle with a little more flour.

Meanwhile, brown the vegetables and aromatics in the frying pan in a little more fat. Pour over 2½ cups of boiling water and stir up the sediment to deglaze. Add the contents of the pan to the casserole. The beef should have had at least 10 minutes' browning and the flour will have darkened and blotched on the surface. Add the wine marinade and stock or an equivalent amount of bouillon and water and stir all together.

Turn up the heat to medium, bring to a bubble, and immediately turning down the heat to achieve the barest simmer. Cover and cook 4 hours for cheek, 1½ hours for shank. Occasionally take off the lid and skim and stir. Note that the only salt and pepper used so far is the small amount in the seasoned flour.

At the end of this time, add the bacon in a piece and cook a further 1 hour before testing the beef to make sure it is cooked as described above.

Remove the casserole from the heat and transfer the beef and bacon to a tray using a slotted spoon. Pass the sauce through the conical strainer to take out the aromatics and vegetables and pass a second time through a finer strainer back into the casserole.

Cut the bacon into lardon strips (see page 187) and fry these gently in the frying pan until golden. Add the pearl onions and continue to cook until they too are golden and then tip both into the sauce. Do not wash the pan, but turn up the heat and sauté the mushrooms until browned. Add these to the sauce.

If serving immediately, slice the ox cheeks thickly, return them to the sauce, and simmer 15 minutes. Taste the sauce and season if necessary. Otherwise wrap the meat and refrigerate; let the sauce cool before refrigerating. Both can be held in this way up to 3 days and then gently reheated before being served.

Serving

Serve on large warmed plates sprinkled with chopped flat-leaf parsley and accompanied by mashed potatoes. This recipe is really a cross between a *daube* and a *bourguignonne*, the best kind of winter grub.

Truffled Poached Chicken

A kind friend has given you a black truffle weighing about 2 ounces, or you have spent a lot of money buying one. What to do with it? French classic cuisine is full of truffles, sliced and slipped under the breast skin of a chicken and poached, or in a rich sauce with a Dover sole baked whole en croûte.

I think a truffled poached chicken is quite the nicest way of enjoying this very rare and special treat, infusing the bird and the broth with its inimitable and all-pervasive flavor. The truffle is something that interacts with other food, elevating ordinary ingredients to another plane. The alchemy of the black arts indeed.

Ingredients (for 4)

1 black truffle, weighing about 2 ounces
3-pound free-range chicken
2 medium carrots
1 onion
4 medium leeks
1 stick (¹/₂ cup) unsalted butter
bouquet garni of celery, parsley stems, 8 black peppercorns, and a sprig of thyme, all tied in a cheesecloth bag
about 2¹/₂ quarts Chicken Stock (see page 19) or water, or a mixture of the two
salt and pepper

Utensils

large saucepan
bowl
sauté pan
colander or strainer

Mise en Place

Prepare the chicken: Gently scrub the truffle, then peel it, reserving the trimmings. Slice it very thinly • Work your hand under the chicken's breast skin, pulling it away from the breast on both sides and working down to pull the skin away from the legs. Slip the truffle slices under the skin, distributing them evenly on both sides, making sure some slices are located under the leg skin as well as under the breast skin.

Peel the carrots • Trim the onion, but leave its skin on • Wash and trim the leeks • Remove the butter from the refrigerator to let it soften.

Cooking

Put the bird in a large pan, surround it with the carrots, onion, and bouquet garni, and cover with chicken stock or water or a combination of the two. Bring to a boil and skim. Then turn down the heat to achieve the barest simmer. Season with salt and pepper.

Poach uncovered, skimming from time to time, for 1 hour. Remove the chicken and put in a warm place to drain and cool.

Strain the stock into a large bowl, clean the saucepan, and return the stock to it. Put on high heat. As it comes to a boil, skim the scum that will be generated, and continue to boil while you cook the leeks.

Put a large pan of lightly salted water on to heat. Cut the leeks into 1-inch pieces and wash again in a colander. Blanch the leeks in the rapidly boiling water for 3 minutes (they should be slightly underdone) and refresh in cold water.

Mince the truffle peelings and add to the softened butter in a small bowl with some salt and pepper, mashing them all together.

Put the leeks in a sauté pan over medium heat and add the truffled butter. Stew gently until the butter is melted and the leeks are hot.

Serving

Serve the broth first in soup plates, then serve the warm chicken as a separate main course on warmed plates with the leeks.

VEGETABLES

Five-Spice Greens

The precise type of greens is not important, though dark-green and slightly bitter leaves like collards or mustard greens are preferable to sweeter and lighter vegetables. Napa cabbage is not suitable. Cantonese chefs would cook this dish in a wok, but I prefer to use a large and heavy frying pan.

This is also an excellent method for cooking spinach or broccoli.

Ingredients (for 4)

1 pound hearty seasonal greens
1 garlic clove
2 tablespoons sunflower oil
1 teaspoon five-spice powder
about 2 teaspoons sesame oil
about 1 tablespoon Kikkoman soy
  sauce
salt

Utensils

large saucepan
colander
wok or heavy frying pan

Mise en Place

Remove stems and blanch the leaves in a large pan of fast-boiling salted water for 2 minutes. Refresh in cold water, drain, and gently squeeze out excess moisture. Chill until ready to cook • Slice the garlic into very thin rounds.

Cooking

Put the sunflower oil in the wok or large heavy frying pan and place over medium heat. Fry the garlic in this for 1 minute, being careful not to let it brown (which makes it bitter).

Turn the heat up and throw in the greens. Toss once, sprinkle over the five-spice powder, and toss again. Dribble over some sesame oil and soy sauce to taste.

Serving

Serve at once, piping hot. If you let it stand, the oil will separate and it will not taste as good.

Turnip, Rutabaga, and Carrot Purée

Not entirely entrancing when individually puréed, these three root vegetables in combination are altogether more intriguing. The food processor makes preparation a rapid and painless exercise.

Ingredients (for 4)

1/2 pound turnips
1/2 pound rutabaga
1/2 pound carrots
1 onion
1/4 nutmeg
2 tablespoons butter
1 tablespoon heavy whipping cream
salt and pepper

Utensils

saucepan
colander
food processor

Mise en Place

Put a large pan of salted water on to heat • Peel the vegetables, including the onion, and cut them into chunks • Grate the nutmeg.

Cooking

Cook the vegetables in the boiling water until all are tender. Drain in the colander and put straight into the food processor.

Add the butter, cream, nutmeg, and some salt and pepper and process to a smooth purée.

This can be eaten at once or left to cool and then refrigerated. Then reheat in a double boiler, beating in a little more cream just before serving.

Rösti

Making rösti properly takes lots of butter, but produces a perfect partner for any grilled meat. Use any large potatoes to make one of Switzerland's great dishes.

Instead of butter you can use ghee, which is clarified butter sold in cans in Indian markets. It produces good results, but is very expensive.

Clarifying your own butter is easy: Put the butter in a heavy pan and melt over low heat. As it melts it will start to throw scum to the surface. Skim this off as it rises. After 10 or 15 minutes, particles will start to brown and rise. Skim again, then strain the liquid butter through a fine strainer or cheesecloth.

Ingredients (for 4)
2 pounds potatoes
2 sticks (1 cup) butter (or $^3/_4$ cup ghee)
salt and pepper

Utensils
large saucepan
colander
grater
bowl
4 blini pans or one larger sauté pan with an ovenproof handle

Mise en Place
Parcook the potatoes: In a large pan of boiling salted water, simmer the potatoes in their skins until nearly done. Drain, then run cold water over them until they are cool enough to handle. Peel.

Preheat the oven to its highest setting • If using butter, clarify it as described above • Grate the potatoes coarsely into a bowl and pour over the butter. Season and mix. Pack the mixture well into the blini pans or sauté pan with the back of a spoon.

Cooking
Bake until brown and crisp on the top. Remove from the oven and unmold by putting a plate on top of the pan, then inverting the pan while holding the plate.

Bubble and Squeak

This English classic was originally devised to use up leftover potatoes and cabbage. It was invariably served on Mondays, with reheated slices of meat from the Sunday roast. A pretty unattractive prospect, particularly when the meat and vegetables had been overcooked the first time around. The potato and cabbage cake would also have been cooked in beef drippings or lard.

This version is altogether more civilized and is particularly good with cold ham and fried eggs or with any grilled meat. The potato should be quite dry and any greens will do, though I prefer collards or spinach to cabbage.

Ingredients (for 4)
2 thick slices of bacon
6 ounces spinach or seasonal greens
2 cups mashed potato
1 egg
salt and pepper
flour, for coating
2 tablespoons butter
1 tablespoon olive oil

Utensils
grill pan or roasting pan with rack
saucepan
colander
bowl
heavy frying pan
metal spatula

Mise en Place
Preheat the oven to 400°F. Bake the bacon on a rack in the oven, then drain on paper towels and cut into small dice • Blanch the greens in a pan of boiling salted water for 2 minutes and refresh in cold water. Drain, pat dry, and chop coarsely • Put the greens into a bowl with the mashed potato, bacon dice, and egg and mix together with a fork to bind. Season with pepper and very little salt (the bacon should give all the salt needed) • Mold into 4 patties and flour lightly.

Cooking
Melt the butter with the oil in a frying pan over low heat. When hot, gently put in the patties. Do not push or turn, but let cook 10 minutes before turning over with a spatula. They will be crisp and brown. Fry the other side 10 minutes. That's it.

DESSERTS

Panettone Bread and Butter Pudding

Bread and butter pudding has enjoyed something of a renaissance in recent times. In this recipe the bread element has diminished and been replaced with panettone, *the light and delicious dome-shaped Italian yeast cake studded with candied orange and lemon peel and raisins.* Panettone *is traditionally eaten at Christmas, but is available all year around from Italian grocers. It is difficult to cut when fresh, as it is so spongy; cut the* panettone *in half the day before cooking to let it to dry out slightly.*

The milk has been enriched with cream and eggs to make a smooth custard, and extra raisins are plumped with grappa to give a distinctively Italian kick to the finished amalgamation. If you don't have grappa (an eau-de-vie *made from the pulp left after crushing muscat grapes for wine), use brandy or dark rum.*

It is a good idea to keep some raisins in a jar of grappa or brandy in the kitchen. They make a nice addition to a lot of dishes, savory as well as sweet.

Ingredients (for 4)

*1 vanilla bean, or 1 teaspoon vanilla
    extract*
*about 1 stick ($^1/_2$ cup) unsalted
    butter*
2$^1/_2$ cups whole milk
2$^1/_2$ cups heavy whipping cream
4 eggs
$^3/_4$ cup sugar
*6 slices of panettone (the size will
    depend on your dish and how you
    slice your cake)*
*$^1/_3$ cup golden raisins. soaked
    overnight in grappa*
*$^1/_4$ cup strained apricot jam
    (optional)*
confectioners' sugar
*more whipping cream, to serve
    (optional)*
seasonal berries (optional)

Utensils

*glazed baking dish about 2-inches
    deep and large enough to hold a
    single layer of panettone
    sandwiches*
bowl
thick-bottomed saucepan
large roasting pan

Mise en Place

Make the pudding the day before serving: Preheat the oven to 325°F • If using, split the vanilla bean by cutting lengthwise in half from just below the stem and then again to make four strips still joined at the top • Butter the baking dish.

Cooking

Put the milk and cream in a saucepan with the vanilla bean, if using, and place over low heat to extract flavor.

Beat the eggs with the sugar in a bowl until they make a smooth foaming mixture.

Butter the panettone slices and make 3 sandwiches with the grappa-soaked raisins as a filling. You can cut these into smaller sandwiches, or use a cookie cutter to make rounds.

Arrange these in the baking dish. (If you have a round baking dish of the right size, consider cutting the panettone across to make one large sandwich.) Spread the sandwiches with apricot jam, if using.

Bring the milk and cream mixture to a boil, stirring in the vanilla extract, if using. Pour over the eggs and sugar (through a strainer, if using a vanilla bean), whisking to make a custard. Ladle this carefully over the bread and let soak 15 minutes.

Place the dish in a roasting pan and pour in water to come half-way up the sides. Bake until firm but pliant to the touch, about 45 minutes. It will be golden brown on top with a slight crust.

Let cool, then chill overnight.

Serving

Sprinkle the top with confectioners' sugar before serving. Serve with cold cream and berries if you don't feel this is over-egging the pudding!

Panforte and Reggiano Parmesan

Sometimes lack of time dictates as easy a dessert as possible. Fruit salad is always popular, but still takes time and patience. A bowl of fruit – or even one fruit selected for its perfection – never disappoints. The combination of panforte *and Reggiano Parmesan is a lovely and unusual alternative.*

Panforte *is available from Italian grocers in both black and white varieties. It is a rich, hard, compressed flat cake from Sienna, full of nuts and honey and with a spicing reminiscent of incense. It was first made around the twelfth century and in its flavors one can taste history, for it is made to precisely the same recipe today as it was then.*

A small wedge of panforte *and a chunk of Parmesan make the perfect end to any meal, particularly with a glass of tawny port or Vin Santo. A good farmhouse Cheddar also goes well with* panforte.

Ingredients (for 8-12)

1 frozen Pâte Sucrée Tart Shell (see page 25), still in its loose-bottomed pan

Vanilla Ice Cream (see page 28), to serve

FOR THE STREUSEL TOPPING:

6 tablespoons flour

6 tablespoons brown sugar, preferably Barbados

6 tablespoons finely ground blanched almonds

3 tablespoons softened unsalted butter

FOR THE BLACK CURRANT AND APPLE FILLING:

1 cup black currants (fresh or frozen)

6 large tart apples, preferably Granny Smiths

6 tablespoons butter

$^1/_3$ cup sugar

2 tablespoons apple brandy (optional)

Utensils

large bowl

strainer

heavy sauté pan

small saucepan

spatula

Black Currant & Apple Streusel Tart

Combine crisp tart apples and black currants on an almond-enriched sweet pastry with a crunchy topping and you have something quite irresistible. The inspiration for this recipe comes from the kitchen of French master chef, Joël Robuchon, very much a three-star incarnation. From a cook's point of view this recipe also scores by eliminating blind baking of the pastry shell – always a tedious business – and uses frozen black currants, one of the few fruits not to suffer from this treatment. Robuchon's pâtissier, Philippe Gobet, used Golden Delicious. I have never understood the French love for these over-sweet apples – which I find insipid – and I prefer to use a tart apple such as Granny Smiths.

Mise en Place

First prepare the streusel topping: Sift the flour into a bowl with the brown sugar and almonds and combine them using your fingers. Add the butter and continue to work for several minutes until thoroughly blended in and the mixture is very crumbly. Let rest about 20 minutes.

Preheat the oven to 375°F.

Prepare the filling: If the black currants are frozen, thaw in a strainer to let any excess moisture drain. Peel, core, and dice the apples into 1-inch chunks.

Cooking

Over medium heat, sauté the apples in a heavy pan with the butter and sugar, tossing to coat and cooking until just tender (which will take between 10 and 15 minutes). They should be golden brown.

If using apple brandy, warm it in a small pan. Ignite it and pour over the apples, stirring in. The mixture should not be too wet. If it is, drain briefly in a strainer.

Take the pastry shell from the freezer, put it on a baking sheet,and spoon in the apples, pressing down to make them level. Sprinkle the black currants over and cover evenly with the streusel topping. Use a spatula to smooth the surface flat.

Bake until the topping is golden brown, about 25 minutes. If it is not, check every 5 minutes until done.

Serving
Serve warm with a scoop of vanilla ice cream.

Ingredients (for 4)

FOR THE DOUGH:

3 cups flour
3/4 cups sugar
*2 sticks (1 cup) + 1 tablespoon
    butter*
2 eggs
1 teaspoon grated lemon zest
pinch of salt
confectioners' sugar, to dust

FOR THE FILLING:

*1 heaped teaspoon of China tea (or
    1 tea bag)*
3 1/3 cups sugar
12 prunes
2 pounds Granny Smith apples
1 1/3 cups pine nuts

Utensils

food processor
heatproof bowl
large saucepan
rolling pin
circular cookie cutter
pastry brush
baking sheet

Ravioli San Giuseppe

The nearest thing I can think of to come close to the Renaissance taste of this unusual dessert is a really good mince pie. The ravioli are fiddly to make and, unusually for ravioli, are baked in the oven, but are well worth the effort.

There are various ways you can ring the changes on the filling: For example, try substituting fresh or dried figs for the prunes, or dried apricots or dates.

Mise en Place

First make the dough: Put the flour and sugar into the food processor. Working at full speed, add the butter in pieces until incorporated. Then add the eggs, the lemon zest, and a pinch of salt. (The addition of salt is an odd thing: It makes all the difference to the taste, but you should not be able to taste it in the cooked ravioli. If you can then you are in trouble.) The dough should be just holding together. Scrape it onto a sheet of plastic wrap, form into a cylinder, and chill. The high butter content means it will keep well in the refrigerator.

Make the filling: Make weak China tea in the heatproof bowl, sweeten it well with 2 or 3 teaspoons of the sugar, and soak the prunes in it. (You need to sweeten it or the natural sugar in the fruit leaches out into the tea, leaving you with rather pointless prunes.) You can now buy some really good Californian prunes that have been dried and then partially reconstituted; these take very little soaking. If using very dry prunes, however, soak them for several hours.

Peel, core, and slice the apples (no need to be too fussy as they are going to be cooked until they disintegrate) • Toast the pine nuts briefly under the broiler, watching them throughout (throwing away burnt pine nuts is an expensive and unamusing exercise).

Cooking

Put a couple of spoonfuls of water into a large saucepan, add the remaining sugar, and put to melt over low heat, stirring from time to time. When the sugar has melted, add the apple slices and stir in.

Increase the heat to medium and cook until the apples are candied. Do not stir or you will only have a spoon coated with an impossibly sticky hot mess. The mixture should be ready after 15 minutes, when it will be quite dry (the water from the apples having evaporated because of the high temperature of the sugar).

Drain the prunes and mince them, removing the pits. Add the minced prunes with the toasted pine nuts to the pan, immediately taking it off the heat. Let cool slightly before scraping the contents into a jar. This will also amalgamate the nuts and prunes.

Preheat the oven to 350°F and butter a baking sheet.

Now assemble the ravioli: Cut slices of dough off the end of the cylinder and roll out slightly on a lightly floured surface. Then, using a circular cutter or upended glass, cut out as many neat circles as you can. Put a spoonful of candied filling on each circle, slightly off-center. Brush the edges with a little water, fold over to make a half circle, and crimp the edges to make a firm seal.

Holding Point – the ravioli will keep in the refrigerator for 2 days or freeze well, while the filling keeps for ages in a jar because of the high sugar content.

Arrange the ravioli on the prepared baking sheet and bake 10–12 minutes, turning once after 5 minutes. Beware: They burn easily.

Serving

Dust the ravioli with confectioners' sugar and serve with a dollop of chilled whipped cream or vanilla ice cream. A word of warning: When they come out of the oven the filling is incandescent so, to avoid your guests burning their mouths rather badly, do not rush to the table.

Compote of Winter Fruits

I serve these seasonal fruits poached in a spicy red wine syrup with a slice of Sauternes and Olive Oil Cake (see page 100) to give a textured contrast. Make this compote at least a day ahead of serving – it will keep for a week or more in the refrigerator.

Mise en Place

Make the compote the day before: Use a potato peeler to scrape off the zest from the lemon.

Cooking

Put the wine, all but 3 teaspoons sugar, the vanilla bean, bayleaf, tangerine peel, and spices into a large non-reactive saucepan and bring to a boil, stirring. Skim off the froth that comes to the surface.

Simmer 30 minutes to infuse the spices. Add the lemon zest to the syrup and set aside to cool and mature.

At the same time, make a weak tea by adding $2^1/_2$ cups of boiling water to the tea bag in the heatproof bowl. Then stir in the sugar reserve (you use this to rehydrate the prunes and apricots and the tea needs to be very sweet to keep the natural sugar in the fruit and not leach into the soaking liquid; this would happen if you used unsweetened tea).

Add the prunes and apricots to the tea and warm over very low heat for 10 minutes. Remove from the heat and leave the fruit to plump up.

Peel the pears, holding them by the stems, and rub with the cut face of the lemon to prevent discoloration. Bring the red wine syrup back to a boil, turn down to a gentle simmer, and add the pears. You need to keep the fruit beneath the surface of the liquid and the easiest way to achieve this is to use a lid from a smaller pan to hold them down. Simmer 30 minutes, and remove from heat.

Drain the prunes and apricots and discard the tea. Remove the lid from the syrup (it will be very sticky) and add them to the pears. Replace the lid and let cool completely before refrigerating overnight.

The compote is now ready to serve. I prefer to leave the spices in, but if you do so warn your guests that they are there for decorative effect. Not everybody likes to crunch on a peppercorn while eating dessert.

Serving

Serve with Olive Oil and Sauternes cake (page 100), or with some crème fraîche or Vanilla Ice Cream (page 28).

Ingredients (for 4)

1 lemon
2 cups red wine
$2^1/_2$ cups sugar
1 vanilla bean
1 bay leaf
1 piece of dried tangerine peel (optional – available from Asian markets)
1 cinnamon stick
12 black peppercorns
8 star anise (optional)
1 Lapsang tea bag
12 prunes
8 dried apricots
4 small pears (firm but not rock-hard, but not ripe enough to eat uncooked)

Utensils

potato peeler
large non-reactive saucepan
large heatproof bowl

Apple, Prune, and Zabaglione Tart

For many people the word zabaglione *conjures up images of the kind of* trattoria *where the host greets you with ejecting teeth and overpowering bonhomie: "Signore, where-a you been for so long? I see you put on a bitt-a weight, but don't worry, on you it looks good." You sit at your table (inevitably "the best in the house," just next to the kitchen service doors) and grimly contemplate the cold antipasto – with its obligatory leaden eggplant – with growing foreboding.*

Forget all that. Here the zabaglione is cooked into a tart of apple and prunes held in a sweet crisp crust. I got the recipe from Rowley Leigh at Kensington Place restaurant. He, in turn, had it from a French guru pâtissier *named Yves Thuries.*

Ingredients (for 8-12)

12 prunes
1 Lapsang tea bag
1/3 cup sugar
6 large tart apples
6 tablespoons butter
2 tablespoons Calvados
1 frozen Pâte Sucrée Tart Shell (see page 25), still in its pan

FOR THE ZABAGLIONE:
7 tablespoons butter
2 eggs
1/2 cup sugar
2 drops of vanilla extract
1 tablespoon Calvados

Utensils

heavy frying pan
wax paper
foil
dried beans for blind baking
baking sheet
spatula
electric mixer
small saucepan
bowl

Mise en Place

Well ahead, prepare the prunes: Make some tea, sweeten with a couple of teaspoons of sugar, and soak the prunes in it as described in the Compote of Winter Fruits (page 185). Once plumped up, pit the drained prunes.

Parcook the peeled and segmented apples with the butter and remaining sugar in a frying pan as described in the Black Currant and Apple Streusel Tart (page 182), drizzling over the Calvados as you do.

Make the pastry shell as described on page 25, or use one you have already made and frozen • Preheat the oven to 400°F • Line the tart shell with wax paper, and then with a double sheet of foil and fill with dried beans to weight. Press down firmly and return to the freezer until ready to bake.

Cooking

Put the pastry shell on a baking sheet and bake 10 minutes, when you should see the visible rim of pastry start to brown.

Remove from the oven and gingerly lift out the foil and beans. Then peel away the wax paper.

Return the pastry to the oven and bake 5 minutes longer. Remove and let cool. Lower the oven temperature to 350°F.

When the apples and prunes are cool, pack them into the pastry shell, but do not overfill as you need to leave room for the custard topping – so no more than three-quarters of the way up.

Make the zabaglione: Melt the butter in a saucepan over very low heat. In a large bowl, beat the eggs with the sugar until stiff. Then, continuing to beat, pour in the hot melted butter in a thin stream, followed by the vanilla and Calvados.

As soon as this is mixed, transfer the custard to a measure and return the tart to the oven on the baking sheet. Only then (when the tart is in place in the oven), carefully pour the custard over the apples and prunes, making sure none runs down the sides of the pastry. (It is easier to avoid slopping by doing this only when the tart is in the oven.)

Bake 10–12 minutes, when the top will be golden brown but still slightly liquid.

Serving

Serve warm.

Glossary

aïoli

The garlic-flavored mayonnaise known as the "butter of Provence," which is an essential accompaniment to many of their fish and vegetable dishes. The feast that consists of a large platter of salt cod and poached vegetables with the sauce is known as *aïoli garni,* and with cold meats it is termed *le grand aïoli* .

al dente

Italian for "to the tooth", this describes food that has been cooked just to the point where it gives slight resistance to the bite. Properly reserved for dried pasta and rice, but now commonly extended to vegetables.

bain marie or water bath

A shallow pan of hot water into which dishes requiring cooking at a low, even temperature are placed prior to being put in the oven. The term is also used to describe a large , shallow pan of water on top of the stove for keeping sauces stable and warm in the professional kitchen.

baking blind

Cooking a pie or tart shell before adding the filling (if there is to be little or no further cooking). It is normal to line such shells first with wax paper and weight them with beans, but freezing the pastry shell first and then baking at the correct temperature enables you to dispense with this complex and time-consuming arrangement.

baron

The saddle and hindquarters of various animals. You are unlikely ever to cook a baron of beef, but may well come across this cut with rabbit or lamb.

beurre manié or kneaded butter

Usually equal parts of butter and flour worked to a paste and stirred in small pieces into a hot sauce or a stew at a late stage to thicken it. Paradoxically, the flour does not taste raw even after brief cooking.

blanching

A brief preparatory cooking of food in copious quantities of boiling water (to fix color, remove pungency or excess saltiness, or partially cook), normally followed by the application of other cooking methods. The cooked food is normally immediately refreshed (see page 189) to arrest the cooking process.

bonito flakes

Intensely flavored flakes of dried tuna flesh, much used as a flavoring condiment in Japanese cooking.

bouquet garni

A small bunch of herbs, usually including one or two bay leaves, some parsley stems and a sprig of thyme, either tied with string or wrapped in a cheesecloth or paper sachet and used to flavor soups, stews, and stocks, then removed before serving. The exact mix of herbs used may vary according to what is being cooked and can include other aromatics, such as celery and carrots.

braising

A method of cooking that involves browning meat (usually tough cuts) and/or vegetables, then adding a small quantity of liquid before covering the pot and slowly simmering until tender.

brunoise

Small dice of celery, carrot, and onions (and sometimes leeks) used in soups and stews where these vegetables are intended to be served rather than strained out of the finished dish.

carpaccio

Fifteenth-century Venetian painter, or a dish invented in Harry's Bar using thinly sliced raw beef and a nasty mayonnaise-based sauce. Now it can mean thin slices of raw beef in almost any guise.

chowder

A North American soup (although thought to be Breton in origin) made with fish or clams and often corn. Almost a stew, the liquid content is usually milk and it is thickened with potatoes.

clarifying

A mystical process whereby egg white, chopped vegetables, and ground meat (or fish) is added to a cold stock, which is then slowly heated and simmered for 1 hour. The egg white attracts all the impurities in the stock, forming a thick crust on the surface. After careful straining, the result is crystal-clear consommé. A tedious and expensive process best ignored.

coating consistency

A liquid is said to have a coating consistency when it will coat the back of a metal spoon and a finger run across it will leave a clear channel. Mainly used when describing sauces and custards.

confit
Traditionally this refers only to lightly salted duck or goose cooked slowly in its own fat and then preserved in that fat (originally a by-product of foie gras production). The term is now widely misapplied on restaurant menus to practically anything, including fish.

coulis
A puréed savory or sweet sauce with one predominant ingredient, such as tomatoes or raspberries.

cutlet or scallop
A thin slice of meat or fish, usually cut across the grain and best cooked quickly.

dashi
Japanese stock made from dried tuna, nori seaweed, and soy sauce. It is the basis of many Japanese dishes and may be bought ready-made in packets. Beware: Large quantities of MSG are commercially standard.

daube
French wine-enriched stew, almost always beef in red wine unless stated otherwise.

deglazing
After sautéing, frying, roasting (or even grilling) meat, poultry, or fish, the cooked food is removed from the pan and a little liquid added (usually wine, spirits, or stock). The residue is boiled vigorously while scraping the pan to incorporate intensely flavored elements stuck to the bottom, thus producing a tasty sauce. In other words, making a gravy without using gravy browning.

filet mignon
A small round steak cut from the thickest part of the bef tenderloin, weighing 4–6 ounces and trimmed of all sinew and fat. A luxurious and expensive beef cut.

fond
Literally "base," this is the French word for any stock.

gratin
A preparation of food cooked in a sauce in a shallow dish and finished in the oven or under the broiler to produce a crust. This usually involves the use of bread crumbs or grated cheese.

julienne
This term refers to any food cut into matchstick-sized strips, most usually vegetables or citrus rind, to be used as a flavoring and/or garnish.

jus
Short for *"jus de viande"* (i.e. meat juices), this term is used for a dressing that is halfway between a gravy and a sauce. It offers the speed of the former with the complex flavors of the latter.

lardons
Strips of bacon, salt pork, or pancetta that are often blanched to remove excessive salt and then either sautéed until crisp for salads or added to casseroles such as *coq au vin* .

macédoine
Big brunoise, or cubed vegetables (or even fruit), most often seen as a salad.

marinating
Most commonly, immersing food in a liquid (the marinade, usually consisting of oil and vinegar, seasonings, and herbs) to flavor, tenderize, and/or prevent food drying out when it is cooked. Occasionally marinades are used to "cook" raw food like *ceviche* or gravlax.

mignonette pepper
Coarsely ground black pepper used in dishes such as *steak au poivre*. The simplest way to achieve the correct texture is to loosen the nut on top of a pepper mill.

mirepoix
Small (1/2-inch) dice of aromatic vegetables such as celery, carrot, and onions, used in stocks and stews; strained and discarded after the flavors have been absorbed into the cooking liquid. There is usually no need to peel the vegetables first.

parboiling
A special case of blanching (see above), the process of partly cooking food by boiling it before applying some other form of cooking, such as potatoes for roasting.

pâte sucrée
Sweet short pastry, used for tarts.

pilaf
Persian in origin, this term describes a rice dish that involves all liquids and flavorings being added together, the rice then being covered and cooked until tender. Very good, but not a risotto.

poaching

Cooking food in a liquid held just below boiling point. This is not a simmer since the liquid should shiver or tremble (*frémir*) rather than bubble. Suitable for delicate foods, such as fish and poultry.

reducing

The process of boiling down a sauce, stock, or gravy to concentrate the flavor. Impurities are thrown to the surface and can be skimmed off.

refreshing

Plunging any cooked foods briefly into very cold or ice water to arrest the cooking process. Do not leave food more than a minute in the water or flavors will be leached out.

risotto

Italian dish of Arborio (or similar) rice: The rice is first sautéed in butter or oil and then hot stock is added a ladleful at a time until the rice is cooked *al dente* . Other flavoring and garnishing ingredients (such as mushrooms, saffron, and cheese) are added at various stages during the process.

roux

Flour and fat cooked together before the addition of hot liquid. Used primarily as the thickening agent in sauces, any roux must be cooked with the liquid for a relatively long period to eliminate the flavor of the raw flour.

salmis

Classic French way of cooking duck and game birds whereby the bird is first roasted whole and then cut up for subsequent stewing in a rich sauce. The rare breast may be served first, without any further cooking, as a separate dish.

saltimbocca

Meaning "jump in the mouth," presumably because the Italians found it so tasty, this dish traditionally consists of a veal cutlet topped with a slice of prosciutto and a sage leaf, quickly sautéed and finished with a simple Marsala sauce. This combination of ham and sage with meat can be used successfully with other foods, including fish.

sashimi

Japanese raw fish preparation usually served with soy sauce, wasabi, and various vegetables. Not the same thing as *sushi* , which is primarily vinegared sticky rice wrapped in seaweed, sometimes with fish attached.

sautéing

From the French for "to jump," this means the shallow frying of (usually smallish pieces of) food in an open pan with fat to brown and cook until done. The food is usually turned regularly to ensure uniform browning and the process may be brief or lengthy, depending on the tenderness of the food. Liquid is anathema and should only be added after the primary ingredient is finished and removed from the pan. See deglazing.

steaming

The cooking of food over boiling water or aromatic stock with no direct contact other than with the generated steam. Suitable for fish and other delicate food. The current appeal of steaming vegetables is a mystery since the more rapid process of blanching is vastly preferable from every point of view (including nutritional).

stewing

The slow simmering of food in liquid with or without initial browning. This essential process, involving an exchange of flavors between the various ingredients, plays a vital role in casseroles, soups, and stocks.

stir-frying

Chinese technique whereby small pieces of food are rapidly fried over high heat with a small amount of (often flavored) oil while tossing and stirring. A wok is not essential.

suprême

The skinless breast half with wing bone of a fowl. (The term is sometimes also used to glamorize fish fillets on restaurant menus.)

sweating

Preliminary slow cooking (usually onions and other vegetables) in oil or fat to extract moisture and flavor, normally without browning. An essential first step when making vegetable soups.

terrine

An ovenproof, usually loaf-shaped, mold often used to facilitate the assembly of chopped raw (and sometimes cooked) food. Dishes cooked in this way are sometimes called *pâtés* , even without the benefit of a pastry crust.

Index